CURRENT ISSUES IN

CURRENT ISSUES IN ECONOMICS

General Editor: David Greenaway

Series Standing Order
If you would like to receive future titles in this series as they are
published, you can make use of our standing order facility. To place a
standing order please contact your bookseller or, in case of difficulty,
write to us at the address below with your name and address and the
name of the series. Please state with which title you wish to begin your
standing order. (If you live outside the United Kingdom we may not
have the rights for your area, in which case we will forward your order
to the publisher concerned.)

Customer Services Department, Macmillan Distribution Ltd
Houndmills, Basingstoke, Hampshire, RG21 2XS, England.

Current Issues in Labour Economics

Edited by

David Sapsford

Senior Lecturer in Economics
University of East Anglia

and

Zafiris Tzannatos

Senior Lecturer in Economics
University of Buckingham

MACMILLAN

First published 1990

Published by
MACMILLAN EDUCATION LTD
Houndmills, Basingstoke, Hampshire RG21 2XS
and London
Companies and representatives
throughout the world

Printed in Hong Kong

British Library Cataloguing in Publication Data
Current issues in labour economics. —Current issues
in economics
1. Employment. Labour
I. Sapsford, David   II. Tzannatos, Zafiris, *1953*–
III. Series
331
ISBN 0–333–45353–0 (hardcover)
ISBN 0–333–45354–9 (paperback)

Contents

v

List of Figures

List of Tables

Series Editor's Preface

The *Current Issues* Series has slightly unusual origins. *Current Issues in International Trade*, which Macmillan published in 1987 and which turned out to be the pilot for the series, was in fact 'conceived' in the Horton Hospital, Banbury, and 'delivered' (in the sense of completed) in the Hilton International in Nicosia! The reader may be struck by the thought that a more worthwhile and enjoyable production process would start and finish the other way around. I agree! Be that as it may, that is how the series started.

As I said in the preface to *Current Issues in International Trade* the reason for its creation was the difficulty of finding suitable references on 'frontier' subjects for undergraduate students. Many of the issues which excite professional economists and which dominate the journal literature take quite a time to percolate down into texts, hence the need for a volume of Current Issues. The reception which *Current Issues in International Trade* received persuaded me that it may be worth doing something similar for the other subject areas we teach. Macmillan agreed with my judgement, hence the Series. Thus each volume in this Series is intended to take readers to the 'frontier' of the particular subject area. Each volume contains ten essays, nine of which deal with specific current issues, and one which provides a general overview, setting the relevant current issues in the context of other recent developments.

As Series Editor the main challenge I faced was finding suitable editors for each of the volumes – the best people are generally the busiest! I believe however that I have been fortunate in having such an impressive and experienced team of editors with the necessary skills and reputation to persuade first-class authors to participate. I would like to thank all of them for their cooperation and assistance in the development of the Series. Like me, all of them will, I am sure, hope that this Series provides a useful service to undergraduate and postgraduate students as well as faculty.

With regard to the present volume, David Sapsford and Zafiris Tzannatos have presented us with a volume of essays that go right to the heart of recent developments in economic analysis. The evident inability of the labour market to adjust quickly and smoothly to recent shocks has stimulated enormous interest in labour-market economics. In this volume we are exposed to implicit-contract theory, job-search models, bargaining theory, profit-sharing models, institutionalist perspectives and as many other current issues again. The reader who would like to see *every* current issue covered will be disappointed; those who wish to see most of the important current issues dealt with should not. The coverage of topics is comprehensive and their treatment thorough. Moreover the coverage nicely complements that of other volumes in the Series.

Overall I think the editors of this volume have done a fine job in assembling such an able and distinguished body of contributors who in turn, have delivered an impressive collection of essays. David Sapsford and Zafiris Tzannatos provide an overview of the essays in their introductory chapter and it is quite unnecessary for me to say anything further to preempt this, save the hope that users gain as much from the volume as I have in reading it.

DAVID GREENAWAY

Notes on the Contributors

George Alogoskoufis is Senior Lecturer in Economics at Birkbeck College, University of London.

Alessandro Cigno is Professor of Economics at the University of Pisa.

Saul Estrin is Lecturer in Economics at the London School of Economics.

Alan Manning is Lecturer in Economics at Birkbeck College, University of London.

C. J. McKenna is Associate Professor of Economics at University of Guelph, Canada.

Robert McNabb is Lecturer in Economics at the University of Wales College, Cardiff.

Paul Ryan is Fellow of King's College, Cambridge.

David Sapsford is Senior Lecturer in Economics at the University of East Anglia.

Zafiris Tzannatos is Senior Lecturer in Economics at the University of Buckingham.

Alistair Ulph is Professor of Economics at the University of Southampton.

David Ulph is Professor of Economics at the University of Bristol.

Sushil Wadhwani is Lecturer in Economics at the London School of Economics.

1 Labour Economics: An Overview of Some Recent Theoretical and Empirical Developments

DAVID SAPSFORD and **ZAFIRIS TZANNATOS**

1.1 INTRODUCTION

It has long been recognised that the need for a 'special' theory of the labour market arises because of the 'peculiar' properties of labour which distinguish it from other commodities to which the usual theory of value may be applied (see, for example, Marshall, 1890; Hicks, 1932). Many important and exciting developments have taken place in the economics of the labour market over the past twenty-five years or so. Labour economics has by now established itself not only as a major subject in its own right, but also as one of considerable importance to the other main branches of economics, including both macro- and microeconomics. The purpose of the current volume is to provide readers with a coverage of the major recent developments which have occurred in labour economics, the majority of which have yet to find a place in set texts or other material readily accessible to students. Each chapter in this book has been specially prepared by an acknowledged expert in the relevant field, with the intention of providing both students and teachers of labour economics with a clear, comprehensive and up-to-date coverage of the topic in question. Our objective in this introductory chapter is to set the scene for the

1

material which follows, by providing a brief overview of the major theoretical and empirical developments which have occurred in the subject over recent years.

1.2   LABOUR DEMAND AND SUPPLY

The determinants of the demand for labour attracted greater attention in the early literature than the determinants of supply, with the development and refinements of marginal productivity theory due to such writers as Marshall (1890), Clark (1900) and Cartter (1959). However, two of the earliest and arguably most significant post-war developments in labour-market analysis relate to the supply side of the labour market. The first such development derives from the publications of Becker, Lancaster and Muth in the 1960s. In particular, Gary Becker's (1965) paper 'A Theory of the Allocation of Time' explicitly recognised the household as the relevant decision-making unit regarding the related questions of labour-force participation and hours-of-work decisions, on the one hand, and home production and consumption decisions, on the other. Becker's model integrated the production, consumption and labour-supply decisions within a household framework and demonstrated quite clearly, how utility-maximising behaviour by households can determine not only the division of each member's available time between market and non-market activities, but also their chosen mix as between home-produced and market-pur-chased goods and their chosen division of labour as between various household members in the performance of the range of alternative tasks. Becker's model proved to be very influential in the labour-supply literature and provided the theoretical underpinning for a large number of theoretical and empirical studies which have appeared in the study of labour supply since the mid-1960s (see Killingsworth, 1983, for a survey). In addition, Becker's model provided a framework within which economic analysis could fruitfully be employed in the study of a wide variety of household activities, including questions of marriage and divorce, optimal family size and so forth. In Chapter 2, Alessandro Cigno discusses and develops the Becker-type framework in a variety of directions and explores its implications for a range of issues, including the allocation of time in multi-person households and the sexual division of labour.

The second supply-side development is the human-capital approach, which basically focuses attention on questions relating to the *quality* of labour. Although the origins of the human-capital approach can be traced back a great deal further (e.g. to Adam Smith, 1776), studies by both Mincer (1958) and Becker (1964) redefined the issue in a more concrete way and proved to be especially influential in the post-war literature. The human-capital approach, which views education and training as forms of investment in the individual, has implications for a wide variety of issues in labour economics relating to the structure of earnings, a number of which are discussed in Chapters 3,7 and 8 of this volume.

1.3 INCOMPLETE INFORMATION AND LABOUR CONTRACTS

Over the post-war period considerable attention has been directed towards the analysis of the functioning of labour markets which are characterised by imperfect information regarding both job opportunities and labour availability. Under such circumstances it has been argued that an amount of market search will be undertaken by labour-market participants, the objective of which is to obtain an improvement in their information regarding available alternatives. Thus it was argued that when in possession of only imperfect information regarding available opportunities, it is rational for both the worker when looking for a job and the employer when seeking to fill a vacancy to engage in some form of information-gathering or search exercise. As Pissarides (1985) points out, it had long been recognised by economists that the problem of the selection of the optimal amount of such search was essentially a capital and investment theoretic problem. However, it was not until developments in both human-capital theory and the theory of choice under uncertainty had progressed sufficiently far that formal models of the search process began to appear: most notably the studies by Stigler (1962) and Alchian (1970). Search models have progressed a long way from these early studies and search theory has proved useful in shedding light on a range of issues:

including both the microfoundation of Keynesian theory and Phillips-curve dynamics. In Chapter 3, C. J. McKenna provides a highly accessible review of both the basic model of labour-market search and a range of the various refinements to the basic model which have been proposed in the recent literature.

The inability of standard competitive analysis to provide a convincing explanation for the observed behaviour of wages and employment, in general, and the existence of both involuntary unemployment and rigid money wages, in particular, has led to the development of various so-called implicit-contract theories of the labour market (Baily, 1974; D. F. Gordon, 1974; Azariadis, 1975). Implicit-contract models were first proposed in the early 1970s and the basic idea behind them is that risk-neutral firms provide some degree of insurance to risk-averse workers against fluctuations across time in the workers' marginal productivity. The consequence of this situation is that wages become less flexible than under the hammer of the Walrasian auctioneer and in the extreme case even become totally rigid. The implicit-contract literature has grown very rapidly and in Chapter 4, Alan Manning outlines the major theoretical developments which have taken place and assesses the extent to which implicit-contract theory has proved successful in explaining the observed behaviour of wages and employment.

1.4 TRADE UNIONS AND THE LABOUR MARKET

In 1975, Johnson conducted a survey of the contents of a wide range of professional journals in economics and concluded that the study of trade unions had become a Cinderella topic within the labour-economics literature. This state of affairs however, was soon to change, for by the early 1980s the literature on the economic analysis of trade unions had expanded very rapidly. Several related themes have emerged in this recent trade-union literature and two might be singled out as especially important. First, considerable attention has been directed towards analysing the nature of trade-union objectives, a question earlier considered in the so-called Ross–Dunlop debate of the 1940s and 1950s (for a convenient summary of this debate see Mitchell, 1972) with important results emerging in both the theoretical and empirical contexts (see Oswald, 1982, and Dertouzos and Pencavel, 1981, respectively). Second, following McDonald and Solow's (1981) 'rediscovery' of the efficient bargaining model (originally formulated some three decades earlier by both Leontief, 1946, and Fellner, 1951) with its axiom of Pareto efficiency, considerable attention has been directed towards developing the efficient bargaining model and evaluating its theoretical and empirical performance relative to other models of union behaviour, especially the so-called monopoly-union model (Ashenfelter and Brown, 1986; MaCurdy and Pencavel, 1986). In Chapter 5 Alistair and David Ulph provide a comprehensive review of recent analytical and empirical developments in the economic analysis of trade unions.

Over the past two decades much attention has also been devoted to modelling the bargaining process which takes place between unions and employers, not only in the context of wage determination but also in order to shed light on the reasons why strikes, as breakdowns in union–employer negotiation, occur. Chapter 6 provides a survey of recent work relating to this issue.

1.5 NON-HOMOGENEOUS LABOUR

Arising out of their dissatisfaction with the conventional approach to labour-market analysis (with its emphasis on homogeneous labour and competitive market analysis) several authors have proposed an alternative approach, which subdivides the aggregate labour market into two sorts of submarkets: the primary sector (characterised by high wages, good working conditions, employment stability, job security, heirarchical structure and so forth) and the secondary sector (characterised by low wages, poor working conditions, poor opportunities for advancement, highly variable employment, ease of entry and so on). In Chapter 7 Robert McNabb and Paul Ryan discuss the various alternative segmentation models which have been proposed in the literature and provide a detailed evaluation of the empirical evidence relating to the segmentation hypothesis.

Recognition of the non-homogeneous nature of labour also led economists to direct their attention to the questions of labour-market discrimination. As will be seen in Chapter 8, a number of different views exist regarding the nature and alternative forms of discrimination. The modern economists' analysis of discrimination has its origins in Becker's (1957) model. Although, as will be seen below, Becker's analysis is not without its shortcomings it has nonetheless served as a point of departure for the numerous studies which followed. The post-war period has seen the adoption by a number of countries of policies designed to provide equality of opportunity for people of different races, sex or other group characteristics and Chapter 8 provides a detailed coverage of the rapidly expanding literature on the economics of discrimination which, amongst other things, seeks to evaluate the effectiveness of such equal-opportunity policies.

1.6 MACROECONOMIC ASPECTS

As noted above, labour economics is a discipline of vital concern to other areas of economics, including macroeconomics, and the final two chapters of this book consider some of the major contributions which labour economics has made in the modern macro field. In Chapter 9 George Alogoskoufis explores the role of the labour market in the context of the open economy, and illustrates the interrelationships which exist between wage rigidity, international competitiveness and macroeconomic policy.

Over recent years a number of economists have argued very forcefully that problems of the stagflationary sort can only be solved by altering in a fairly fundamental way the methods by which pay is actually fixed. In the forefront of this field is the proposal that a system of economy-wide profit-sharing be introduced in place of the more traditional system of wage determination (Weitzman, 1984). In the final chapter of this book Saul Estrin and Sushil Wadhwani discuss in detail both the theoretical arguments underlying the proposal for the introduction of a system of profit-related pay and the empirical evidence relating to its effectiveness.

2 Home-Production and the Allocation of Time

ALESSANDRO CIGNO

2.1 INTRODUCTION

The home-production approach to the analysis of household behaviour draws its origins from Gary Becker's insight that market commodities are not consumed in their raw state,[1] but transformed into utility-giving final goods,[2] not transferable from one household to another, by the application of the consumer's own time. For example, a meal at home requires various ingredients and appliances to prepare it, and time in which to prepare and consume it. We may, therefore, think of the good 'home meal' as having been produced by household members using as inputs market commodities and their own time. Such a product will have different characteristics and generally yield different utility from a restaurant meal. Typically, it will also have different monetary and time costs. Its costs and characteristics will also vary according to the number of people involved and to the relationship that exists among them: cooking for two is generally more efficient than cooking for one, and eating alone or in the company of strangers is not the same as sitting down to a family dinner!

The home-production approach has considerable generality and includes as a special case the standard consumer model of microeconomic theory, where commodities bought from the market are assumed to be consumed without any further processing and without any expenditure of the consumer's own time. Another special case is the income–leisure model, widely used in labour economics and macroeconomics, according to which the good 'leisure' is domestically produced by time alone, without any input of commodities. In this chapter we examine the implications of the home-production approach for the allocation of time and, in particular, for the supply of labour.

2.2   ONE-PERSON HOUSEHOLDS

Let us start by considering a person j living on his or her own. For present purposes, we may take the relative market prices of commodities as constant, so that (by Hicks's composite-commodity theorem) we can aggregate all commodities bought by j into a single input, which will be denoted by I_j. Similarly, we shall abstract from the presence of 'lumpy' items of expenditure, to be discussed later, and assume that home-production takes place under constant returns to scale. Marginal costs will then be constant, thus allowing us to treat all home-produced goods as a single output, to be denoted by X_j.

The production possibilities open to j are summed up by the *home-production junction* $F(\ )$, so that

$$X_j = F(H_j, I_j) \tag{2.1}$$

where H_j denotes the amount of time devoted to home-production. Having assumed constant returns and assuming further, that H_j and I_j are both essential to home-production but substitutable for each other at a diminishing marginal rate, it follows that this function is linear-homogeneous and strictly quasi-concave with isoquants that do not cut the axes.

The choice of values for the variables figuring in (2.1) is subject to a number of restrictions. First, they must all be non-negative. Second, home-time must satisfy

$$H_j \leqslant T \tag{2.2}$$

where T is j's total time. Third, the input of commodities (using commodities as *numéraire*) must be equal to income,

$$I_j = w_j L_j + V_j \tag{2.3}$$

where w_j and V_j are, respectively, j's wage rate and property income, expressed in terms of commodities, and L_j is j's labour supply. Finally, since leisure is subsumed in X_j, labour and home-time must add up to T, so that

$$L_j \equiv T - H_j \tag{2.4}$$

In general, j will be interested in both the size and the composition of the home-product, but for our immediate purposes it may be assumed that the output mix is given, so that only the output size remains to be chosen. H_j and I_j will then be chosen so as to maximise (2.1) subject to (2.2) and to a *budget constraint*:

$$w_j H_j + I_j = w_j T + V_j \equiv Y_j \tag{2.5}$$

obtained by substituting (2.4) into (2.3) and rearranging terms. Y_j is j's *full income*.

How will time be allocated? The rate of return to L_j is the market-wage rate w_j. The rate of return to H_j, which we shall call the *shadow-wage rate*, is none other than the marginal rate of substitution of commodities for home-time:

$$w^*_j \equiv \frac{F_H}{F_I} \tag{2.6}$$

where F_H is the marginal product of home-time, and F_I the marginal product of commodities. If the shadow-wage rate exceeds the wage rate for all H_j less than T, then j's time will be used exclusively for home-production, and I_j will be equal to V_j. Otherwise, j will engage in home-production up to the point where w^*_j is equal to w_j, and use the rest of the time to raise income. Therefore, in general:

$$(w^*_j - w_j)(T - H_j) = 0 \tag{2.7}$$

The two possible outcomes are illustrated in Figure 2.1, where the budget constraint is shown as a straight line (truncated at T) and the home-production function is represented by its highest achievable isoquant. In panel (a), the slope of the isoquant at T, w^*_j, is higher than the slope of the budget line (w_j) so the labour supply

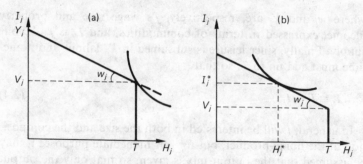

FIGURE 2.1   The allocation of time in one-person households

(L_j) is set equal to zero. In panel (b), by contrast, L_j is positive because the two slopes are equalised before H_j has reached T.

Now suppose that unearned income increases to V_j' (see Figure 2.2). If j's time is already fully committed to home-production $(H_j = T)$, the additional income will be spent entirely to buy more commodities, as shown in Figure 2.2(a). Otherwise, H_j will rise as shown in Figure 2.2(b). I_j will rise too, but by less than $(V_j' - V_j)$, because the unearned income rise is partly offset by a fall in earnings. For small changes in V_j, we may write

$$\frac{V_j}{I_j}\frac{\partial I_j}{\partial V_j} = \frac{V_j}{Y_j}\,\varepsilon_{yi} \qquad \varepsilon_{yi} > 0 \tag{2.8}$$

and

$$\frac{V_j}{H_j}\frac{\partial H_j}{\partial V_j} = \frac{V_j}{Y_j}\,\varepsilon_{yj} \qquad \varepsilon_{yj} \geqslant 0 \tag{2.9}$$

where ε_{yi} and ε_{yj} denote full income elasticities of, respectively, commodities and home-time.

Suppose, next, that the wage rate increases. If (2.2) is binding, then nothing else will happen. Otherwise, I_j will rise because the cross-substitution effect $(I_j' - I_j^\circ)$, and the income effect $(I_j'' - I_j)$ are both positive, while H_j may fall (as in Figure 2.3) or rise, depending on whether the negative substitution effect $(H_j' - H_j^\circ)$ dominates or is dominated by the positive income effect $(H_j'' - H_j')$. But, whether it falls or rises in absolute terms, H_j will always change by less than

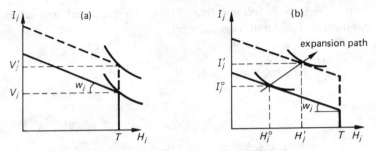

FIGURE 2.2 Changes in unearned income

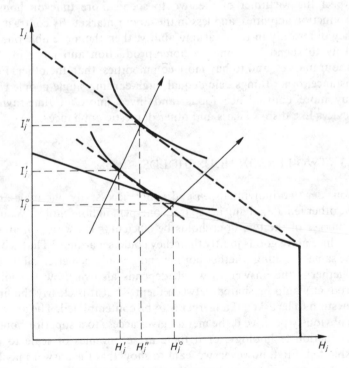

FIGURE 2.3 Changes in wage rates

I_j, from which it follows that X_j will be produced less time-intensively. For small wage changes:

$$\frac{w_j}{I_j} \frac{\partial I_j}{\partial w_j} = \varepsilon_{hi} + \frac{w_j L_j}{Y_j} \varepsilon_{yi}, \qquad \varepsilon_{hi} \geqslant 0, \tag{2.10}$$

and

$$\frac{w_j}{H_j} \frac{\partial H_j}{\partial w_j} = \varepsilon_{hh} + \frac{w_j L_j}{Y_j} \varepsilon_{yj}, \qquad \varepsilon_{hh} \leqslant 0, \tag{2.11}$$

where ε_{hi} and ε_{hh} denote wage-elasticities of, respectively, commodities and home-time, holding the output of goods constant.

Thus, in conclusion, if we compare two single persons differing from each other only in terms of their property income, we can expect the wealthier of the two to spend more time on home-production activities, and less in the labour market. By contrast, if they differ only in their earning ability, then the more able one is likely to spend less time on home-production and more in the labour market, and to buy more commodities, than the other. For instance, other things being equal, high-earning single people will buy more convenience foods, and invest more in time-saving devices like dish-washers and other domestic appliances.

2.3 TWO-PERSON HOUSEHOLDS

Consider two individuals, m and f (not necessarily one male and the other female), living in separate one-person households. Would a merger of the two households be efficient – i.e. would m and f produce more goods jointly than they could separately? That is not the same as asking whether both m and f would be better-off living together – the answer to which depends also on how the joint product would be shared between them – but it is clearly the first question to be asked if a merger is to be contemplated. The answer is obviously positive if the merger gives access to a superior home-production technology, or if there are economies of scale to be exploited. First, however, we want to show that the answer may be positive even if there are no such advantages – i.e. even if the merged household has to operate with exactly the same, constant-returns-to-scale technology already available to each of the one-person households.

Suppose, for example, that m's one-person output, maximised subject to m's one-person budget constraint, is equal to f's, similarly maximised, one-person output. Suppose, further, that V_m is less than V_f, and w_m more than w_f, so that m's efficient one-person input mix is less time-intensive than f's. In Figure 2.4a, m's output is maximised at the point P, with coordinates (H_m^*, I_m^*), and f's at the point Q, with coordinates (H_f^*, I_f^*).

Now, consider the midpoint, R, of the line segment joining P to Q. Since R lies on a higher isoquant, output at that point is higher than at either P or Q. R is unattainable by either m or f acting independently, because it lies above their respective one-person budget constraints (represented by broken lines). It can be reached, however, by the two acting in concert: all they need to do is exchange $\frac{1}{2}(I_m^* - I_f^*)$ of m's income for $\frac{1}{2}(H_f^* - H_m^*)$ of f's time. By collaboration, m and f could thus increase their combined (and, as it happens, individual) output, while still remaining in separate one-person households.[3]

They could do even better, however, by outright merger. To see that, consider a composite household, endowed with $\frac{1}{2}(V_m, V_f)$ units of property income, $\frac{1}{2}T$ units of time attracting the higher wage rate w_m, and $\frac{1}{2}T$ units of time attracting the lower wage rate w_f. Given constant returns to scale, the maximised output of such a household will be half that of the two-person household that would result from the merger. As shown in Figure 2.4a, the composite household will locate itself at point S of its budget boundary (represented by a continuous line) where output is higher than at R. By merging, m and f would thus have more goods to share between them than they would have, even with collaboration, if they stayed apart.

For another example, suppose that m and f have the same wage rate. If they also have the same unearned income, it is obvious that they have nothing to gain from either cooperation or merger. The same would be true – so long as the time constraint were not binding on either of them – if m and f had different property incomes, but still the same wage rate. As shown by Figure 2.4b, if V_f is higher than V_m, and the individual time constraint is at T, then m's one-person output is maximised at P, and f's at Q. Since the input mix is the same at both those points, there is clearly no

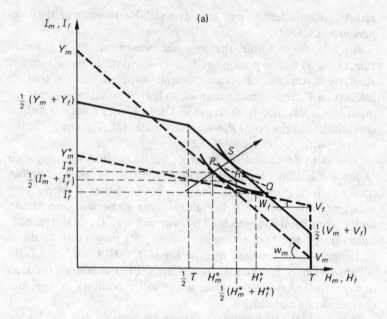

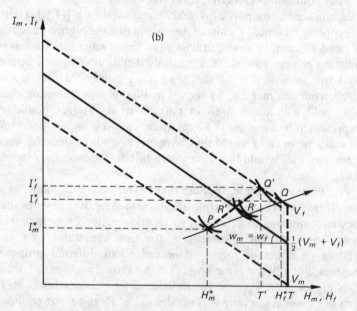

FIGURE 2.4 Two-person households

scope for improving the mix by either exchanging inputs or pooling resources.

Not so, however, if the individual time constraint is at T', and thus binding on f's one-person household. The latter, in this case, maximises its output at Q', where the input mix is less time-intensive than at P. By cooperation, m and f could both move to R', but that would not do them any good, because output at that point is just the arithmetic mean of output at P and Q'.[4] On the other hand, by merging, m and f could jointly produce twice the output associated with point R and thus more than twice that associated with point R'. It is then clear that merger may enhance productivity even in a case where the potential partners differ only in their property endowments.

Notice that, in each of the cases considered, the merged household produces at least as much as the two component households put together. Where it produces more, it is because the parties can pursue their comparative advantages more fully than they could without the merger. That does not mean, however, that the greater efficiency is always associated with greater division of labour between the parties. It was so in the case with w_m greater than w_f, because in that case it was efficient for f to replace m, as far as possible, in home-based activities. It was not so in the case with V_f greater than V_m (and the time constraint at T'), because the whole point of merger, there, was to allow f to do exactly the same as m! In general, however, the efficiency gain is greater where the parties to the merger have different comparative advantages.

Let us now look at the allocation of time in a two-person household in more general terms. The joint output of goods is determined by

$$X_{mf} = F(H_{mf}, I_{mf})$$ (2.12)

where

$$H_{mf} = H_m + H_f$$ (2.13)

denotes the joint input of home-time, and I_{mf} the joint input of commodities. The two household members will have a common interest in maximising (2.12), subject to the time constraints (2.2) for $j = m, f$, and to the joint budget constraint

$$w_m H_m + w_f H_f + I_{mf} = V_m + V_f + (w_m + w_f)T \equiv Y_m + Y_f \qquad (2.14)$$

A solution will again satisfy (2.7), for $j = m,f$. As in one-person households, an individual will thus participate in both market and home activities if and only if that individual's wage and shadow-wage rates are equal. In a two-person household, however, it is possible that *one* member will have a wage rate higher than the shadow-wage rate (common to both members of the household) and will thus specialise completely in paid work, leaving all the domestic chores to the other. That would obviously be impossible in a one-person household.

Figure 2.5 illustrates the possible outcomes for the case where the household members have different wage rates. We shall continue to assume that w_m is the larger of the two, but only the subscripts would need to change if the opposite were true. In panel (a), the efficient level of the joint home-time is H_{mf}^*, less than T, and

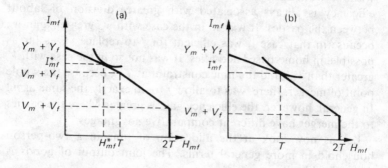

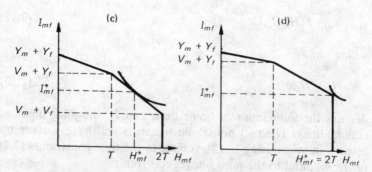

FIGURE 2.5 Specialisation in two-person households

$$w_f = w_f^* = w_m^* < w_m \tag{2.15}$$

Since the cheaper time will be used first in the home, this means that m specialises completely in paid work ($L_m = T$), while f spends some time at home ($H_f = H_{mf}^*$) and some in the market ($L_f = T - H_{mf}^*$). In panel (b), H_{mf}^* equals T, and

$$w_f < w_f^* = w_m^* < w_m \tag{2.16}$$

Here, both members are fully specialised: f at home($H_f = T$) and m in the market ($L_m = T$). In panel (c), H_{mf}^* is more than T but less than $2T$, and

$$w_f < w_f^* = w_m^* = w_m \tag{2.17}$$

Hence, f is fully specialised in home work ($H_f = T$), while m spends some time at home ($H_m = H_{mf}^* - T$) and some in paid work ($L_m = 2T - H_{mf}^*$). In panel (d), finally, H_{mf}^* is equal to $2T$, and

$$w_f < w_m < w_f^* = w_m^* \tag{2.18}$$

There, m and f have so much property between them, that they can both dedicate themselves exclusively to home activities ($H_m = H_f = T$).

In the case where m and f command the same wage rate, the only possibility is

$$w_f = w_m < w_f^* = w_m^* \tag{2.19}$$

in which case both partners are fully specialised in home-production. What we could not have is a situation where the common wage rate is greater than the common shadow-wage rate, because both household members would then specialise completely in paid work, and no goods would be produced. Nor would there be any point, in the absence of scale economies, in setting up a two-person household if the common wage rate were equal to the common shadow-wage rate, because both partners would then be sharing equally in both activities, and thus producing no more than they could produce separately. In conclusion, *at least one* household member will always be fully specialised in one or other of the two activities.

A rise in either V_m or V_f will lift the budget constraint, increasing I_{mf} and, unless both partners are fully specialised in home production, H_{mf}. A rise in the lower of the two wage rates, w_f, will rotate the first segment of the budget-line clockwise (see Figure 2.6). Therefore, H_{mf} and I_{mf} will be affected if f participates in both home and market activities, but not otherwise. A rise in w_m, on the other hand, will rotate the whole budget-line (see Figure 2.7). Therefore, both H_{mf} and I_{mf} may be affected as long as at least one member of the household does some paid work. While a rise in property income is likely to reduce the household's total labour supply $(L_m + L_f)$, it is thus clear that a wage rise may or may not increase it, and that the effect may be different according to which of the two wage rates has changed.

2.4 SEXUAL DIVISION OF LABOUR

Now imagine a situation where the merger of two individual households enlarges the set of home-production possibilities. Suppose, in other words, that the members of this two-person household can not only produce more of the same goods that they could produce on their own, but also produce other goods (companionship, familiarity, love, children) that they could not produce on their own. A simple way of formalising this idea is to write

$$H_{mf} = G^{mf}(H_m, H_f) > H_m + H_f \qquad (2.20)$$

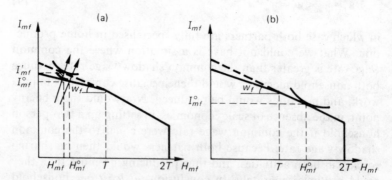

FIGURE 2.6 Two-person households and wage changes: case 1

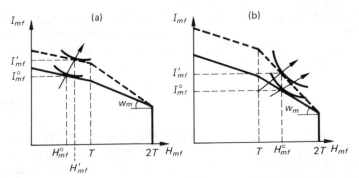

FIGURE 2.7 Two-person households and wage changes: case 2

where $G^{mf}(\ )$ may be interpreted as another kind of home-production function.[5] It is thus as if m and f produced first an intermediate good H_{mf} by time alone in accordance with (2.20) and then combined that with commodities to produce final goods in accordance with (2.12).

We shall concentrate our attention on a special type of two-person household, the conventional nuclear family, consisting initially of a man, m, and a woman, f (here, gender matters). Such a household type lies at the opposite end of the spectrum from the purely business-like arrangement examined in the last section, where the only advantage of communal living was to replace the individual budget constraints with a less-restricting joint budget. But much of what follows applies also to the in-between cases (close friendships, loose marriages).

Suppose that $G^{mf}(\ )$ has the same general properties as $F(\ )$, including the one that both inputs, while substitutable for each other at a diminishing rate, are essential to production. That immediately rules out the possibility of either partner choosing to specialise completely in market work (or how would they keep each other company, let alone have children?). Unlike $F(\ )$, however, $G^{mf}(\ )$ is specific to those particular m and f: a different pair, with different personal characteristics, might relate differently, or not at all (in which case the joint home-time would be just the sum of its parts).

Given (2.12) and (2.20) m and f will again have a common interest in making their output of final goods as large as possible, subject to a time constraint (2.2) for each of them, and to the common budget constraint (2.14). As in the situation examined in the last section, an output-maximising allocation of time will again satisfy (2.7) for $j = m,f$. But, since the shadow-wage rates are now given by

$$w_j^* = \frac{F_H}{F_I} \, G_j^{mf} \tag{2.21}$$

where G_j^{mf} is the marginal product of H_j in terms of H_{mf}, there is no reason, in general, why w_m^* should be equal to w_f^*. Consequently, it does not necessarily follow that at least one of the partners must specialise completely in one activity.

The organisation of home-production can be better understood if we break the optimisation process into two stages. We start by looking for the time-mix that minimises the income foregone $(w_m H_m + w_f H_m)$ in order to attain a desired level of intermediate production H_{mf}, subject to (2.20), and to (2.2) for $j = m,f$. A solution to this cost-minimising exercise will either equate the marginal rate of technical substitution of H_m for H_f to the wage ratio,

$$\frac{G_m^{mf}}{G_f^{mf}} = \frac{w_m}{w_f} \tag{2.22}$$

or set the time of at least one of the partners equal to T. The possibilities are illustrated in Figure 2.8, where the curve is the isoquant of $G^{mf}(\ )$ corresponding to the desired output of the intermediate good, H_{mf}.

In panel (a), the isoquant is symmetric around the 45°-line, implying that m and f are interchangeable in their domestic roles. In that case, the partners will share domestic activities equally between them (point P) if their wage rates are the same, unequally (e.g. at point Q) if not. But, there is no reason to expect that male and female domestic roles are indeed interchangeable – think, for example, of the woman's role in child-bearing.

In panel (b), by contrast, it is assumed that her home-time can be more readily substituted for his, than his for hers. Consequently, it would be efficient for her to spend more time at home than him (e.g. to locate at point Q) even if her wage rate were equal to his, and for both to contribute equal shares (point P) only if w_f were sufficiently higher than w_m.[6]

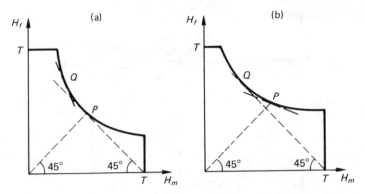

FIGURE 2.8 Organisation of home production

Now let $W^{mf}(H_{mf}, w_m, w_f)$ denote the minimised cost of H_{mf}, at the given values of w_m and w_f. Its partial derivative with respect to w_j, W_j^{mf}, is the demand for H_j conditional on the stated value of H_{mf}. The partial derivative with respect to H_{mf}, $w_{mf} \equiv W_H^{mf}$, is the marginal cost (in lost income) of H_{mf}. We can thus think of w_{mf} as the 'price' charged by the household department producing the intermediate good to the household department producing the final good.

Given constant returns, w_{mf} is independent of H_{mf} up to the point where H_f is fully used for home-production. This is shown in Figure 2.9, where H_m and H_f are combined in the same proportion, satisfying (2.22), and the income foregone thus rises in proportion to H_{mf}, up to the point $\bar{H}_{mf} \equiv G^{mf}(\bar{H}_m, T)$. Further increases in the intermediate output are possible only by raising the ratio of H_m to H_f, and thus pushing their marginal rate of technical substitution below the wage ratio. If H_{mf} is raised beyond $\bar{H}_{mf}$, its marginal cost will then rise until, at $\bar{\bar{H}}_{mf} \equiv G^{mf}(T, T)$, H_{mf} can grow no more, and w_{mf} goes to infinity. Clearly, w_{mf} is increasing in both w_m and w_f up to $H_{mf} = \bar{H}_{mf}$, but independent of w_f beyond that.

We now look for the combination of commodities and joint home-time that makes the output of final goods as large as possible. The second stage of the optimisation process is to maximise (2.12), subject to the budget constraint, which can now be written as

$$W^{mf}(H_{mf}, w_m, w_f) + I_{mf} = Y_m + Y_f \qquad (2.14')$$

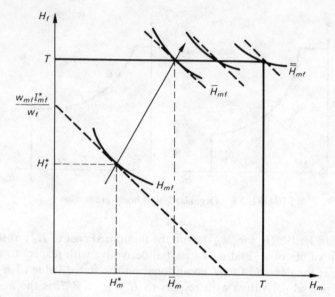

FIGURE 2.9 Organisation of home production: stage 1

At a maximum output point, either the marginal rate of technical substitution of H_{mf} for I_{mf} is equal to the marginal cost of the intermediate product,

$$\frac{F_H}{F_I} = w_{mf} \tag{2.23}$$

or the time of at least one of the partners is entirely committed to home-production. That is illustrated in Figure 2.10, where the concave-to-the-origin curve, with absolute slope w_{mf}, represents the budget constraint, and the convex-to-the-origin curve is an iso-quant of $F(\ )$. Efficiency may require both partners to share in both market and home activities as in panel (a), or f to dedicate herself completely to the latter as in panels (b) and (c), or both to do so as in panel (d), but in no circumstances will either of them specialise completely in the former.

Finally, we look for the effects of changes in V_j or w_j. A rise in property income lifts the budget line. I_{mf} thus increases, as does H_j if $j = m, f$ is not already fully committed to homely pursuits. For small changes in V_j:

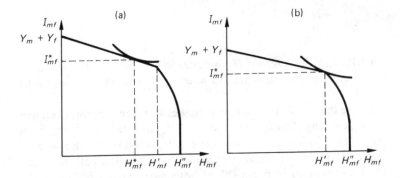

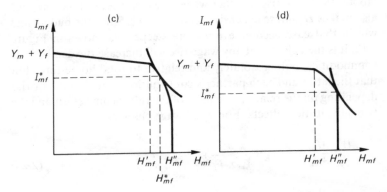

FIGURE 2.10   **Organisation of home production: stage 2**

$$\frac{V_j}{I_{mf}}\frac{\partial I_{mf}}{\partial V_j} = \frac{V_j}{Y_m + Y_f}\,\varepsilon_{yi} \tag{2.24}$$

$$\frac{V_j}{H_m}\frac{\partial H_m}{\partial V_j} = \frac{V_j}{Y_m + Y_f}\frac{\gamma_m}{\varepsilon_m}\,\varepsilon_{yh} \tag{2.25}$$

and

$$\frac{V_j}{H_f}\frac{\partial H_f}{\partial V_j} = \frac{V_j}{Y_m + Y_f}\frac{\gamma_f}{\varepsilon_f}\,\varepsilon_{yh} \tag{2.26}$$

where $\varepsilon_{yh} \geqslant 0$ and $\varepsilon_{yi} > 0$ are the full-income elasticities of H_{mf} and I_{mf}, respectively, $\gamma_j \geqslant 0$ is the elasticity of w_{mf} to w_j, and

$$\varepsilon_j \equiv \frac{w_j H_j}{w_{mf} H_{mf}} \tag{2.27}$$

Clearly, ε_{yh} will be zero if H_{mf} is equal to $\bar{H}_{mf}$, while γ_j will be equal to either ε_j or zero according to whether H_j is less than or equal to T.

A rise in w_f, if H_f is less than T, makes H_f more expensive relative to H_m, causing the expansion path of H_{mf} to rotate clockwise as in panel (a) of Figure 2.11. Conversely, if H_m is less than T, a rise in w_m makes H_f relatively cheaper, causing the expansion path to rotate the other way as in panel (b). If both partners participate in the labour market, a rise in either wage rate increases full income, but also makes H_{mf} more expensive relative or Y_m. Since the budget line will in that case become everywhere steeper, as shown in Figure 2.12, it is then clear that any wage rise will increase the demand for commodities, both absolutely and relative to total home-time, but that the latter and each partner's contribution to it may fall or rise depending on the relative strengths of the full-income effect and the two substitution effects. For small wage changes:

$$\frac{W_m}{I_m} \frac{\vartheta I_{mf}}{\vartheta w_m} = \gamma_m \varepsilon_{hi} + \frac{w_m L_f}{Y_m + Y_f} \varepsilon_{yi} \tag{2.28}$$

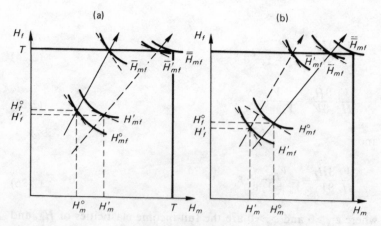

FIGURE 2.11   A rise in w_f

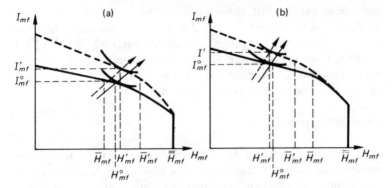

FIGURE 2.12 A rise in either w_m or w_f

$$\frac{W_m}{H_m} \frac{\partial H_m}{\partial w_m} = \frac{\gamma_m}{\varepsilon_m} \left[\gamma_m \varepsilon_{hh} + \frac{w_m L_m}{Y_m + Y_f} \varepsilon_{yh} \right] + \eta_{mm} \qquad (2.29)$$

$$\frac{w_m}{H_f} \frac{\partial H_f}{\partial w_m} = \frac{\gamma_f}{\varepsilon_f} \left[\gamma_m \varepsilon_{hh} + \frac{w_m L_m}{Y_m + Y_f} \varepsilon_{yh} \right] + \eta_{mf} \qquad (2.30)$$

$$\frac{w_f}{I_{mf}} \frac{\partial I_{mf}}{\partial w_f} = \gamma_f \varepsilon_{hi} + \frac{w_f L_f}{Y_m + Y_f} \varepsilon_{yi} \qquad (2.31)$$

$$\frac{w_f}{H_f} \frac{\partial H_f}{\partial w_f} = \frac{\gamma_f}{\varepsilon_f} \left[\gamma_f \varepsilon_{hh} + \frac{w_f L_f}{Y_m + Y_f} \varepsilon_{yh} \right] + \eta_{ff} \qquad (2.32)$$

and

$$\frac{w_f}{H_m} \frac{\partial H_m}{\partial w_d} = \frac{\gamma_m}{\varepsilon_m} \left[\gamma_f \varepsilon_{hh} + \frac{w_f L_f}{Y_m + Y_f} \varepsilon_{yh} \right] + \eta_{fm} \qquad (2.33)$$

where $\varepsilon_{hh} \leqslant 0$ denotes again the elasticity of H_{mf} to w_{mf}, and $\varepsilon_{hi} > 0$ the cross elasticity of I_{mf} to w_{mf}, holding X_{mf} constant, while $\eta_{jj} \leqslant 0$ represents the elasticity of H_j to w_j, and $\eta_{jk} \geqslant 0$ the cross-elasticity of H_k to w_j, holding H_{mf} constant $(j,k = m,f)$.

Suppose that γ_f is greater than γ_m (and thus η_{ff} more negative than η_{mm}) – in other words, that the isoquants of $G^{mf}(\ )$ look like the one in Figure 2.8b. Suppose, also, that w_f is no greater than w_m. If w_f is so low (or y_f so high) that f is completely specialised in home production, then a small wage change will have no effect on her labour supply. But, if both partners participate in the labour market, then (2.29) and (2.32) tell us that her own-wage elasticity of home-time is more negative than his. Similarly, (2.30) and (2.33) tell us that his cross-wage elasticity of home-time is more positive than hers, and (2.28) and (2.31) that her wage elasticity of commodity demand is more positive than his.

Some implications

A number of important implications flow from these theoretical results. One is that if married women have a comparative advantage in home-production over their husbands ($\gamma_f > \gamma_m$ and $w_f \leqslant w_m$), then their labour supply will be zero up to a certain wage level. Once that threshold is cleared, however, their labour supply will rise proportionately more in response to a rise in wage rates for women than the labour supply of their husbands would in response to a rise in wage rates for men. Furthermore, the labour supply as a whole will be more responsive to changes in wage rates for females than in those for males. Such a phenomenon is well-documented, suggesting that the comparative advantage in question – whatever its causes – does exist.[7]

The elasticity differential and threshold effect help to explain why the gradual rise of wage rates for females towards equality with wage rates for males in industrialised countries has brought with it such a drastic narrowing of the gap between male and female labour market participation rates.[8] It also helps to explain the very rapid diffusion of convenience foods and domestic time-saving appliances, and the sharp fall in time-consuming activities, such as having children,[9] since the Second World War.

Yet another implication of the elasticity differential between married men and women is that a government interested in maximising tax revenues (or minimising the distortionary consequences of any desired level of tax revenue) should tax married men's earnings more heavily than those of married women.[10] Fiscal practices such as 'income splitting', whereby each spouse's taxable income is equal to half the couple's joint income, should therefore be abandoned. On the other hand, if married women's marginal tax rates were reduced, that would be equivalent to a rise in wage rates for females and thus accentuate the move away from time-intensive activities like child-rearing, and that may be thought undesirable. Optimal taxation, in a context where parents decide how many children to have and when to have them, is a difficult business.[11]

2.5 SCALE ECONOMIES AND TRANSACTION COSTS

Economies of scale, or increasing returns, are usually modelled by directly postulating a cost-function concave in output, or a production-function convex in any linear combination of inputs. That, however, does not throw much light on the mechanisms whereby inputs might be better utilised in larger units. Rather than follow that route, therefore, we shall maintain the assumption that $F(\ )$ is linear-homogeneous, and model particular sources of scale economies explicitly.

One such source, division of labour, we have already examined in some detail. Another has to do with items of household expenditure – the house itself, some of the furniture, domestic appliances, etc. – which from the point of view of members of the same household have 'public good' characteristics. Where such items are present, the per-capita cost of any desired level of per-capita output may decrease as the number of household members increases.

In order to separate savings made possible by cost-sharing, from efficiency gains associated with division of labour, we shall now assume that all members of the same household are identical. Indeed, since everyone will be doing the same things, we shall dispense with person-identifying subscripts altogether. Thus, I will now be used to stand for the per-capita income and expenditure of the household in question, H for the per-capita level of home-time, and $X = F(H,I)$ for the per-capita output of goods. N will denote the number of household members.

Total household expenditure is not, in general, NI, but

$$E = N^\gamma I, \qquad 0 \leqslant \gamma \leqslant 1 \tag{2.34}$$

where γ may be interpreted as a *congestion* parameter: the smaller γ, the greater scope for cost-sharing. If γ equals zero, that means that the commodities bought by the household are pure public goods (I equals E, whatever N). If γ equals unity, it means that those commodities are pure private goods (I is equal to the Nth part of E).

For any given N, the per-capita cost of X, $(Hw + IN^{\gamma-1})$, is minimised where either H is equal to T, or the common shadow-wage rate is equal to the opportunity-cost of home-time:

$$w^* \equiv \frac{F_H}{F_I} = wN^{1-\gamma} \tag{2.35}$$

Let $C(w,N,X)$ denote the minimum cost of producing X, in a household of N members, if the market wage rate is w. By the envelope theorem,

$$C_N = -(1-\gamma)I\,N^{\gamma-2} \tag{2.36}$$

Therefore, if γ is less than unity, the minimum cost of X falls as N rises.

In the absence of other considerations, the efficient household size would thus be either indeterminate (if $\gamma = 1$) or arbitrarily large (if $\gamma < 1$). One way of making the household size finite and determinate is to bring into the picture *transaction costs*. If two or more people are contemplating setting up home together, they must spend time and money finding out about one another first, and then negotiating the division of tasks and distribution of goods. These initial transaction costs will recur every time that something new is learned about a member's capabilities, or that there is a change in market prices (wages). Additional transaction costs will arise from the need to check that every member keeps to the agreements, and to punish defaulters.[12]

Transaction costs rise with the size and complexity of the organisation which generates them. They will thus increase with the degree of diversity among household members, and with household size. Assuming that per-capita transaction costs increase in proportion to N, say by a factor of t, total costs per person will then be minimised at $N = 1$ if γ is unity, or where

$$-C_N = t \tag{2.37}$$

if γ is less than unity the lower t, the larger N (Figure 2.13). If w increases, per capita income expenditure I will be substituted for H

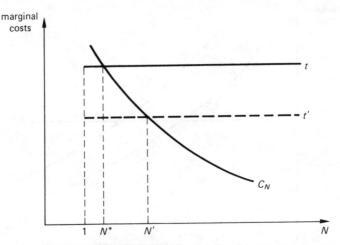

FIGURE 2.13 Household size and transaction costs

in the production of X. For γ less than unity, C_N will then rise in size, and the optimal N will become larger (Figure 2.14).

Another way of determining the household size is to postulate that the utility of each household member, denoted by U, depends directly on N, as well as X,

$$U = U(X,N) \qquad (2.38)$$

This line of argument is associated with Ermisch (1981) who assumes that U increases with N up to a certain point, where companionship turns into an intrusion on privacy, and then decreases. Although not substantially different from the transaction cost approach – all it does is measure the cost of increasing household size directly in terms of utility, rather than of commodities – its comparative statics implications can be quite different.

Maximising (2.38) subject to the per-capita budget constraint,

$$C(w,N,X) = V + wT \equiv Y , \qquad (2.39)$$

requires that the marginal rate of substitution of X for N be equated to the negative of the opportunity cost of privacy:

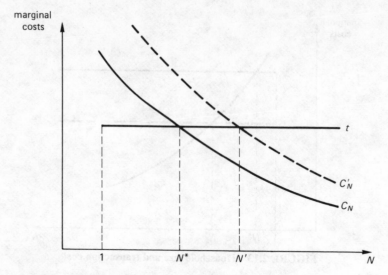

FIGURE 2.14 **Household size and transaction costs: the effect of a wage increase**

$$\frac{U_N}{U_X} = \frac{C_N}{C_X} \tag{2.40}$$

where C_X is the marginal cost of X. As illustrated in Figure 2.15a, if γ is unity, the per-capita consumption of home-produced goods is independent of household size, and there is thus no point in expanding the household size beyond where people cease to be a good (i.e. where the marginal rate of substitution of N for X is zero). If, on the other hand, there is scope for cost sharing ($\gamma < 1$), as in Figure 2.15b, then it is worth trading some privacy for other goods.

Now consider the effect of a wage increase. As the opportunity-cost of home-time rises with w, per capita expenditure I will be substituted for H in the production of X. The marginal cost of home-produced goods will consequently rise less than the full income. If there is no scope for domestic cost-sharing ($\gamma = 1$), however, the opportunity-cost of privacy is identically zero. As shown in Figure 2.16a, N is then unaffected by the wage change. If, on the other hand, there is scope for cost-sharing ($\gamma < 1$), then the opportunity-cost of privacy is positive and may increase or de-

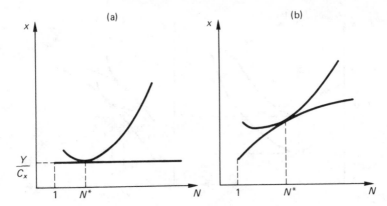

FIGURE 2.15 Utility maximisation and household size

crease.[13] If it decreases, as in Figure 2.16b, the substitution effect on N is negative and, since the full-income effect is also negative because N is a 'bad'; household size will definitely fall. If the opportunity-cost of privacy increases, the substitution and the full-income effect have opposite sign, but the net result *may* still be a fall in N as shown in Figure 2.16c.

The empirical evidence suggests that household size decreases as real wages rise.[14] In other words, higher earners tend to have smaller households, and generalised wage rises tend to reduce the size of the average household. It may consequently be inferred that cost-sharing is a consideration in household formation, and that there is some degree of substitutability between privacy and other goods.

2.6 CONCLUSION

The home-production approach to the analysis of household behaviour yields a number of interesting insights that cannot be obtained by more conventional methods. One area where the approach is particularly fruitful is, as we have seen, that of time allocation in multi-person households, and of differential responses to wage changes by persons of different sex. Another important area of application, very fully explored by Becker (1960, 1981) and many others, but barely touched upon here, is that of

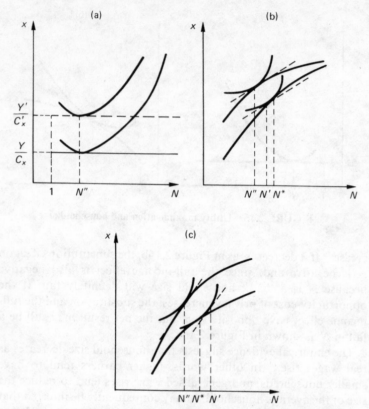

FIGURE 2.16 Utility maximisation and household size: the effect of a wage
increase

fertility decisions and their interactions with female labour-market
participation (see also Willis, 1973, and Cigno, 1983, 1986).
Nevertheless we have explored the approach in sufficient depth to
gain some appreciation of how this framework can permit us to use
economic analysis to gain insights into several important features
of the labour market.

3 The Theory of Search in Labour Markets

C. J. McKENNA

3.1 INTRODUCTION

This chapter studies the main results of the theory of search in labour markets. Since most work in the literature is concerned with job search by workers, this will also be our main concern. Perhaps because of the technical difficulties involved in formulating models of job search, all but the most elementary ideas associated with the approach are omitted from undergraduate labour-economics textbooks. This is a pity, since job-search models have proved a useful vehicle for the study of a variety of problems and, once the veneer of theoretical abstraction has been penetrated, the results are readily explained.

The most natural context for search arises in markets in which agents have incomplete information about market opportunities. In such markets, and if circumstances allow it, an amount of search and 'shopping' around is justified so that information is improved and also so that the best alternatives may be located. Search activity is clearly missing from most market analyses studied by undergraduates. The reasons for this are the assumption of complete certainty and the 'static' or 'single-period' nature of many of the problems. The classic topic of labour supply which figures prominently in all labour texts is an example. The analysis is single-period (how many hours of work to supply in a day) and there is no uncertainty (in particular the wage rate available is known). Search theory is therefore characterised by uncertainty and dynamics, extending over several periods.

The aims of this chapter are twofold. The idea is both to give a flavour of the basic search model, its derivation and results, and to leave the reader with a clear impression of the problems and issues which continue to attract interest in this area.

The first of these aims forms the substance of the following section in which the basic approaches to and results of job-search theory are outlined. The elemental job-search model describes the behaviour of an unemployed worker faced with a distribution of wage offers from which the searcher attempts to find the largest such offer, given that search is costly. Various refinements of the basic model are studied in turn.

3.2 JOB SEARCH BY WORKERS

We start by considering two plausible characteristics of job-search by workers. Abstract characterisations are necessary because, in practice, workers are faced with a large number of job-search methods. Typically, no single method is used and so a combination of visits to Jobcentres, thumbing through newspapers, personal enquiries and personal contacts are used. Stripped to essentials, however, search methods used in practice have several features in common. First, there is an element of 'sampling': that is, because of the impossibility of locating all job offers in reasonable time, a decision must be made as to which firms are to be approached. Should you follow up a particular newspaper advertisement first, or a tip from a friend, or try a casual enquiry? Second, there is the problem of how many firms to sample and how intensive search is to be. This, of course, is related to how costly search is. The 'amount' of search is best thought of as having two dimensions – one *intensive* and the other *extensive*. If we think of time as being divided into equal intervals or 'periods' (days, weeks, etc.) then we may associate the *intensity* of search with the amount of activity within a period, whilst we associate the *extensive* dimension with the number of periods over which search is to be carried out. The amount of search, in both these senses, is in general endogenous and governed by the perceived benefits of search relative to search cost.

Whilst a host of subsidiary questions need to be answered when constructing a search model (such as the worker's objective, the total permissible time-horizon and so on) the issues of 'sampling' and the amount of search seem to be central. To make things more concrete, consider the following story.

Before setting out on a day's searching an individual decides on how many firms to approach before calling off the search. We assume that the firms are sufficiently close together geographically so as to make it possible to sample a very large number during the course of a day. Moreover, we assume that the individual is concerned not merely with finding a vacancy, but with finding a job offering a high wage – the higher the wage, the better. Since the searcher has decided that a job must be chosen by the end of the day's search, the problem is obviously to choose the number of firms to be sampled and then to select the highest wage from amongst the firms approached. Search is the only way of finding out any particular firm's wage offer, although the *distribution* of offers is assumed to be known, and it costs a fixed known amount to sample each firm. In the absence of further guides on which firm to choose, the searcher selects the sample *randomly*. Once the desired number of firms has been approached, and only then, does the worker select the highest wage offer (at no additional cost) and on application to the firm is certain to be offered the job.

Although highly stylised (and even contrived), this story at least contains the key ingredients that we might expect to motivate search. There are costs of search but also gains to search represented by the wage offer distribution. Furthermore we expect intuitively that larger sample sizes are more likely to contain higher wages and hence offer greater expected rewards. A simple numerical example from Joll *et al.* (1983) will serve to illustrate how the costs and (expected) returns to search combine to determine the best or *optimal* sample size for the searcher to take.

Suppose that there are 155 firms in a locality offering weekly wages of between £120 and £160. Table 3.1 shows the assumed distribution. Column (1) shows the weekly wages on offer, column (2) the number of firms offering each wage and finally, since each firm is selected randomly the relative frequency of each wage is interpreted as the probability of obtaining each wage, $Pr(W)$.

Table 3.1 provides all the information required to calculate the expected return to search – hence the importance of knowing the wage-offer distribution. Given the nature of the search process assumed – random selection of a fixed number – the problem is to

TABLE 3.1   Costs and returns to search

(1) Weekly wage, W(£)	(2) Number of firms	(3) Relative frequency, or $Pr(W)$
120	2	$2/155 = 0.0129$
125	7	$7/155 = 0.0452$
130	14	$14/155 = 0.0903$
135	28	$28/155 = 0.1806$
140	40	$40/155 = 0.2581$
145	26	$26/155 = 0.1677$
150	20	$20/155 = 0.1290$
155	15	$15/155 = 0.0968$
160	3	$3/155 = 0.0194$
	155	1.0000

choose the size of sample which gives the greatest *expected* return net of search costs. For each possible sample size, we need to calculate the expected return. Several things require clarification here. First each sample size has associated with it an *expected* return. Selecting a particular sample size does not guarantee a unique return. For example, consider a sample of size 1. From Table 3.1 we see that *any* of the wages in column (1) could constitute our sample depending on the 'luck of the draw'. We may be lucky enough to draw £160 or unlucky enough to draw £120. But what can we *expect* to obtain by sampling the distribution randomly once? This expected return is simply the expected (or *mean*) value of the distribution, $E(W)$. The formula for the mean, using elementary statistics, is:

$$E(W) = \sum_{i=1}^{9} [W_i \, Pr(W = W_i)]$$
$$= 141.2225$$

Although £141.2225 is not available in the market, we infer from this that a single sample of size one can be expected to offer a wage of £140. We develop the idea of the expected value further presently.

A second issue is the nature of the *return* contained in a sample of whatever size. Our story tells us that the searcher is only

interested in the *maximum* wage in any given sample. The expected
return of interest then relates to the expected maximum of samples
of any given size. We denote this quantity as $E(\max\ W|n)$ (reads;
expected maximum wage given samples of size n). In the case of
samples of size 1, the maximum wage is the only wage in the sample
and so:

$$E(\max\ W|n=1) = E(W) = £141.2225$$

To calculate other expected sample maxima we proceed as
follows. Consider samples of size 2 and list all possible samples.
Column (1) of Table 3.2 does this for selected samples. Taking
account of order and assuming sampling with replacement calculate the probability of drawing each sample. In the case of the
sample (120, 125) the probability is the product,
$\Pr(W=120) \times \Pr(W=125) = 0.0129 \times 0.0452 = 0.00058308$. Table
3.2, column 2 shows some of the results.

TABLE 3.2   Expected maximum wage offer from samples of size 2

(1) Wages in samples of size 2	(2) Probability of sample	(3) Maximum wage of each sample	(4) (2) × (3)
(120 , 120)	0.00016641	120	0.0199692
(120 , 125)	0.00058308	125	0.0728850
(125 , 120)	0.00058308	125	0.0728850
(125 , 130)	0.00116487	130	0.1514331
(130 , 125)	0.00116487	130	0.1514331
.	.	.	.
.	.	.	.
(160 , 160)	0.00037636	160	0.0602176
	1.00000000	$E(\max\ w|n=2) = 146.0451200$	

Column (4) takes the product of the probability of each sample
and the maximum wage in each sample. The sum of all items in this
column represents the quantity of interest – the expected maximum
wage offer from samples of size 2. (We have omitted most of the
possible samples as there are 81 possible samples of size 2.)

A similar procedure is possible for samples of size 3, 4 and so on, although the computations become more cumbersome and require a short computer programme to complete in reasonable time. Table 3.3 produces the expected maximum of samples up to size 4, in colum (2).

Notice from Table 3.3 that the expected maximum wage from samples of size 2 is larger than that from samples of size 1, or

$$E(\max W|n=2) > E(\max W|n=1)$$

so that our intuition about increased (expected) benefits from increased sample size is correct. Clearly, as n becomes larger, $E(\max W|n)$ will approach £160 – the highest wage available. Notice however from Table 3.3 that the *additional* expected return to increasing the sample size falls so that there are diminishing marginal returns to increasing the sample size.

We have explored here the possible returns from taking samples of varying sizes although the searcher's actual choice will be constrained by the search costs. We may model costs quite simply by assuming that each selection involves a fixed known cost c. Hence a sample of size 2 costs $2c$ whilst a sample of size 4 costs $4c$ and so on. For the purposes of our example we have selected $c = £2$. The total search cost for each sample is shown in column (3) of Table 3.3. The final column shows the net expected return for each sample size, $R(n)$. The searcher maximises $R(n)$ at $n = 3$. Denote

TABLE 3.3   Expected maximum wage offer from samples up to size 4

(1) Sample size, n	(2) $E(\max W/n)$	(3) Search cost, cn	(4) Expected net return $R(n)$, (2)–(3)
1	141.2225	2	139.2225
2	146.0451	4	142.0451
3	148.4724	6	142.4724
4	150.0097	8	142.0097
.	.	.	.
.	.	.	.
.	.	.	.

this 'best' or 'optimal' sample size by n^*, then the maximum the individual can expect to obtain from searching is achieved by sampling just three firms during the course of the day and the expected maximum return thereby generated is:

$$R(n^*) = £142.47$$

Given the search procedure, this is the best the individual can do. The determination of n^*, shown in Figure 3.1 is where the (positive) gap between $E[\max W|n]$ and cn is largest. (Note that the curves in Figure 3.1 are 'smooth', suggesting that n takes a continuum of values rather than being an integer. This simplification is of little consequence and does not materially alter the main conclusions of the model.) It is apparent that the optimal amount of search equates (as nearly as possible) the marginal cost of one additional selection, c, with the marginal expected return, $E(\max W|n) - E(\max W|n-1)$; this is suggested by the equality of the slope of the total cost curve and the slope of the expected maximum wage curve.

It is natural to ask how the optimal amount of search changes with changes in the market environment. The effects of two changes are easily verified in the model. First an increase in the (marginal) search cost, c, reduces the amount of search-lowering,

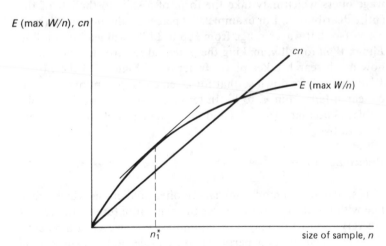

FIGURE 3.1 Optimal search

n^*. Given unchanged opportunities offered by the distribution of wage offers an increase in the search cost will clearly make search less worthwhile. The most direct way to see this is to consider Figure 3.2, where initially the amount of search is n_0^* when the search cost is c_0 and then falls to n_1^* as the search cost increases to c_1.

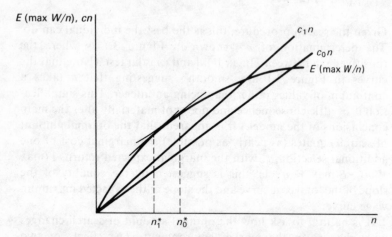

FIGURE 3.2 Optimal search and an increase in search cost

Second we may envisage a general (and *real*) deterioration in wage offers which may take the form of a shift to the left of the entire distribution. For example a 20 percent reduction in *all* (real) wages (so that wages range from £96 to £128) will lead to a fall in $E[\max W|n]$ for all n, making the potential rewards less no matter how much search takes place. In terms of Figure 3.3 the $E(\max W|n)$ curve shifts down so that for given costs the optimal amount of search falls from n_0^* to n_1^*. In terms of our numerical example, Table 3.3 becomes Table 3.4 and the optimal sample size falls from three to two.

Reservation wages

This simple search model appears to offer predictions which are in line with intuition and moreover the general nature of the results are very robust to changes in assumptions. However, a moment's thought reveals that the particular search rule – take the maximum from a predetermined sample of size n – is not a satisfactory

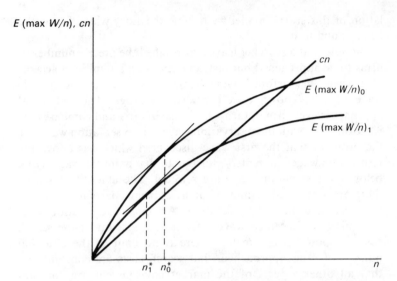

FIGURE 3.3   **Optimal search and a reduction in wages**

TABLE 3.4   **Expected maximum wage offers and a reduction in wages**

(1) Sample size, n	(2) $E(\max W|n)$	(3) Search cost, cn	(4) Expected return $R(n)$, (2)–(3)
1	112.9780	2	110.9780
2	116.8361	4	112.8361
3	118.7779	6	112.7779
4	120.0078	8	112.0078
.	.	.	.
.	.	.	.
.	.	.	.

description of how most agents would behave. For most of us, whilst we might have an idea of the maximum number of firms it would be worthwhile approaching during a day, there will be a desire to stop short of that number if a 'sufficiently high' wage offer were discovered. The most widely used model of job-search takes this view and, of course, is designed to solve the problem of what is meant by 'sufficiently high'. Before we look at a particular formulation of this search model we outline the story which forms the background to it.

Suppose that a searcher leaves unspecified the precise number of firms to be approached but instead decides on a minimum acceptable wage offer before leaving home. This minimum acceptable wage offer is known as the *reservation wage*. The individual approaches each firm in turn – i.e. *sequentially* – and compares the wage on offer, with the reservation wage. The reservation wage has the property that the first wage discovered which lies above the reservation wage is accepted whilst up to that point the wages lying below the reservation wage are rejected. The amount of search therefore is not predetermined but arises from a particular reservation wage and the luck of the draw. An *optimal* reservation wage maximises the accepted wage offer taking account of the search cost. Suppose, as before that there is no limit to the potential number of firms approached, that search costs are constant and that all other aspects of the market environment are constant throughout the period. Then, at any point in time during the course of the day, the expected return to further search is constant. The key concept is that of the reservation wage, r^*, which causes the searcher to behave so that:

> if an offer w is found and $w > r^*$ then accept w;
> if an offer w is found and $w < r^*$ search again and reject w.

The simplest way of deriving the reservation wage is to observe that if a wage is observed which is precisely equal to r^*, then the searcher is indifferent between accepting and rejecting the offer. This implies an equality between the expected return to search and return to accepting a $w = r^*$. We have already argued that (given a reservation wage in use) the return to search is constant under our assumptions. It is clear that if search is a worthwhile activity, the wage-offer distribution must contain sufficient inducement, say by having a high mean, relative to the search cost. For reasons we discuss presently we assume that the (constant) return to search, R, is positive. On the other hand, the return to accepting a wage is higher the higher that wage is. In the very simple model with discounting, if w is accepted and the job taken for an indefinitely long period the present value of the job, and hence the return to accepting w, is simply w/i where i is the rate of discount. The reservation wage, r^*, therefore satisfies

$$R = \frac{r^*}{i}$$

which simply says that the reservation wage is that wage which, if discounted, would make acceptance (receiving r^*/i) and rejection (receiving R) equally attractive alternatives. This position is illustrated in Figure 3.4.

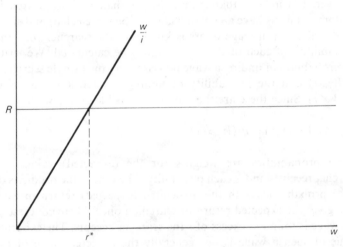

FIGURE 3.4   The reservation wage

We see immediately that given our assumption about R and the fact that the return to job acceptance is increasing in the wage rate, the reservation wage exists and is unique. Although, r^* is an 'indifference' wage the convention is that a job paying exactly r^* would be accepted. Hence, we have the *sequential* rule:

accept w if $w \geqslant r^*$;
reject w if $w < r^*$.

We can see how the optimal reservation wage is obtained by

using a simple illustration based on the wage distribution used in the fixed sample rule case. For the moment we ignore discounting.

To set up a model we need to specify the return to search. In fact we specify the return to searching once, since we are uncertain about how long search is actually going to last but by assumption at least one search is worthwhile. Let r denote the reservation wage and let $R(r)$ denote the return to searching once, when the reservation wage is r. Remember that r has the property that if a wage offer is at least as great as r it will be accepted whilst a wage less than r is rejected in favour of searching once again. On searching once there are only two possibilities; either the wage discovered is no less than r or it is less than r. Since search is random (all firms have an equal chance of being selected) and since the distribution of wage offers is known to the searcher then the probabilities of each of these events may be calculated. We write the probability of finding a wage no less than r on a single search as $Pr(W \geqslant r)$ and the probability of finding a wage less than r as $Pr(W < r)$. Since these are the only two possible events we have:

$$Pr(W < r) = 1 - Pr(W \geqslant r)$$

These probabilities are weights for the (expected) values the searcher receives under each possibility. The sum of the products of these probabilities with the associated (expected) return in each case gives the expected return to searching once. More concretely, if a wage is found in excess of r the searcher accepts. The expected value of such a wage is not generally the expected value of the entire distribution but only the expected value of those wages greater than or equal to r. We denote this expected value as $E(W|W \geqslant r)$ (read; the expected wage amongst all wages no less than r). If the randomly selected wage is less than r, the searcher rejects that wage in favour of continued search, and the return in this case is the return to searching once more which, given the stable environment, is equal to the expected return to searching the first time, $R(r)$. The expected return to searching once is therefore:

$$R(r) = E(W|W \geqslant r)Pr(W \geqslant r) + R(r)[1 - Pr(W \geqslant r)] - c \qquad (3.1)$$

where, in any event the searcher incurs the search cost, c. The expected return to searching once using a reservation wage, r, is the mean (expected) wage of all wages no less than r (i.e. the expected acceptable wage) multiplied by the probability of finding such a wage, *plus* the expected return to searching once more multiplied by the probability that an unacceptable wage is found, *less* the cost of the first search. I emphasise that the return to searching once and the return to searching again in the event of failing to find a $W \geqslant r$ are equal to $R(r)$ under our assumptions. Equation (3.1) is easily solved for $R(r)$ to give:

$$R(r) = E(W | W \geqslant r) - \frac{c}{Pr(W \geqslant r)} \tag{3.2}$$

The *optimal* reservation wage, r^*, is that which maximises (3.2). Clearly any of the possible wages available is a candidate for being the reservation wage and so by evaluating equation (3.2) for each possible wage in our earlier numerical example we will be able to find that reservation wage which maximises $R(r)$. The required computations again only make use of elementary statistics. First, the calculation of the probability $Pr(W \geqslant r)$ is straightforward as the sum of the probabilities associated with all wage offers equal to r and above. That is:

$$Pr(W \geqslant r) = \sum_{W \geqslant r} Pr(W) \tag{3.3}$$

Second, the formula for the *conditional* mean $E(W | W \geqslant r)$ is:

$$E[W | W \geqslant r] = \frac{\sum_{W \geqslant r} W Pr [W]}{\sum_{W \geqslant r} Pr [W]} \tag{3.4}$$

We perform these calculations for the two lowest wages in our example distribution from Table 3.1. First, assume $r = 120$, then *all* wages are greater than or equal to r, so that $\sum_{W \geqslant 120} Pr(W) = 1$, and the conditional mean is just the mean of the distribution;

$$E(W | W \geqslant 120) = \sum_{W \geqslant 120} W Pr(W) = E(W) = 141.2225 \tag{3.5}$$

Second assume $r = 125$, then, $\sum\limits_{W \geqslant 125} Pr(W) = 0.9871$, while (4) becomes,

$$E(W \mid W \geqslant 125) = \frac{139.6745}{0.9871} = 141.4998$$

$$(3.6)$$

Continuing in this way we may calculate $R(r)$ for each assumed value of r. Assuming the search cost is £2 per search as before we may construct Table 3.5.

TABLE 3.5   The optimal reservation wage

(1) r	(2) $E(W \mid W \geqslant r)$	(3) $c/Pr[W \geqslant r]$	(4) = (2) − (3) $R(r)$
120	141.2225	2.0000	139.2225
125	141.4998	2.0261	139.4737
130	142.2916	2.1234	140.1682
135	143.5950	2.3485	141.2465
140	145.9083	2.9806	142.9277
145	149.6016	4.8438	144.7678
150	152.7588	8.1566	144.5922
155	155.8003	17.2117	138.5886
160	160.0000	103.0928	56.9072

It is apparent that the expected return to search, $R(r)$ is maximised when the reservation wage chosen is £145. The *optimal* reservation wage in this case is therefore £145, and the search rule says that if at any stage a wage W is discovered then:

if $W \geqslant £145$ accept W and stop searching;
if $W < £145$ reject W and continue searching with expected return $R(145)$.

More generally, if r^* is the optimal reservation wage the optimal search rule is:

if $W \geqslant r^*$ accept and stop searching
if $W < r^*$ reject and continue search with expected return $R(r^*)$

Importance of the sequential search model

Before we pursue the implications of this model and before we discuss some of its developments, we should establish why the *sequential*-search model has dominated the job-search literature. There are two main reasons. First, it is easy to see the sequential search model extending over time so that not all search takes place *within* a period. This makes for some interesting implications of search for the duration of unemployment, length of job tenure and so on. Second, there are good reasons for expecting the sequential-search rule to be superior to the fixed-sample-size rule. Certainly, under the assumptions of this section so far, the sequential-search model improves on the fixed-sample-size model in terms of the maximum expected return generated. Our example illustrates this. From Table 3.3 we see that the maximum return to search possible under the fixed-sample-size procedure is $R(n^*) = R(3) = 142.4724$. Table 3.5 on the other hand, shows that with the same wage offers available, the same probability distribution of wage offers and the same unit-search costs, the sequential-search procedure generates a higher maximum expected return to search, $R(r^*) = R(145) = 144.7687$. We conclude from this that the sequential rule is superior to the fixed-sample rule in this case. The intuition behind this was alluded to earlier – cost savings are possible by stopping search as soon as a high enough wage is found and it is unnecessary to continue to assemble a predetermined sample. It turns out that as well as being true in our case this superiority is true under a large variety of market circumstances.

Some implications of the model

We can now proceed to study some implications of this model. Suppose that exactly one firm may be approached in each period so that $Pr(W < r^*)$ is the probability that a searcher must sample one more firm. If, as we have implicitly assumed, the searcher is unemployed until a suitable income is found then $Pr(W < r^*)$ is the probability that the searcher will experience at least one more period of unemployment. Returning now to equation (3.2), the equation for the expected return to search, we see that this is composed of two terms. The first is the total expected income generated by accepting the first offer for which $W \geqslant r$ and the second has the interpretation of the total expected cost of behaving in this way. This second term may therefore be thought of as the product of two terms; the per period search cost, c, and the expected number of periods of search, $1/Pr(W \geq r)$. This interpretation of (3.2) makes clear the trade-off involved in choosing the optimal reservation wage. A higher r increases the first term in (3.2) but also, by lowering $Pr(W \geq r)$, increases the second term. Under our new interpretation of search extending over a number of periods, since $1/Pr(W \geq r)$ is the expected number of periods of search before a suitable offer is found and since the searcher is assumed to be unemployed, it follows that $1/Pr(W \geq r)$ is the expected duration of a spell of unemployment. The expected duration of unemployment is therefore the inverse of the probability of leaving unemployment since leaving unemployment is equivalent to finding a suitable job.

This simple theory of job-search attributes spells of unemployment to lack of success in locating a suitable wage. The key feature which brings this about is the reservation wage and so the behaviour of this value as market circumstances change is of supreme importance. One result is immediately available with respect to the reservation wage. This is stated without formal proof, although the intuition is very strong. An increase in the search cost, c, reduces r^*, thereby increasing the probability of leaving unemployment $Pr(W \geq r^*)$ and reducing the expected duration of search, $1/Pr(W \geq r^*)$. The mechanism behind this is simply that an increase in c lowers the return to search and prompts a desire to terminate search sooner, which in turn is brought about by a fall in r^*. In terms of Figure 3.5 an increase in c lowers the return to search R and lowers r^* from r_0^* to r_1^*. Note that as far as the duration of search is concerned this result is similar to that of the fixed sample rule, although the mechanism is different. In both cases an increase in the cost of search lowers the amount of search taking place.

The assumption that the return to search is positive is motivated by decisions by individuals to participate. The participation decision fits into the job-search model in the following way. For an individual who is deciding to participate, the return to search is the expected return to market activity since it represents the expected income generated by pursuing the (optimal) reservation-wage rule net of expected total search costs. If the return to continued non-market activity is zero, then search is worthwhile if the return to

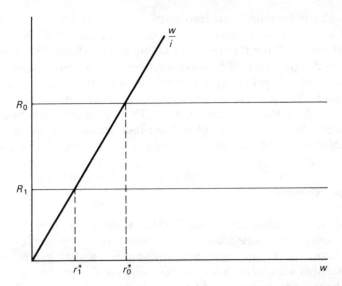

FIGURE 3.5   Search costs, reservation wages and duration of search

search is positive. Thus, in this situation $R > 0$ is a necessary and sufficient condition for participation. In the static theory of labour supply, non-participation is associated with the leisure preference, and this may easily be incorporated into the non-participation decision by assuming that the value of leisure associated with non-market activity is positive, say b. In this case $R > 0$ is no longer sufficient to induce participation and we may need $R > b$ to make search worthwhile.

One criticism often levelled against the simple job-search theory is that since in practice search costs are negligible the theory is unlikely to have empirical relevance. In the model presented in our example, c represents all costs of search, and the direct search costs may be small. Moreover search cost may be totally offset by unemployment and social-security payments for the unemployed. The simple model predicts in this case that search will continue indefinitely or until the highest wage is located. That this is not observed in practice even when direct search costs are negligible may be explained in a number of ways. One explanation has already figured in our more general treatment of the simple job-search model and takes the form of an *indirect* search cost. If individuals discount future income-streams then an indirect search cost arises because continued search delays the receipt of employment income. Since the size of the discount rate reflects degrees of impatience (impatient individuals discount more heavily and prefer their income sooner rather than later) then a high discount rate will be associated with a low reservation wage and hence a high probability of leaving unemployment. That this is the relationship between the rate of discount and the reservation wage has been established in the literature and, because of its difficulty, is not proven here.

Some extensions

Two other explanations for the limited nature of search even with low direct search costs require us to consider two extensions of the simple model. First, it is argued that search is undertaken not to locate high wage offers but to locate *vacancies*. In this case, search continues not because only 'unsatisfactory' wages have been located but because no vacancies have been unearthed, and search will end when a vacacy is found. Search as a response to job-rationing is clearly a plausible feature of labour markets in excess supply. Consideration of this need not lead to an abandonment of the reservation wage concept, however, and job-rationing may be introduced into the simple model by assuming that instead of one wage offer being received each period, there is a probability, p, that at most one offer will be received. If p is low then the searcher is more severely constrained by job availability than if p is higher. Models exist along these lines and show that p and the reservation wage are positively related. A low probability of receiving an offer makes the individual more likely to accept any offer which may be received by setting a low reservation wage. This result is clearly supported by intuition. Notice that the probability of leaving unemployment in this case is the product of the probability of locating an offer and the probability that the offer is acceptable, $p[1 - F(r)]$.

A second explanation for search with small direct search costs is arrived at by assuming an entirely different informational environment to that of the simple model. Suppose that, rather than knowing the distibution of offers for certain an individual must undertake some search in order to find about market opportunities. Models of so-called 'adaptive search' have studied this type of problem and suggest that since search is, under these circumstances, a way of gathering information, search will cease when the value of additional information is less than the value of stopping search and accepting one of the discovered wage offers.

Finally, on this issue of search costs it is possible to counter the argument that direct search costs are negligible by arguing that individuals must not only finance their search activity but must also consume, maintain housing and so on whilst unemployed. These expenses soon account for any state transfer payment and constitute a real search cost. In this case it is the searcher's budget constraint which binds to bring search to an end.

It is clear from this discussion that many 'real world' issues may be brought to bear on the simple search model. These issues have consequently led to many reformulations of the job-search problem. (For further discussion see McKenna, 1985, 1987.)

One obvious feature of the real world not accounted for in the simple model is that time itself is a scarce resource. It is important therefore to see what implications flow from relaxing the assumption of an infinite time-horizon. Restricting the number of possible periods of search now cause the return to search at any point in time to depend on whether or not previously discovered wage offers may be taken up. Whether the *recall* option may be used to accept wage offers found in earlier periods of search plays a crucial role in finite-horizon search models. A particularly important result is that if no recall is possible the return to search is no longer constant over time and the reservation wage becomes time-dependent. The intuition here is obvious enough. As the horizon approaches the earnings opportunities with *any* accepted wage falls. Thus the (discounted) return of the distribution of wages falls as time lapses. If search does not become correspondingly cheaper at the margin (i.e. if search costs are constant) the net value of continued search falls as the time-horizon is approached. The corollary of this, that the reservation wage falls over time, is merely a reflection of the desire of the searcher to increase the probability of discontinuing increasingly less productive search. In the finite-horizon no-recall model then, the reservation wage falls over time and the probability of leaving unemployment increases.

On the job-search

In the simplest models job-search is an activity associated with unemployment, with the implication that search for improved job offers by employed workers is prohibitively high. In practice, few people leave jobs voluntarily before having an alternative lined up which suggests that 'on-the-job' search may be a common activity. Allowing for this possibility complicates the job-search model in a number of ways. First, the decision to accept a job does not necessarily mean the abandonment of search, and whilst a new wage might be accepted it may not be sufficiently high to make further search in the new job unnecessary. This is formalised not by having a single reservation wage but by having two reservation wages, say r_L and r_u, where r_L is the smallest acceptable wage and r_u the smallest wage which would make further search not worthwhile. The worker's strategy in this case might take the form:

> if $W < r_L$, reject new wage offer, W, and continue search
> if $r_L \leqslant W < r_u$, accept new wage offer, W, and continue search in the new job
> if $W \geqslant r_u$, accept new wage offer, W, and discontinue search

We can imagine that the lower reservation wage r_L will be at least as high as the current wage offer and will generally exceed it if the searcher wishes to recoup search costs. Moreover, r_L is likely to depend also on possible costs of removal.

This important extension of the job-search model, to allow for on-the-job search provides an explanation of voluntary turnover by workers, since the decision to accept a wage greater than r_L is clearly a decision to quit the present job. However, on-the-job search is not the only explanation of voluntary turnover, and quits also arise when workers find themselves in a job which fails to live up to initial expectations. This extension of the simple model starts by noting that a job package typically involves more than simply a wage offer. There are many non-wage attributes which contribute to workers' utility such as job-safety, job-security, pension schemes, work-place environment and so on. We then note that not all of the non-wage attributes are readily observable at the time of job-acceptance. Whilst pension schemes and some of the more superficial workplace characteristics may be observed simply by inspection, others can only be discovered by experience. This leads to the possibility that a job accepted on the basis of its observable characteristics may subsequently be rejected as some unpleasant and, presumably, unanticipated, characteristics come to light. In many cases in which the job turns out to be only moderately disappointing, the discovery may simply initiate on-the-job search for an alternative. In the extreme, however, the discovery of some unpleasant characteristic may induce a quit immediately in favour of search unemployment. It is this extreme case which has received attention in the literature. There is at present no model which incorporates both on-the-job search and experience characteristics.

Apart from the possibility of inducing quits the existence of job characteristics which might cause disutility to be incurred also suggests the possibility that the reservation wage rule might not apply. Remember that the reservation wage rule is derived from a model in which higher wages are unambiguously preferred to lower wages. A counter-example to this is suggested by an extensive form of the theory of compensating wages. It is a well-known proposition dating back to Adam Smith that a competitive labour market in which jobs differ according to the 'agreeableness' or 'disagreeableness' of working conditions will generate compensating wage differentials so that the *net* attractiveness of all jobs are equal. Under certainty the correlation between wage and non-wage attributes will be perfect and negative. Generally, though, in such markets high wages will be a signal that undesirable conditions may be associated with the job, in which case a high wage may not necessarily be preferred to a lower one. Hence there may be no single wage (reservation wage) which an individual can use to separate 'good' jobs worth accepting from 'bad' jobs which are not, and we have a case of the inapplicability of the reservation-wage rule.

Happily, none of this invalidates the general approach of search theory, but it does mean that the mechanics of the problem become more tricky. The literature has established a variety of conditions under which the reservation-wage rule is preserved. Furthermore, this discussion is not meant to imply that the reservation-wage rule and compensating wage differences are necessarily incompatible. For example, a negative correlation between wage and non-wage job attributes is not sufficient to invalidate the reservation-wage rule. A more complete analysis of compensating differences under uncertainty will be needed before a full picture is possible.

We have covered many of the most important extensions of job search theory here, and hope that the reader has a feel for the types of issues on which the search approach can shed light. However, these models tell only one side of the story, and we now go on to consider what role the firm plays in the search market and hence what we can expect market equilibrium to look like.

3.3   FIRMS AND MARKET EQUILIBRIUM

As in the static models of undergraduate labour economics, the 'supply' side of search markets has attracted more attention than the 'demand' side. However, the generation of job-offers and firms' decisions are crucial to an understanding of wage structure and turnover in labour markets. Moreover, the full story of market equilibrium can only be told once the demand side has been specified.

As a minimum, a theory of the firm in a search market must explain three things. These are the wage offer, vacancy creation (or the employment decision) and turnover or contract duration. We will discuss each of these and their consequences for market equilibrium.

Wages

In simple search models it is the wage-offer decision by firms which attracts most attention. This is because of the crucial role played by the wage-offer distribution in the job-search story. Any theory of wage determination must explain why firms make different wage offers, and persist in doing so. If all firms offer the same wage, the simple job-search model becomes trivial and there is no point in workers searching. This immediately rules out wage determination by the Walrasian auctioneer, where individual firms take the market wage as given. For simplicity we also rule our wage determination by bargaining. This leads to wage-setting behaviour in which firms post a wage offer on a take-it-or-leave-it basis. Wage-setting behaviour is a feature of monopsony, and we may think of firms operating in a market where wage-location is costly for workers, to have more monopsony power in the sense that any one firm can expect to regulate labour supply by varying the wage offer. A high wage offer is more likely to be found acceptable by searchers using the reservation-wage rule, and so the wage offer chosen by the firm will represent a trade-off between filling the vacancy more quickly (to reduce vacancy costs, including lost output) and keeping employment costs down. Hence, given that employment costs depend positively on the wage offer and expected vacancy costs depend negatively on the wage offer, the profit-maximising wage offer may easily be determined. Suppose for simplicity that the firm's revenue is independent of the wage offer, so that the price is a constant, and output of the worker is independent of the wage offer w. Then, under these conditions profit-maximisation occurs at the same wage as cost-minimisation. Costs in turn will be minimised where the sum of employment costs and vacancy costs are a minimum. Figure 3.6 illustrates this situation. The firm's optimal wage offer is w^*.

It is obvious why employment costs should be increasing in the wage. To see precisely why expected vacancy costs are decreasing in the wage offer, suppose that the firm incurs a fixed cost k for each period the vacancy is unfilled, and suppose further that $q(w)$ is the probability that the vacancy is filled in any period. Then

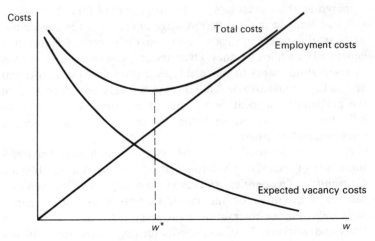

FIGURE 3.6 The firm's optimal wage offer

$(1 - q(w))$ is the probability that the vacancy is left unfilled and the expected number of periods during which the vacancy is unfilled is (using a similar argument to that used earlier) $1/q(w)$. Total expected vacancy costs will then be $k/q(w)$, and so the assumption that these fall with w imply that $q(w)$ *increases* with w. Clearly, the probability $q(w)$ is implied by workers' behaviour. Workers behave in such a way that a higher wage offer is more likely to be accepted by a randomly searching worker. This is certainly the case if workers have different reservation wages, because the higher is a wage offer the greater the number of reservation wages which will be below it and hence the higher the probability that a worker approaching the firm will find the wage offer acceptable. Thus in the same way that a distribution of wage offers is required for workers' search to be non-trivial, it appears that a distribution of workers' reservation wages is required for a firm to use its wage offer to regulate supply and hence to determine its optimal wage offer.

It is now possible to see the importance of studying the typical firm's wage-offer decision. It is clear that if all firms face the same distribution of workers' reservation wages, face the same price and vacancy cost, and if all workers and jobs are equally productive, then all firms will arrive at the same wage-offer decision. This result is incompatible with our model of job-search by workers since it implies no distribution of wage offers and no incentive to search. Apparently, there must be some heterogeneity of some kind which will lead firms to make different wage offers. Two obvious candidates are differences in vacancy costs and differences in the product generated by a filled vacancy. Of course, we still need a distribution of reservation wages to make the wage-offer decision non-trivial and so there must also be differences in workers' search costs or in the probability of locating an offer in discount rates to lead to different reservation wages being chosen by workers facing the same wage-offer distribution.

A non-trivial equilibrium in this simple search model requires some sort of underlying heterogeneity. Moreover the equilibrium distribution of wage offers and reservation wages must be such that there is no incentive for one individual firm or worker to change their wage offer or reservation wage given the behaviour of other firms and workers. That is, the equilibrium distributions form a Nash-equilibrium. Figure 3.7 shows a schema of how the underly-

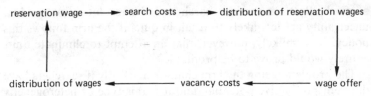

FIGURE 3.7   Equilibrium distribution of wage offers and reservation wages

ing distribution of, say, search and vacancy costs give rise to the equilibrium distribution of wage offers and reservation wages.

The literature on equilibrium search with wage dispersion is therefore composed of models in which some sort of heterogeneity on each side of the market plays a crucial role. (See McKenna, 1987, for a summary of the issues and models.)

Vacancies and turnover

The simplest case to consider is when a new firm is established. The firm has no turnover history and simply seeks to fill each vacancy with a suitable worker at an appropriate wage. The number of vacancies is determined by production technology and the size of the firm. In a market of searching workers the time to fill each vacancy is random and, in general, will depend on the firm's wage offer (as we have seen) and its recruitment policy. If all workers are equally productive, as in the last section, the recruitment policy is trivial in that any worker attracted by the wage offer is accepted. If workers are not equally productive then the firm must either establish the productivity of an applicant before hiring, hire in ignorance of, or uncertainty about, productivity and make adjustments afterwards, or invest in some information-gathering at the time of hire and respond appropriately when actual productivity is perceived. In practice the last-mentioned option is the method most widely used and largely depends on the existence of signals – easily observed but not totally accurate indications of likely productivity such as qualifications, references and so on.

A firm's wage and employment policy in general should take account of the fact that subsequent quits are likely. If quits are at all costly then the firm will want to make its own job-offer relatively more attractive than if no quits took place. This is achieved by raising its wage offer and improving other conditions

of work. Both on-the-job search and the resolution of residual
uncertainty are less likely to result in quits if the firm follows this
policy. It is unlikely, however, that an attempt to eliminate quits
entirely would prove to be profitable.

The problem facing the firm changes markedly if searchers have
different productive potential, and it is this type of heterogeneity
which makes firms exercise choice between job applicants, so far as
possible to employ the most productive workers. Generally, productivity is not simply a characteristic of a worker, and it is the
quality of the job-match which produces differences in productivity. Putting the right workers in the right job is a central
allocative role for any labour market. Hires are made on the basis
of the expected productivity of the match, and given that the actual
productivity may differ from that expected, the firm may want to
revise its contractual terms, particularly if it is disappointed. The
literature distinguishes between two types of adjustment, either of
which might induce turnover. First, the firm might indulge in wage
adjustment in which case it is said to operate in a 'flexwage'
environment (Pissarides, 1976). In practice, firms face many constraints on their ability to invoke a downward wage revision in line
with productivity. The 'institutional' constraints arise from trade-
union agreements and contracts. However, an important economic
constraint is the possibility that a downward revision will induce
the employee to search, on the job, and subsequently to leave the
firm with a costly vacancy. Second, the firm may operate in a
'fixwage' environment in which case rather than lower the wage to
increase the net revenue from a match, the firm will determine a
reservation profit-level. An employee whose productivity in the job
is insufficient to generate a profit-level at least as great as the
reservation profit at the given wage will be dismissed thus creating
involuntary turnover.

Market equilibrium

What then are the broad features we might expect to characterise
search-labour-market equilibrium?

Job-searchers generally face two problems. They must locate
vacancies, and they must search for higher wages. For the second
of these activities to be worthwhile use of time and resources there

must be a non-degenerate distribution of wage offers in equilibrium. We have already seen some conditions required for this. Equilibrium in search markets is also likely to be characterised by turnover, so that equilibrium will not merely determine the stock of vacancies and the stock of unemployed but also the flows into and out of jobs. To keep technical difficulties to a minimum, studies of the equilibrium turnover properties of search markets have tended to keep the problem of wage-search in the background and have concentrated instead on search as a process of finding vacancies. One natural characterisation of equilibrium in these turnover models is that of the *steady-state*. In a steady-state the flows into and out of jobs are such that the stocks of vacancies, jobs and of unemployed searchers are all constant. This implies particular – i.e. equilibrium – flow-rates into and out of jobs. At the heart of these models is the *search technology* – the process which brings searchers into contact with vacancies. For example, the number of job-matches made in any period, x, will depend on both the number of active searchers, u, and the number of vacancies, v. In fact x will increase with both u and v because more unemployed means that a given number of vacancies are more likely to be filled, while more vacancies means that a given number of unemployed are more likely to find jobs.

One discovery made by these equilibrium models is that the amount of job-formation or the amount of search and vacancy-creation may not be *efficient* in the sense that private decisions on these matters have associated externalities. For example, a decision to create a new vacancy in equilibrium will be a marginal private decision for the firm. In equilibrium a firm will be indifferent between opening up a new vacancy and not. Society, however, may not be indifferent. The new vacancy creates added competition for other vacancies or congestion which is not taken into account in the private decision. On the other hand the new vacancy bestows an unaccounted for benefit on searchers, making job-finding easier. The social optimum may not coincide with the equilibrium number of vacancies and unemployed. This raises the possibility that there may be too few searchers in equilibrium in relation to the number of vacancies and too little search taking place (Pissarides, 1984).

Other externalities might arise in markets with wage-dispersion. If wage-information obtained by a searcher can be observed by others then an external economy has passed between the cost-bearing searcher and neighbouring 'free-riders'. This, too, would imply, from society's point of view, too little search taking place.

3.4 JOB SEARCH AND UNEMPLOYMENT

Search theories of the labour market offer a large number of hypotheses which are testable, at least in principle. The determinants of quits, job tenure, the extent of on-the-job search, etc., are all potential topics for empirical study. However, it is unemployment and unemployment duration which has attracted and continues to attract considerable interest.

In many countries, including the UK, more people now experience unemployment spells than in the early 1960s. Moreover, the spells seem to be of longer duration. These factors combine to make recorded unemployment during the 1980s much higher than during any period since 1945. To what extent is increased search activity responsible for this? Or, more generally, how useful is the search framework in studying the increase in unemployment? Consider the search theory as it applies to the duration of unemployment.

The key relationship for the empirical search model is the probability of leaving unemployment:

$$\theta(t) = p(t)\{1 - F[r(t)]\}$$

where $p(t)$ is the probability of locating a vacancy at time t and $\{1 - F[r(t)]\}$ the probability of accepting the offer in time t. The function $\theta(t)$ is often described as the escape rate and allowance is made for the fact that it might change as unemployment continues by making it time-dependent. There are a variety of ways of obtaining estimates of $\theta(t)$ some of which involve first obtaining estimates of the reservation wage, $r(t)$ and some of which avoid this (see McKenna, 1985, or Narendranathan and Nickell, 1985, for further details). We are not concerned here with the econometric details, but it is important to establish on what in general $\theta(t)$ depends, and also its behaviour over time.

It is apparent from the equation that $\theta(t)$ is composed of two interrelated terms. We might regard $p(t)$ as reflecting predominantly demand conditions, since more vacancies will generally mean a higher value of $p(t)$. However, $p(t)$ will also depend on search intensity. The less the effort which searchers put into searching, the lower is $p(t)$. Second, $\theta(t)$ is affected by a whole range of variables indirectly, via their effect on $r(t)$. Some of these variables, such as unemployment benefit, search costs, discount rates, as well as time itself, are suggested by the theory. Others such as age, sex, ethnic origin, skill, regional location and so on will also affect $\theta(t)$ though these are not suggested directly by the theoretical model.

The effect of unemployment benefit on $\theta(t)$ has received great attention. The argument is that an increase in benefit acts as an increased search subsidy, increasing $r(t)$ and hence lowering $\theta(t)$. Estimates of this effect are very sensitive to assumptions about the level and form of benefit. Most studies use the *replacement ratio* – the ratio benefit to post-tax earnings – as reflecting the search subsidy. An often-quoted statistic for the UK is based on the work of Nickell (1979) who finds an elasticity of re-employment probability with respect to the replacement ratio of around -0.6. Atkinson *et al.* (1984) have produced a variety of estimates based on different replacement ratio assumptions and different subsamples. Estimates of the elasticity vary from -0.12 to less than -1.0. One result of these studies is the importance of distinguishing the younger unemployed from the older and long-term unemployed. The 'disincentive' effects of benefits for younger people are more marked than for older and long-term (generally in excess of 1 year) unemployment.

In our discussion in section 3.2 we discovered a number of reasons why the probability of leaving unemployment increases over time. The mechanism is via the reservation wage. An approaching horizon, liquidity constraints, pessimism about prospects and so on are likely to lower the reservation wage and hence increase the probability of leaving unemployment. Most evidence on the behaviour of $\theta(t)$ over time is directly counter to this. That $\theta(t)$ displays negative time-dependence suggests that the effect of any downward movement of the reservation wage is swamped by other factors such as job-availability or lowered search-intensity because of discouragement. These factors are likely to be particularly important for the old and the long-term unemployed.

Some evidence by Bean, Layard and Nickell (1987) confirms the view that, at least for the UK, the rise in unemployment through the 1970s and 1980s is largely due to reduced search-intensity and (more so) to demand. Whether reduced search-intensity is a reaction to a liberal benefit system or simply a sign of discouragement is impossible to say using our models of search theory alone. Most economists appear to agree that an across-the-board reduction in benefits is unlikely to have a great impact on unemployment, although some rescheduling to reduce the disincentive effects among sensitive groups may reduce unemployment among those groups.

3.5 CONCLUSION

This chapter has aimed to give a flavour of the theoretical richness of job-search models and the light they can shed on important issues. The emphasis has been on providing an introduction or 'tastier'. The empirical aspects of search models and the properties of search-market equilibrium, including its implications for macroeconomic adjustments still attract much interest in professional journals. The reader interested in some detail is referred to the surveys by McKenna (1985) and (1987) and Mortensen (1986).

4 Implicit-Contract Theory

ALAN MANNING

4.1 INTRODUCTION

The origins of implicit-contract theory lie in the belief that observed movements in wages and employment cannot be adequately explained by a competitive spot labour-market in which wages are always equal to the marginal product of labour and the labour market is always in equilibrium.

Implicit-contract theory is one attempt, although not the only one,[1] at producing a model of the labour market more capable of explaining observed phenomena. Implicit-contract models were originally proposed by Baily (1974), Gordon (1974) and Azariadis (1975). But the ideas spawned an enormous literature (for excellent surveys see Azariadis and Stiglitz (1983), Rosen (1985), and Hart and Holstrom (1986)).

Among the stylised facts which have been the targets for implicit-contract theory are:

1. the observation that over the cycle wages are 'rigid', while employment varies;
2. the existence of involuntary unemployment in the sense that unemployed workers would like jobs even at a wage slightly below the current level;
3. the existence of involuntary unemployment in the sense that employment is at a lower level than it would be in a competitive labour market.

It should be stressed at the outset that implicit-contract theory has many other potential applications (some of which will be mentioned below); that not all the proponents of implicit-contract theory have claimed that the theory can explain the stylised facts presented above, and that even the validity of the aformentioned stylised facts is questioned by some economists. But these stylised facts do represent some of the most important issues in macroeconomics, and we shall be largely concerned with evaluating whether implicit-contract theory can provide convincing explanations of them.

The plan of this chapter is as follows: in section 4.2 we will outline the reasons why implicit contracts might exist. In section 4.3 we present a simple model of implicit contracts which will be used to show the potential problems in using implicit-contract theory to explain the stylised facts presented above. Section 4.4 discusses the problem of enforceability of contracts, and in section 4.5 we briefly discuss the more recent development of asymmetric information implicit-contract models.

4.2 WHY DO IMPLICIT CONTRACTS EXIST?

The basic idea of implicit contracts is that in their dealings employers are less risk-averse than workers and so it can be profitable for employers to offer workers an employment contract which involves some insurance elements. For example, a contract may offer workers some insurance against fluctuations in their marginal product of labour which, in a competitive labour market, would lead to fluctuations in the wage.

In this description, several questions arise. First, why do workers need employers to offer them insurance: why can they not obtain insurance from a specialist insurance company (as is done for other risks, e.g. house and car insurance)? There are several reasons for this which particularly apply to risks which workers might face in the labour market. To take a specific example, suppose there is a chance that a worker's skill will no longer be valued in the future. Being risk-averse, the worker would like to insure him/herself against this risk by obtaining an insurance contract which pays out in the event of unemployment. There are likely to be several problems in obtaining such insurance from an insurance company. For example, the insurance company may find it very difficult to distinguish when the worker is unemployed because his/her skill is now obsolete (which is no fault of the worker) from when the worker is unemployed because the worker is low quality or has behaved in such a way as to lose his/her job.[2] In both cases someone who is in a better position to judge whether the worker has been unlucky or negligent in losing his/her job is the worker's employer. So the employer may be able to offer insurance to workers against certain labour-market risks that cannot be offered by specialist insurance companies.

Second, why are employers likely to be less risk-averse than workers? One reason is that it is generally difficult to diversify assets which take the form of human capital, i.e. workers generally work for only one employer at a time. On the other hand, owners of capital who represent the employers can divide their capital among many different firms through the stock market, and by this diversification obtain insurance against the risks faced by individual firms. As human capital cannot be split up in this way, workers cannot obtain insurance in a similar manner.

Third, why are implicit contracts so-called? If employers are to offer workers insurance one cannot wait until after the event one wants to insure against has occurred (one does not insure one's car after it has been stolen). The worker and employer must agree to a contract in advance so that there may be some type of long-term attachment of workers to firms. Furthermore this contract must specify what will happen in the event of various contingencies (which will be discussed in detail later) e.g. whether the labour market situation is good or bad. However, the labour contracts we observe in the real world do not seem to be as complicated as this, so that such contracts, if they exist are not explicitly written down; they must remain as *implicit* agreements between worker and employer. The fact that these contracts are implicit rather than explicit raises important issues of enforceability. Explicit contracts can be generally enforced through the courts as their terms are written down. But the implementation of implicit contracts must rest on the desire of the parties concerned not to break the contract. The question of enforceability will be discussed in section 4.4

4.3   A SIMPLE IMPLICIT-CONTRACT MODEL

In this section we will present a simple one-period implicit-contract model which can be used to address most of the important issues raised by implicit-contract theory. Most implicit-contract theory is fairly technical in nature but to keep the mathematics to the minimum, formal proofs of the propositions have been consigned to the Appendix to this chapter. In the main body of the text I will simply describe the main results and provide intuitive explanations for them.

We will consider a model in which an employer employs a number of identical workers. We will assume that the firm has a production function $f(L)$ where L is employment which exhibits decreasing returns to scale, and that it sells output at an exogenously given price p. So if the employer employs L workers at a wage w, profits will be given by:

$$\pi = pf(L) - wL \qquad (4.1)$$

We will assume for convenience that the employer is risk-neutral so that under uncertainty the employer will be concerned with maximising expected profits.

The workers will be assumed to have a utility function of the form $u(w,h)$ where w is the wage and h the hours worked. For simplicity we will assume that if the worker does work, hours are fixed at unity, and this cannot be varied. Define

$$u(w) = U(w,1) \qquad v(b) = U(b,0) \qquad (4.2)$$

$u(w)$ represents the utility from wage w if the worker does work and $v(b)$ the utility from unemployment benefit b if the worker does not work. These functions may differ as income is valued differently when workers are employed and when they are unemployed. This difference will be of some importance later. As workers are assumed to dislike working we will have $u(w) < v(w)$ for all w so workers will only choose to work if w is larger than b.

Define w^* to be the wage at which workers are just indifferent between working and non-working, i.e. $u(w^*) = v(b)$. We will use w^* later. Call w^* the *reservation wage*, as it is the wage at which workers are just indifferent between working and not working.

We will assume that workers are risk-averse so that both $u(\ )$ and $v(\ )$ are strictly concave functions, i.e. their second derivatives are negative (see Hey, 1979, if these concepts are not familiar).

First let us briefly consider what would happen if wages and employment were determined in a competitive spot labour market. Given the output price p and the market wage rate w, employers would choose the level of employment so that the revenue product of labour was equal to the real wage: i.e. choose L so that

$$f'(L) = \frac{w}{p} \tag{4.3}$$

On the labour-supply side all workers would choose to work so long as $w \geqslant w^*$. In such a labour market fluctuations in the product price will lead to fluctuations in the demand for labour curve and consequent fluctuations in wages and employment or both.[3] This leads to fluctuations in the utility of workers. As workers are risk-averse they will want to insure themselves against these risks, and as employers are assumed to be risk-neutral, they will be prepared to offer such insurance. Note also that in a competitive labour market, the wage of workers can never fall below w^* so that from (4.3) the marginal product of labour will never be below (w^*/p).

Before we model the way in which employers might offer insurance to workers we will be more precise about the uncertainty faced by the employer. Assume that it is only the output price that fluctuates and that it can take one of a number of possible values $(p_1 \ldots p_n)$. Let the probability of p_i occurring be α_i where for consistency $\sum_{i=1}^{n} \alpha_i = 1$.

Assume that before the output price is known the employer signs a contract with N workers. This contract specifies the wage paid to workers if they are employed w_i, and the number of workers employed L_i, for any realisation of the firm's output price p_i. Denote a contract by (w_i, L_i) $i = 1, \ldots, n$. It is conventional to call a contract of this type a *contingent contract* as it tells us the wage paid to workers and the employment level contingent on the realisation of the firm's output price. For the moment assume that any such contingent contract is enforceable, i.e. it is effectively explicit. As the firm is assumed to be risk-neutral the employer's expected utility from this contract is simply the expected profits of it. Using (4.1), this is given by

$$E\pi = \sum_{i=1}^{n} \alpha_i \, [p_i \, f(L_i) - w_i \, L_i] \tag{4.4}$$

On the other hand, using (4.2) the worker's expected utility is given by:

$$EU = \sum_{i=1}^{n} \alpha_i \, [\frac{L_i}{N} \, u(w_i) + \frac{N - L_i}{N} \, v(b)] \tag{4.5}$$

In this formulation we have assued that all workers have an equal chance of employment so that if L out of N workers are employed this probability is L/N. If employed the workers receive $u(w_i)$. The probability of being unemployed is $(N - L_i)/N$ in which case the workers receive utility $v(b)$.[4]

The constraints on the employer's choice of contract are the following. First, workers must receive a level of expected utility that is at least as high as that obtainable elsewhere. Let us call this level $\bar{U}$; we will not model it further. Second, we will assume that the employer cannot employ any more labour than that contracted for, i.e. we must have $L_i \leqslant N$. So we can write the employer's choice of the optimal employment contract as being the choice of (w_i, L_i) $i = 1, \ldots, n$ and N to solve the following constrained maximisation problem:

$$\max E\pi = \sum_{i=1}^{v} \alpha_i \, [p_i \, f(L_i) - w_i . L_i]$$

subject to:

$$EU = \sum_{i=1}^{n} \alpha_i \, [\frac{L_i}{N} . u(w_i) + \frac{N - L_i}{N} . v(b) \geqslant \bar{U} \tag{4.6}$$

$$L_i \leqslant N \qquad i = 1, \ldots, n$$

The formal analysis of this constrained maximisation problem is contained in the Appendix, but one of the important results is stated below:

Proposition 4.1(i)

In the optimal contract which solves (4.6) the wage is rigid and does not vary with the firm's output price.

Proof See Appendix.

This is the celebrated rigid-wage result of implicit-contract theory; wages do not fluctuate in response to fluctuations in the firm's output price. The intuition for this result is as follows. The risk-averse workers do not like fluctuation in their wages but the risk-neutral employers only care about the average wage bill. Both parties can be made better-off by replacing a fluctuating wage with a fixed-contract wage which has a slightly lower average value.

To see this, suppose that there are only two possible values of the output price p_1 and p_2. Let p_1 occur with probability α and p_2 with probability $(1-\alpha)$. Suppose the employer has decided to employ the worker whatever the output price, so the only decision left for the employer is what wages are to be paid to the worker in the two states. Denote these wages by w_1 and w_2. If these wages are high enough to attract the worker to the firm, they must satisfy:

$$\alpha.u(w_1)+(1-\alpha).u(w_2)=\bar{u} \qquad (4.7)$$

so that this firm's employment contract offers the same level of expected utility as other firms. The combinations of w_1 and w_2 which satisfy (4.7) are represented by the indifference curve in Figure 4.1. The slope of this indifference curve is $\dfrac{-\alpha.u'(w_1)}{(1-\alpha).u'(w_2)}$.

Given that the employment decision has been made, the employer wants to choose w_1 and w_2 to minimise the expected labour costs of employing the worker. Expected labour costs are given by $(\alpha.w_1+(1-\alpha).w_2)$. Iso-cost curves are also drawn on Figure 4.1. They are straight lines with a slope of $-\frac{\alpha}{(1-\alpha)}$.

The optimal contract is the point E where the iso-cost curve is tangential to the worker's indifference curve. This occurs at a point on the 45° line, i.e. at a point where $w_1=w_2$. So the worker's wage will be the same whatever the firm's output price.

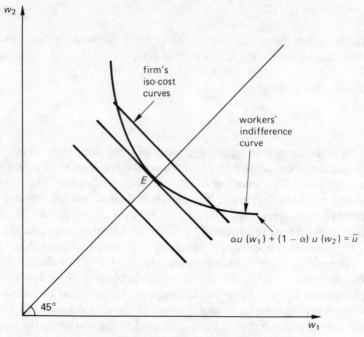

FIGURE 4.1 The optimal contract

So it appears that implicit-contract theory can explain wage-stickiness, one of the stylised facts of the labour market mentioned in the introduction. However, one should be clear about the nature of this wage-stickiness result. It means that employers will stabilise the real income of workers. This implies that if there are variations in the aggregate price level (which are not in the model above) which affect the real value of the worker's wage then the nominal wage paid to workers will be indexed to this aggregate price level. Thus the real consumption wage is constant and the real product wage varies with fluctuations in the output price.

Second, the duration of the wage-stickiness will only be the duration of the contract. Suppose that the fall in the output price today is a permanent downward shock. Although wages fixed by contract will not respond in this period, when the contracts are renegotiated next period they will fully take into account the lower demand for labour and the negotiated wage will be lower. So wage rigidity lasts only as long as the length of wage contracts.[5]

Third, the wage rigidity result depends crucially on the assumption that the employer is risk-neutral. If the employer is risk-averse then wages will not be rigid; they will vary with the firm's output price.[6]

Finally it should be remembered that although if wages are fixed in a competitive labour market fluctuations in the marginal product of labour will be reflected in fluctuations in employment, this is not necessarily true in an implicit-contract model as the wage is not necessarily equal to the marginal product of labour. In fact, it is possible to prove the following proposition.

Proposition 4.1 (ii)

For any value of the firm's output price, employment will always be higher with an implicit contract than it would be in a competitive labour market.

Proof See Appendix.

This over-employment result was first pointed out by Akerlof and Miyazaki (1980) and Pissarides (1981). The intuition for the result is as follows.

For any value of the firm's output price, the wage and employment level in that state will be chosen to be efficient in the sense that there is no other combination of wage and employment level which makes both the employer and the worker better-off. If the price of output in the state under consideration is p and the wage paid is w, and L out of N workers are employed, then the expected utility of workers in this state will, from (4.5) be given by:

$$\frac{L}{N}.u(w) + \frac{(N-L)}{N}.v(b) \tag{4.8}$$

This captures the fact that the worker expects to be employed with probability L/N and unemployed with probability $(N-L)/N$. Indifference curves for the worker in w–L space are drawn in Figure 4.2.

The firm's profit in this state will from (4.1) be given by

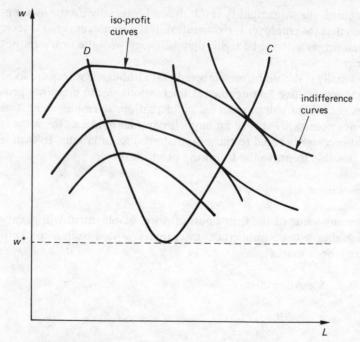

FIGURE 4.2   Employment: implicit contracts versus the competitive labour market

$pf(L) - wL$. The firm's isoprofit curves are also drawn in Figure 4.2.

If the contract is efficient, we must have a combination of w and L for which the workers' indifference curves are tangential to the employer's isoprofit curves. The set of these points is represented by the upward-sloping line AC. This line is formally analogous to the contract curve in the efficient bargain theory of trade union behaviour.

Now in a spot-market employment always lies on the labour-demand curve given by (4.3). This relationship between w and L is represented by the downward-sloping line AD. Now, we know that with implicit contracts we must always be on a point on AC while with a competitive spot-labour market we must always be on AD. As the level of employment on AC is never below that on AD, employment must be higher with implicit contracts than in a competitive labour market. This proves the proposition described above.

This argument also shows that although implicit contracts may lead to arrangements like rigid wages which are commonly thought of as being indicative of inefficiencies, implicit contracts are in fact efficient given that workers need to buy insurance from their employers. So it is not clear that the government should intervene to make wages less rigid.

The very simple implicit-contract model presented in this section has produced two of the classic results in this area; rigid wages and overemployment relative to the competitive level. However it has been a very simple model in a number of respects.

First we assumed that the decision to work is a $(0,1)$ decision; there can be no variation in hours. If we introduce hours as an additional choice variable in our model, we find that all workers should work the same number of hours so that any unemployment is in the form of work-sharing rather than lay-offs. This is simply another consequence of the fact that workers want to be insured against fluctuations in their utility. However, this prediction is the opposite of what seems to happen in the real world where lay-offs rather than work-sharing seem the norm. Feldstein (1976) and Baily (1977) present modifications of the model integrating it with the social-security system to produce more realistic results. The basic idea is that workers in the USA only receive government unemployment benefit if they are wholly unemployed and receive nothing if they work even a small number of hours. This creates an incentive to lay off some workers rather than reduce the hours of all workers.

Second, the only payments made by the employer to workers have been in the form of wage payments made to workers when they are employed. But as workers desire to stabilise their incomes they would like to receive payments from the firm when they are unemployed as well. So there will be a demand for unemployment benefit paid by the employer to the workers. In the model presented above we did not allow for this. What is the consequence if we do so?

Assume that when unemployed each worker receives unemployment benefit of s, on top of the government unemployment benefit of b. s can vary with the firm's output price so if the output price is p_i, then denote the benefit paid by the employer by s_i. When unemployed workers now receive utility of $v(b+s_i)$ rather than the $v(b)$ as before. In addition the firm's profit in any state is now given by:

$$\pi_i = p_i.f(L_i) - w_i.L_i - (N - L_i).s_i \tag{4.9}$$

(Equation 4.9) captures the idea that employers make payments not only to those workers they employ but also to those with whom they have signed a contract, but whom they do not employ.

Taking account of the changes introduced by assuming that employers can pay unemployment benefit, we can rewrite the problem of choosing the optimal contract in (4.6) in the following way. The employer must now choose (w_i, s_i, L_i) $i = 1, \ldots, n$ and N to solve the following constrained maximisation problem:

$$\max E\pi = \sum_{i=1}^{n} \alpha_i \left[p_i.f(L_i) - w_i.L_i - s_i (N - L_i) \right]$$

subject to:

$$Eu = \sum_{i=1}^{n} \alpha_i \left[\frac{L_i}{N} u(w_i) + \frac{N - L_i}{N} v(b + s_i) \right] \geqslant \bar{u} \tag{4.10}$$

$$L_i \leqslant N \qquad i = 1, \ldots, n$$

As before, the technical analysis of this problem is presented in the Appendix. The main results are summarised in the following Proposition.

Proposition 4.2(i)

When the employer can pay unemployment benefit, we have the following results:

(a) the wage paid by the employer does not vary with the firm's output price, i.e. $w_i = \bar{w}$ for all i.
(b) the level of unemployment benefit paid by the employer does not vary with the firm's output price i.e. $s_i = \bar{s}$ for all i.
(c) the level of the wage and unemployment benefit are set so as to equate the marginal utility of income of workers both when employed and unemployed i.e. $u'(\bar{w}) = v'(b + \bar{s})$.

Proof See Appendix.

From part (a) of this proposition note that, as before, the wage is rigid. The explanation of this is exactly the same as before: workers dislike risk but employers only care about the average wage bill. Part (b) of the proposition tells us that we also have a rigid unemployment benefit result; again this is the result of the workers' desire for insurance.

Part (c) of the proposition is more novel. The intuitive explanation for it is the following. Suppose the employer has £1 to give to the workers who have to choose whether to have this as a wage or unemployment benefit. They will choose to divide it in such a way that the marginal utility of income when employed and unemployed is the same so that no change in the division of the pound will increase utility.

Note that the fact that marginal utilities of income are equal does *not* necessarily mean that the worker's income will be the same both when employed and when unemployed. Nor does it mean that the levels of utility will be the same for employed and unemployed workers. The reason for this is that the utility functions $u(\ )$ and $v(\ )$ are different.

In fact we can show that it is optimal in certain circumstances to make employed workers worse off than unemployed ones. This will be the case for any utility function in which leisure is a normal good (which is taken to be the usual case). In such a case we do not have involuntary unemployment where those unemployed would like to be employed, but involuntary employment where those who are employed are worse-off than their unemployed counterparts. This does raise potential problems; if this was the case all workers would try to be the unemployed ones, and this may have adverse consequences for work effort.[7]

Turning now to the optimal employment rule, we can show that for some specifications of the worker utility function the over-employment result of Proposition 1(ii) disappears. Now, employment with implicit contracts will be the same as it would be in a competitive labour market. However, it is still difficult to explain why employment might be lower than in a competitive labour market.

In this section we have presented two simple implicit-contract models, one in which the employer does not pay unemployment benefits, and one in which s/he does. Which is to be preferred? The model itself predicts that it will be profitable for the employer to pay unemployment benefit, but Oswald (1986) finds that very few employers actually do so.[8]

How successful are these simple models in replicating phenomena observed in the real world? Both models generated real-consumption wage rigidity, but they do not always generate less employment than would be observed in a competitive spot labour market, and they do not always generate involuntary unemployment in the sense that unemployed workers are worse-off than those employed. However it should be stressed that precise results in all these areas depend crucially on the assumptions made about the risk aversion of employer and workers, and the utility function of workers.

But the most important point to realise is that whereas it is common to think of real-world phenomena like wage rigidity and unemployment as representing inefficiencies, the optimal contracts described above are always efficient, given the imperfect nature of insurance markets, which leads workers to desire insurance from their employers.

4.4   ENFORCING IMPLICIT CONTRACTS

The previous section presented a model of implicit contracts based on the assumption that the contract agreed could be enforced. Given that optimal contracts do not seem to be observed in reality, the mechanism by which these 'implicit' contracts are enforced is unclear. This section aims to outline some of the ways in which this might be done.

To illustrate the problems that might arise if contracts cannot be enforced by a court, suppose that after the output price has been realised it is possible for workers to sell their labour on a spot market and for the employer to dispense with his/her existing workers and hire new workers at the spot-market wage. Suppose that neither worker nor employer can be bound to a contract they have signed.

If the spot-market wage turns out to be greater than the wage specified in the contract then the worker will leave to earn more elsewhere. If the spot-market wage is less than the wage specified in the contract then the employer will replace the existing worker with an outside worker. If the marginal product of labour is below the contract wage the employer will want to fire the worker.

So if neither worker nor employer can commit themselves in advance not to break the contract then the contract will collapse; the only enforceable contract is one in which the contract wage is always equal to the spot-market wage, and the marginal product of labour is equal to this wage, i.e. the contract is the same as a spot market.

What ways out of this are there?

One of the earliest approaches (e.g. Baily, 1974) was to assume the existence of mobility costs for workers and costs for the employer of replacing workers.[9] If these costs are large enough then one can enforce a contract with wages different from the spot-market wage as long as the difference is not large enough to make it worthwhile for either the worker to leave or the employer to replace the worker. However, this cannot prevent the employer from laying-off workers when the marginal product of labour is below the wage. This acts as a constraint on the set of feasible contracts although contracts are still desirable – for more details see Bean (1984).[10]

Another approach, taken by Holmstrom (1981), is to look at models where contracts last more than one period. Suppose there is no problem for the firm in committing itself to enforcing a contract but that the workers cannot bind themselves not to leave in the event of a better offer turning up.[11] If contracts last for two periods then workers can offer to work for a low wage in the first period in return for a guarantee of a higher wage in future periods. This high second-period wage removes the incentives for workers to leave in the second period while the low first-period wage ensures that workers do not receive a greater level of expected utility than they could find elsewhere.

Finally another approach, also illustrated by Holmstrom (1981), is reputation effects. If either employer or workers gain a reputation for breaking contracts when it is in their short-term interest to do so, we might expect them to have difficulty in finding employers or workers to sign contracts with them in the future, i.e. they will acquire a bad reputation which is costly to them in the future. This type of effect does allow for implicit contracts to be enforceable although some constraints are generally imposed on the type of contracts that can be enforced.

In the previous section we assumed that any contract could be enforced. But, if implicit contracts really are implicit, and cannot be enforced in the courts, we need to model the problem of enforceability. We have shown how enforceability can be a problem and sketched ways of dealing with it. In general, problems of enforceability may limit the type of implicit contracts that are feasible but do not render implicit contracts useless.

4.5 IMPLICIT CONTRACTS WITH ASYMMETRIC INFORMATION

In the model of the third section although there was initially some uncertainty about the firm's output price, when it was revealed both worker and employer could observe it. This is known as symmetric information.

In response to some of the problems associated with symmetric information implicit-contract models, people began to look at contract models in which one party knew more than the other, i.e. in which there was an asymmetric distribution of information. The literature on implicit contracts with asymmetric information is generally quite technical (for excellent surveys, see Hart, 1984; Azariadis and Stiglitz, 1983; Hart and Holstrom, 1986), so I will concentrate on presenting a very simple example to illustrate the main ideas.

Suppose that an employer has to consider whether to employ a single worker who, if employed, will produce one unit of output which will be sold at a price p. If the wage paid is w, profit will be

$$\pi = p - w$$

We will assume that any contract must satisfy a no-bankruptcy condition that $\pi \geqslant 0$. We assume that the employer is risk-neutral.

Assume that the worker's utility function is given by $u = w$ and that he or she is risk-neutral.[12] Assume that at date 0 a contract is signed and that the output price p is distributed uniformly between zero and one, so that employment is always desirable. Also assume that the worker now chooses the optimal contract subject to offering the employer at least zero-expected profits. This might be because there are lots of potential employers so there is excess demand for labour.

Suppose first of all that we have a situation of symmetric information so that when at date 1 the output price is revealed, it is observed by both employer and worker. This means that the worker's wage demand can depend on the firm's output price. We will write it as $w(p)$.

The worker wants to choose $w(p)$ to solve the following constrained maximisation problem:

$$\max Eu = \int_0^1 [w(p)]\, dp$$

subject:

$$E\pi = \int_0^1 [p - w(p)]\, dp \geqslant 0 \quad p - w(p) \geqslant 0 \tag{4.11}$$

The first constraint says that expected profits must be greater than or equal to zero while the second constraint is the no-bankruptcy condition. Without worrying about the technical details of the solution to (4.11), it should be apparent that the best contract for the worker is $w(p) = p$ for all p so that the employer has zero profits in all states.

Now suppose that only the employer observes the output price at date 1. Accordingly the only way the worker can make the wage dependent on the output price is if the employer communicates his/her observations of the output price to the worker. But there is nothing to make the employer tell the truth, so if the wage-demand of the worker depends on the firm's output price, the employer will always say that the output price is very low in order to obtain a low wage. In the example given above if the worker tried to implement the wage contract $w(p) = p$ the employer would always say that $p = 0$, in which case the wage will also be equal to zero. Even though the worker intended the wage to vary with p it will not do so in practice. Recognising this problem, the only feasible strategy for a rational worker is to set a wage, w, which does not vary with the output price. But the problem with this strategy is that when the output price is very low it will be below this wage, with the consequence that the employer will go bankrupt and the worker will be unemployed.

To find that optimal wage, suppose the worker sets a wage w.

The worker will be employed if $p > w$ which happens with probability $(1 - w)$ (recall the assumption that p is uniformly distributed between zero and one) in which case the worker receives w. If $p < w$ the worker will be unemployed and receive nothing; this happens with probability w. So the expected utility of the worker if s/he sets a wage w will be:

$$Eu = w(1 - w) + 0.w = w(1 - w)$$

Maximising with respect to w yields $w = 0.5$. This means that the worker will be unemployed with probability 0.5. So, this very simple asymmetric information model yields a rigid wage and unemployment as its outcome. The outcome is *ex post* inefficient. This is so because when $p < w$ and the worker is unemployed, workers and employers know that both could be better-off if the wage was lower and the worker employed. However, the worker does not want to obtain a reputation for reducing wages when the output price is low as the employer will then always claim a low price in order to obtain a low wage even when the output price is high. This simple asymmetric-information implicit-contract model therefore has as its outcome a rigid wage, together with unemployment which is too high in that unemployed workers would like to be employed at slightly below the going wage. It seems to explain all the stylised facts set out in the Introduction.

However the conclusions of this very simple asymmetric information model do not necessarily carry over to models with different assumptions. In general the wage rigidity result does not hold if there is a concave production function and employment can vary. And one can present models in which if the worker's utility function is such that leisure is a normal good, the optimal contract has over-employment rather than the under-employment exhibited above.

Finally there are also models with other asymmetries of information. For example, Moore (1985) considered the case in which workers have some private information, while more complicated still is the case where both worker and employer have some private information (see Moore, 1984). However, the important point remains that models with asymmetric information can generate inefficient outcomes which models with symmetric information cannot.

4.6 CONCLUSION

Implicit-contract theory was originally proposed as a practical theory designed to explain the observed behaviour of labour markets. Various proponents of the theory, at various times, have claimed that it can explain wage rigidity and involuntary unemployment. As we have seen, these are only predictions of the theory in certain special cases. Some doubts can even be expressed about whether implicit (or explicit) contracts even exist. However, the idea that because of the imperfect nature of insurance markets, workers desire some insurance from employers which alters the nature of labour markets does seem to be an important point even if it cannot ultimately explain the existence or level of involuntary unemployment.

APPENDIX

Proof of Proposition 4.1(i)

From (4.6), we can write the employer's choice of the optimal employment contract as being the choice of $\{w_i, L_i\}$ $i = 1, \ldots, n$ and N to solve the following constrained maximisation problem:

$$\max E\pi = \sum_{i=1}^{n} \alpha_i [p_i f(L_i) - w_i.L_i]$$

$$\text{s.t.} = \sum_{i=1}^{n} \alpha_i \left[\frac{L_i}{N}. u(w_i) + \frac{(N-L_i)}{N}.v(b)\right] \geq \bar{U} \tag{4A.1}$$

$$L_i \leq N \quad i = 1, \ldots, n$$

Define a Lagrange Multiplier μ for the first constraint and λ_i, $i = 1, \ldots, n$ for the second set of constraints.

The first order condition for the problem in (4A.1) for w_i can be written as:

$$-\alpha_i L_i + \frac{\mu \, \alpha_i L_i}{N} u'(w_i) = 0 \tag{4A.2}$$

which, on simplification, reduces to:

$$u'(w_i) = \frac{N}{\mu} \tag{4A.3}$$

As N, the size of the labour pool is independent of p_i and μ the multiplier on the first constraint in (4A.1) is also independent of p_i. Equation (4A.3) says that the marginal utility of income for an employed worker must be the same in all states, i.e.

$$w_i = \bar{w} \text{ for all } p_i \tag{4A.4}$$

This completes the proof of Proposition 4.1(i).

Proof of Proposition 4.1(ii)

Turning to Proposition 4.1(ii), we need to examine the first-order condition for employment in state i in the problem in (4A.1). This can be written as

$$\alpha_i \left[p_i f'(L_i) - w_i \right] + \frac{\mu \alpha_i}{N} \left[u(w_i) - v(b) \right] - \lambda_i = 0 \tag{4A.5}$$

Now, from (4A.4) and (4A.5) we know that $w_i = \bar{w}$ and that $u'(\bar{w}) = N/\mu$ so that (4A.5) can be written as:

$$p_i f'(L_i) = \bar{w} + \frac{u(\bar{w}) - v(b)}{u'(w)} - \frac{\lambda_i}{\alpha_i} \tag{4A.6}$$

so that marginal product of labour is not equal to the wage. Note that, from the Kuhn–Tucker complementary slackness conditions, if $\lambda_i > 0$ then $L = N$ so all the labour pool will be employed; while if $L < N$, we have $\lambda_i = 0$. We will concentrate on this last case (although there will always be some states in which $L_i = N$).

Now consider a comparison of the level of employment with implicit contracts with the level in a competitive labour market. Recall that with a competitive labour market we had the wage equal to w^* where $v(b) = u(w^*)$ so that workers were just indifferent between working and not working.

Now from the definition of concavity we know that

$$u(\bar{w}) - u(w^*) > u'(\bar{w})(\bar{w} - w^*) \text{ for any } \bar{w}, w^* \tag{4A.7}$$

so that:

$$\frac{u(\bar{w}) - v(b)}{u'(w)} = \frac{u(\bar{w}) - u(w^*)}{u'(w)} \geq \bar{w} - w^* \tag{4A.8}$$

Substituting this in (4A.6) we obtain:

$$p_i f'(L_i) < w^* - \frac{\lambda_i}{\alpha_i} \tag{4A.9}$$

Alan Manning 83

For these states in which $\lambda_i = 0$ (i.e. those states for which $L < N$ so not all workers are employed) we have

$$p_i f'(L_i) < w^* \tag{4A.10}$$

so that the marginal product of labour is always below the competitive wage level. As in the competitive spot market we always have equality between the wage and the marginal product of labour and the wage never below w^*, implying that employment is *higher* with an implicit contract than predicted by a competitive spot labour market model. This does not fit with the third of the stylised facts presented in the Introduction.

Proof of Proposition 4.2(i)

When the employer pays unemployment benefit, we can write the employer's problem as being to solve:

$$\max E\pi = \sum_{i=1}^{n} \alpha_i \, [p_i f(L_i) - w_i.L_i - s_i \, (N - L_i)]$$

$$\text{s.t.} \ Eu = \sum_{i=1}^{n} \alpha_i \, [\frac{L_i}{N} u(w_i) + \frac{(N - L_i)}{N} v(b + s_i)] \geqslant \bar{u} \tag{4A.11}$$

$$L_i \leqslant N \qquad i = 1, \ldots, n$$

As before, define a Lagrange Multiplier μ for the first constraint and multiplier $\lambda_i \, i = 1, \ldots, n$ for the second set of constraints.
The first-order condition for the solution to (4A.11) for w_i is:

$$- \alpha_i L_i + \mu \alpha_i \, \frac{L_i}{N} \, u'(w_i) = 0 \tag{4A.12}$$

which reduces to:

$$u'(w_i) = \frac{N}{\mu} \tag{4A.13}$$

which can be seen to be identical to (4A.5). So, once again the real-consumption wage paid to workers is rigid. This proves 4.2(i) part (a).
But we also now have first-order conditions for s_i the level of unemployment benefit payable by the firm. The first-order condition for the solution to (all) for s_i is:

$$- \alpha_i(N - L_i) + \mu \alpha_i \, \frac{(N - L_i)}{N} v'(b + s_i) = 0 \tag{4A.14}$$

which reduces to:

$$v'(b+s_i) = \frac{N}{\mu} \tag{4A.15}$$

This implies that $(b+s_i)$ must be a constant so that the unemployment benefit paid is independent of the employer's output price. The intuition for this is again that insuring workers against fluctuations in their income is the cheapest way for employers to guarantee workers the required level of expected utility. This proves 4.2(i) part (b).

Comparing (4A.15) with (4A.13) we also have the additional result that:

$$u'(\bar{w}) = v'(b+\bar{s}) \tag{4A.16}$$

so that $\bar{w}$ and $\bar{s}$ are chosen so that the marginal utility of income is the same both when workers are employed and unemployed. This proves 4.2(i) (c).

Note that this does *not* necessarily mean that the worker's income will be the same both when employed and when unemployed. Nor does it mean that the levels of utility will be the same for employed and unemployed workers. The reason for this is that the utility functions $u(\ )$ and $v(\ )$ are different. To illustrate these points we need to return to the specification of $u(\ )$ and $v(\ )$ in (4.2) and to the underlying ability function $u(W,H)$. Suppose that $u(W,H)$ is of the following form:

$$u(w, H) = U(w - rH) \tag{4A.17}$$

r represents the disutility of labour. This is the utility function used by Azariadis (1975). Then from (4.2) we have

$$u(w) = U(w - r)$$

$$v(b) = U(b)$$

so (4A.16) becomes $u'(\bar{w} - r) = u'(b + \bar{s})$ so that for specification of the worker's utility function in (4A.17) we have:

$$\bar{w} - \bar{s} = b + r \tag{4A.18}$$

so that the wage exceeds the unemployment benefit by an amount which exactly compensates for the foregone state unemployment benefit and the disutility of labour. Workers are equally well-off when unemployed as when employed. However, different union utility functions yield different results. Suppose that:

$$u(w, H) = G(w) - H \tag{4A.19}$$

Then we have

$$u(w) = G(w) - 1$$
$$v(b) = G(w)$$

and (4A.16) becomes:

$$u'(\bar{w}) = G'(\bar{w}) = G'(b + \bar{s}) = v'(b + \bar{s}) \tag{4A.20}$$

This implies that $\bar{w} - \bar{s} = b$ so that the wage exceeds the unemployment benefit by an amount which compensates only for the foregone state unemployment benefit. Comparing the utility levels of workers when employed and unemployed we have:

$$u(\bar{w}) = G(\bar{w}) - 1 = G(b + \bar{s}) - 1 < G(b + \bar{s}) = v(b + \bar{s}) \tag{4A.21}$$

so that workers who are employed are *worse*-off than those who are unemployed.

Turning now to the optimal level of employment, the first-order condition for L_i is:

$$\alpha_i \left[p_i(L_i) - w_i + s_i \right] + \frac{\mu \alpha_i}{N} \left[u(w_i) - v(b + s_i) \right] - \lambda_i = 0 \tag{4A.22}$$

which can be rewritten as:

$$p_i f'(L_i) = w_i - s_i - \frac{u(w_i) - v(b + s_i)}{N/\mu} + \frac{\lambda_i}{\alpha_i} \tag{4A.23}$$

To make more sense of (4A.23) let us take a special case, the utility function of (4A.17). For that utility function, we showed that in the optimal contract $u(\bar{w}) = v(b + \bar{s})$ and that $\bar{w} - \bar{s} = b + r$ so that (4A.23) becomes (for any state with $L_i < N$)

$$p_i f'(L_i) = b + r \tag{4A.24}$$

so that the marginal product of labour is set equal to the sum of the disutility of labour and the level of unemployment benefit. Now $(b + r)$ is also the minimum wage for which workers will work so in the earlier notation we have $(b + r) = w^*$. This should be contrasted with (4A.6), the case without employer-paid unemployment benefit. So with unemployment benefits paid by the employer the over-employment result disappears.

5 Union Bargaining: A Survey of Recent Work*

ALISTAIR ULPH and DAVID ULPH

5.1 INTRODUCTION

While economists have had a long-standing interest in the way the presence of trade unions affects the operations of the labour market and hence of the economy, there has been a remarkable upsurge of work in this area since the late 1970s. This was undoubtedly sparked by the recognition that, given the prevalence of collectively negotiated wage agreements, a clear understanding of how unions set wages was an essential part of the urgent need to explain the prevailing very high levels of unemployment.

This renewed attention has had two effects. First, the whole theory of union wage-bargaining has been more fully articulated. Many models have been shown to be just special cases of other more general models, and, as a result two very general classes of model – right-to-manage and efficient-bargain models – have come to dominate the literature. Much of this is reviewed in the recent survey by Oswald (1986). Moreover a start has been made on empirical work to test these alternative theories. Second, the limitations of these simple models of union bargaining have been exposed: for they essentially focus on a single union with a fixed membership bargaining with a single firm with fixed production possibilities, where the only variables of concern are wages and employment. Much of the work at the frontiers of this area has been devoted to exploring how results of the simple models survive when there are multiple unions and multiple firms; when it is recognised that strategic variables on the firm side, such as the level of investment or the level of R&D expenditure, can both affect and be affected by the bargain between the firm and the union; and when it is similarly recognised that on the union's side membership might both affect and be affected by the bargain.

In section 5.2 we will set out in some detail the main elements of what have now become the standard models of union wage determination. We then briefly review some empirical work that has been done to test these alternative theories. This is followed by an outline of their major weaknesses.

Section 5.3 explores the outcome of the bargain when there might be other aspects of work, such as hours of work, or other factors of production such as capital which directly or indirectly affect the union. Section 5.4 examines models where the level of membership is affected by and can also affect the bargain between the firm and the union, while section 5.5 takes up the issues that arise when there may be many firms or many unions involved in bargaining. Section 5.6 summarises the conclusions drawn.

As we will see, the general theme lying behind this latter work is that the major weakness of the simple standard models is that they essentially presuppose that the firm has some power that enables it to make a surplus, while the union has some power which enables it to try to extract some of this surplus. As in recent work by Gale (1986a and b), Binmore and Herrero (1987a and b) and Rubinstein and Wolinsky (1986), the need is to understand where this power comes from in a world where there may be many alternatives open to both firms and workers.

5.2 STANDARD MODELS OF UNION BEHAVIOUR

The simplest traditional models of how such a bargain is made over wages, and, directly or indirectly, over the level of employment, are constructed as follows.

General framework

(1) We focus on the bargain between a single firm and a single union.

(2) This union represents the interests of $m > 0$ identical workers – the union membership – who possess some special skills that are valuable to the firm. We assume that if the firm wishes to bargain with the union representing these workers it must enter into a *closed-shop* agreement that it will only hire workers of this type who are members of this union. As we will see, m does not often play much of a role in traditional models, and this is often assumed to be so large that, not all union members will be employed by this firm. For the moment we also make this assumption.

(3) Any of these workers who are not employed by this firm have the opportunity of earning a 'reservation wage', $r > 0$, in some 'alternative sector' of the economy. This reservation wage is independent of the number of union members who finally receive it. This 'alternative' could represent either full-time employment in some other competitive labour market, or being unemployed and receiving unemployment benefit from the state,[1] or some weighted combination of the two, where the weight will depend on the general level of unemployment in the rest of the economy.[2]

(4) We next have to assume that there is something for the union and the firm to bargain over. What this entails is that the firm must be able to make more profits by hiring union labour (at the reservation wage) than it can by using no union labour at all. This gives the union the power to try to appropriate some of these surplus profits by using the threat of withholding union labour to negotiate a wage above the reservation wage and it is clear that the assumption of a closed shop is crucial to this threat. Of course, in general it cannot appropriate all the surplus since the firm can equally threaten not to employ union workers. Both sides have an incentive to reach an agreement on how this surplus is to be split between them.

For this surplus to exist, a number of conditions must be satisfied.

In the first place, it must not be possible for the firm to simply hire all the workers it needs with these particular skills from the competitive sector. For, if it could, any attempt by the union to drive the wage of its members above the reservation wage, will leave the firm with the more profitable alternative of simply hiring non-union workers. Thus m has to be large relative to the total pool of workers with these skills.

However, this is not sufficient. What we also have to rule out is a situation where there is constant average productivity of labour and the firm is operating in a very competitive output market, so that with free entry price is driven down to the average cost of other firms, which is just the inverse of the average product of labour multiplied by the reservation wage. Now, the fact that the union has already accounted for a large percentage of workers with the requisite skills, may, under some circumstances, go a long way to providing the required entry barriers. But this would not be so in the context of international competition where foreign firms could draw on a completely different labour pool.

This last condition is quite a complex one, being a restriction on the kind of technology open to the firm, and/or the kind of product market within which it is operating. Nevertheless, it clearly goes a long way towards explaining why in some sectors of the economy, such as retailing, unions have been able to make much less impact than in others.

The source of union power is never explicitly modelled in the standard theories. Rather, the assumption that they do have power is captured by assuming, for example, that the firm is operating in a competitive product market, but has a production function displaying sufficient decreasing returns to labour, that the firm can make positive profits when employing labour at the reservation wage. This is the approach we will take, though we could alternatively have assumed constant returns to labour and an imperfectly competitive output market, without making any substantive difference to the conclusions.

Thus we formally assume that we have a firm that is selling its output at a fixed price $p > 0$, and has a production function,[3] specifying that if it hires n union members it can produce output q, where

$$q = f(n) \tag{5.1}$$

$f'(n) > 0$, $f''(n) < 0$ – so marginal products are positive and decreasing.

Moreover we assume that $f(0) = 0$, to capture the idea that the skills that these workers possess are essential to enable the firm to undertake production.[4] Finally we assume that the marginal revenue product of the first worker exceeds the reservation wage – i.e. $pf'(0) > r$ – so the firm can make profits by hiring union members at the reservation wage, and there is therefore a surplus to be bargained over.

Thus if, as the outcome of bargaining with the union, the firm ends up hiring n union workers at a wage of $w \geqslant r$, then, in this example, its profits will be:

$$\pi(n,w;p) \equiv pf(n) - wn \tag{5.2}$$

so, recalling that we are ruling out fixed factors, and have assumed $f(0) = 0$, the gain it will have made from agreeing to this bargain rather than being unable to undertake productions without the union is:

$$G^f(n,w;p) = \pi(n,w;p) \tag{5.3}$$

In Figure 5.1 we represent the *iso-profit* contours of the firm.

Clearly for a given n, profits are higher the lower is the wage. Given diminishing marginal productivity, then, for a given wage, profits initially increase as employment is increased, since marginal revenue product is above the wage. This happens up to the point where profits are maximised – marginal revenue product equals the wage – and thereafter further increases in employment reduce profits. This explains the general inverse-U shape of the curves. Moreover since the locus of turning-points of these curves is the locus of profit-maximising employment levels for different wages, it represents the standard demand curve for labour, and is, as we know from theory, downward-sloping.

(5) We now have to specify the gain to the union from agreeing to a bargain which results in n of its members being employed at a wage w, with the remaining $m-n$ getting the reservation wage r. One crucial issue in specifying this is whether the union attempts to operate some scheme of internal income redistribution amongst its members. We very rarely observe unions doing this, but the problem is that given the way union preferences are typically specified, it would always be optimal for it to run such a scheme, and, as we shall see, some of the conclusions of the theory depend

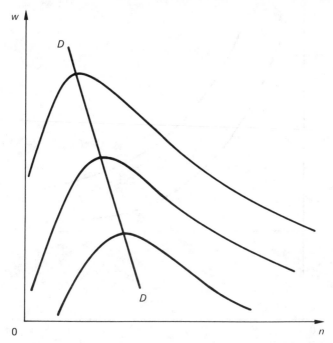

FIGURE 5.1 Iso-profit contours of the firm

critically on the assumption that the union does not redistribute income. So we are in the position that some of the conclusions depend on behaviour which is not fully explained by the model. Nevertheless we will proceed for the moment with the widely employed assumption that there is no internal redistribution.

If we assume that the workers to be employed by the firm are chosen at random from the pool of members, then each member of the union has expected utility

$$U(n,w;r,m) \equiv (n/m)u(w) + [1 - (n/m)]u(r) \tag{5.4}$$

where $u(x)$ is the utility of a worker getting income x for sure.[5] We assume $u'(x) > 0$, $u''(x) \leqslant 0$, so workers are either risk-neutral ($u'' = 0$) or strictly risk-averse ($u'' < 0$).

Assuming that if the union fails to agree with the firm all

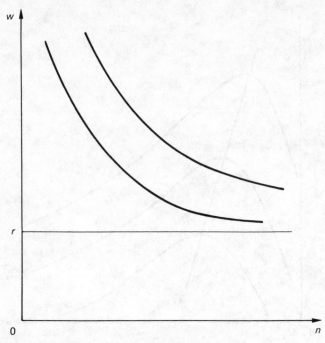

FIGURE 5.2   Union indifference curves

members get employed in the alternative sector at the wage r then the gain to the entire union from getting n of its members employed at the wage w is:

$$G^u(n,w;r) \equiv n[u(w) - u(r)] \qquad (5.5)$$

In Figure 5.2 we represent 'union indifference curves' – the various combinations of w and n that give the union the same value of G^u. Notice these are only defined for $w \geqslant r$, and, given risk-aversion, have the standard shape.

(6) Having now set up the basic ingredients of the bargaining framework, we are in a position to say how the bargain is determined. The first thing is to specify the subject of the bargaining and here there are two very different theories, which we will deal with in two separate subsections.

Right-to-manage models

Here the assumption is that although the union can bargain over the wage, the firm retains the right to determine the number of workers it hires. There are a variety of justifications that have been given for this assumption (see, for example, Nickell and Andrews, 1983) and we will discuss these later on. Given this assumption, then, whatever wage is set in the bargain, the firm will always choose *n* to maximise profits, and so *employment will always lie on the demand curve.*

The simplest version of the right-to-manage model is the *monopoly union model.* Here the wage is chosen unilaterally by the union so as to maximise its utility, subject of course to the constraint that employment must lie on the demand curve. Combining Figures 5.1 and 5.2 we can illustrate this solution in Figure 5.3, where the wage chosen, w^m, occurs at the point where the union indifference curve is tangent to the demand curve.

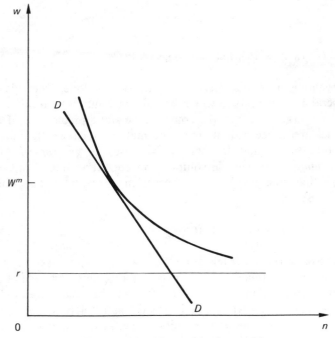

FIGURE 5.3   Monopoly union model

A more general version of the thory, has the wage being set as the outcome of a bargaining process between the firm and the union.

Let $\hat{n}(w/p)$ be the level of employment chosen by the firm when the real wage is w/p, and the maximum profits to which this choice of n gives rise will be written as

$$\hat{\pi}(w;p) \equiv \text{Max } \pi(n,w;p)$$

$$n \geqslant 0$$

where the standard theory of profit maximisation implies[6]

$$\hat{\pi}_w(w;p) = \hat{n}(w/p) \; ; \; \hat{\pi}_p(w;p) = f[\hat{n}(w/p)]$$

Substituting these back into (5.3) and (5.5) we see that the gains to the firm and union from agreeing to any given wage w are

$$\hat{G}^f(w;p) \equiv \hat{\pi}(w;p) \tag{5.6}$$

and

$$\hat{G}^u(w;p,r) \equiv \hat{n}(w/p)[u(w) - u(r)] \tag{5.7}$$

Bargaining now takes place over the wage alone. There is no general agreement as to which bargaining solution to adopt, and, by and large, as far as the comparative static predictions of the model are concerned, it does not matter much which one we choose. In all that follows we will use the *generalised Nash bargaining solution* as our solution concept. According to this, the wage that emerges from the bargaining process is that which maximises:

$$G(w;p,r) \equiv [\hat{G}^u(w;p,r)]^s \cdot [\hat{G}^f(w;p)]^{(1-s)} \tag{5.8}$$

where s is a parameter reflecting the relative bargaining strength of the union. The function $G(w;p.r)$ is just a weighted average of the gains to the union and the firm. If $s = 1$ then the wage that is determined is that which maximises the gain solely to the union, and so is just the monopoly union wage; at the other extreme if $s = 0$ the wage selected will be that which maximises the gain to the firm, and this will clearly just be the reservation wage; as s varies

between 0 and 1 we simply trace out all the wages between the
reservation wage and the monopoly union wage. So the generalised
Nash bargaining solution concept has the advantage that whatever
other solution concept we had used, there always exists some value
of s such that the bargain determined by this alternative concept
can be described as a generalised Nash bargain for that value of s.

What determines the relative bargaining strengths of the two
parties? To understand this requires us to think of a bargaining
process that might generate the Nash bargaining solution as an
outcome. The work of Rubinstein (1982) shows that what might
determine the relative bargaining strength in such a process is the
relative eagerness of the two parties to reach an agreement, and
obviously the party which is keener to reach a settlement is more
likely to settle for a smaller share of the gains. Factors which might
reflect this eagerness to settle would be a party's discount factor
(capturing how long a party would be willing to hold out), or a
party's attitude to risk (capturing a party's wish to be rid of the
uncertainties of the bargaining process and settle). Beyond this
however, economists have not had much to say about what
determines s, and for our purposes we shall simply treat s as a
parameter.

Carrying out the optimisation in (5.8) produces the first-order
condition:

$$\frac{swu'(w)}{[u(w)-u(r)]} = s\varepsilon(\omega) + \frac{(1-s)w\hat{n}(\omega)}{\hat{\pi}(w;p)} \qquad (5.9)$$

where $\omega = w/p$ is the real wage, and $\varepsilon(\omega) = -[\omega\hat{n}'(\omega)/\hat{n}(\omega)]$ is the
elasticity of the demand for labour.

The left-hand side of (5.9) is the percentage increase in a
worker's utility gain (from being employed by the firm rather than
in the alternative sector) brought about by a 1 per cent increase in
w, multiplied by the bargaining strength of the union (the share of
$\hat{G}^u$ in G). It therefore represents the percentage marginal benefit to
G from increasing w. The right-hand side represents the percentage
marginal cost. The first term reflects the percentage reduction in
the number of workers employed as a result of the wage increase –
which is a cost to the union and so is multiplied by s. The second
reflects the percentage reduction in profits, which is a cost to the
firm and so is multiplied by $(1-s)$.

The wage determined by (5.9) depends on the parameters s,r and

p, and can be written $\hat{w}(s,r,p)$. An increase in union strength unambiguously raises $\hat{w}$ with $\hat{w} \to r$ as $s \to 0$, $\hat{w} \to w^m$ as $s \to 1$.

Similarly, an increase in r, by lowering the absolute utility gain from any given wage, raises the percentage marginal gain from a further wage increase that appears on the left-hand side of (5.9), and so raises the wage that is bargained. Bearing in mind the interpretation of r which we had earlier on, this implies that an increase in unemployment in the economy at large will cause unions to moderate wage demands, and hence increase employment.

The most complex issue involves the effect of an increase in p. The difficulty is that an increase in p raises the profits the firm will make from any wage, but simultaneously increases the demand for labour and hence the utility which the union would obtain from any wage. Therefore, how this price increase affects the wage that is ultimately negotiated will depend on whether, at the margin, it is more beneficial to the firm than to the union. At this level of generality either outcome is possible. What will happen in any particular situation will depend on the underlying features of the model. To illustrate this, consider the case where:

$$f(n) = An^\alpha, \tag{5.10}$$

so $f(.)$ has essentially a Cobb–Douglas form. Then it is easily checked that the elasticity of demand is just $\varepsilon = 1/(1-\alpha)$, and so is independent of p. Moreover wages are just a share α of revenue, while profits are a share $(1-\alpha)$, so the second term on the right-hand side of (5.9) is also independent of p. But then (5.9) does not contain p explicitly, and the negotiated wage is independent of p.

This is a striking result, for variations in p can be interpreted as reflecting sectoral shifts in commodity demand, or in labour productivity. Therefore in this class of cases the theory predicts that changes in commodity demand or labour productivity do not affect the wage workers receive, but is absorbed entirely by employment.

These results illustrate the final feature of the right-to-manage models we wish to note, which is that their *testable restriction* is that variables such as the reservation wage and union strength which only affect union preferences, or the bargaining solution, should affect employment only through their effect on the wage rate: i.e. a regression of employment on the wage rate, and the other parameters of the model should detect no significant impact from parameters affecting solely union preferences or the bargaining solution.[7]

Now the reason that is given for rejecting the right-to-manage models, can be illustrated by considering Figure 5.4. Here s lies between 0 and 1, and so the outcome of the bargaining process produces the wage/employment combination represented by the point A on the demand curve. We have drawn the iso-profit curve and the union indifference curve passing through A, and it is clear that if either side were to propose the alternative of increased employment, albeit at a lower wage, as represented by, say, the point B, then the other side would accept it, in preference to A. In other words, A is not a Pareto-efficient outcome, and it is hard to see why rational agents in the process of bargaining, would ever

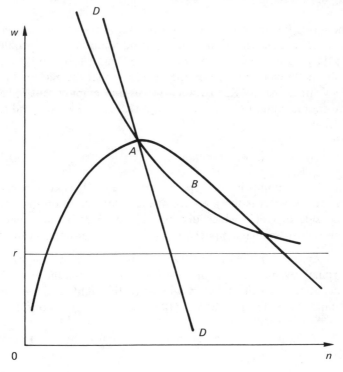

FIGURE 5.4   Inefficiency of the right-to-manage model

settle for an outcome that was not Pareto-efficient. This leads to the second major class of models we want to consider.

Efficient-bargain models

Probably the best-known paper developing an efficient-bargain model of union behaviour is that by McDonald and Solow (1981). The central feature of these models is the requirement that any wage/employment combination that emerges from the bargaining procedure should be *efficient* – that is, should maximise the gain to the firm from the bargain subject to achieving a given level of gain for the union. Thus the (w,n) pair that emerge should solve the problem:

$$\max_{n \geqslant 0, w \geqslant r} pf(n) - wn \quad \text{s.t.} \quad n[u(w) - u(r)] \geqslant \tilde{G}^u$$

where $\tilde{G}^u \geqslant 0$ is some specified level of gain to the union, restricted only by the requirement that the resulting solution to this problem should yield non-negative profits for the firm. All solutions to this problem are characterised by the condition that the marginal rate of substitutional (MRS) between wages and employment for the firm should equal the corresponding MRS for the union, and this becomes

$$pf'(n) = w - [u(w) - u(r)]/u'(w) \tag{5.11}$$

The locus of points in (w,n) space satisfying (5.11) is known as the *contract curve*. It is the presence of the second term on the right-hand side of (5.11) which distinguishes efficient-bargain models from right-to-manage models. It has a number of implications:

(1) Apart from the extreme case where $\tilde{G}^u = 0$, and so $w = r$, the marginal revenue product of labour will be less than the wage that is negotiated, so the solution will lie to the right of the labour-demand curve. The intuition for this should emerge in considering the next two points.

(2) If the union is risk-neutral – i.e. $u'' = 0$ – then $u(x)$ can be written

$$u(x) = a + bx$$

where a and $b > 0$ are constants, and substituting this into (5.11) yields:

$$pf'(n) = r$$

Thus the contract curve is a vertical straight line at the competitive level of employment.

In this case the union does not care if some of its members are paid more than others; it simply wants to maximise the size of the wage surplus $n(w - r)$. It therefore shares the firm's incentive to use labour in the most efficient way – hire it up to the point where marginal revenue product equals the reservation wage – and it then gets as much of these profits as it can by bidding the wage up above r.

Notice that this is precisely the case that would arise if the union ran an income-sharing scheme. For then of course individual union-members face no income risk, and the union simply wants to maximise its total income $wn + (m - n)r$, i.e. to maximise the wage surplus $n(w - r)$.

(3) If the union is risk averse – i.e. $u'' < 0$ – then it is easy to check that (5.11) makes the level of employment an increasing function of the wage – i.e. the contract curve is upward-sloping. This is hardly surprising, since, the greater the wage, the greater the opportunity cost to an individual member of not getting employed by the firm, so the union will wish to offer greater insurance to its members against this risk by increasing employment.

Thus in this case, far from higher wages being obtained by the union at the expense of employment falling further and further below the competitive level, as in right-to-manage models, with efficient bargains, if the union is successful in getting higher wages, it can also offer its members increased employment above the level that would be obtained under competition. Figure 5.5 illustrates the two kinds of contract curve.

So far the theory does not explain where on the contract curve the solution lies. Once again, while there are a number of solution concepts that could be employed, for convenience we will employ the generalised Nash bargaining-solution concept. Doing so implies that the full solution is characterised by (5.11) and

$$pf'(n) - w = [s/(1 - s)] [w - pf(n)/n] \tag{5.12}$$

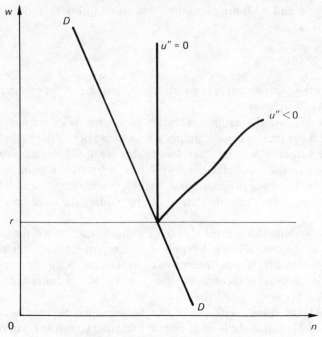

FIGURE 5.5 **The contract curve**

There are two interesting implications of (5.12).

The first is that, in the case of risk-neutrality – case (2) above – the wage gain to the union, $w(n-r)$, is just a share s of the profits the firm would have made in competitive market. In other words, in this case the union just reduces the firms profit by a fraction s, leaving employment unaffected. The profits made by the firm are then just the proportion $(1-s)$ of the profits it would have made facing a competitive labour market.

The second implication is that in the case of the Cobb–Douglas production function, (5.10), (5.12) can be solved to get

$$pf'(n) = \alpha w/[s + \alpha(1-s)] \qquad (5.13)$$

which, on substituting back into (5.11) produces an equation in w alone which does not contain p.

The comparative statics properties of the model are as follows:

(a) An increase in s increases w and, if there is risk-aversion, also increases n. This is just a straightforward move out along the contract curve.

(b) An increase in the reservation wage, shifts the contract curve to the left, and results in a higher wage and lower employment. Had there been no changes in wages and employment, then the increase in r would simply have eroded the union's gain from the bargain. The union will not bear all this loss, but passes some of it on to the firm in the form of a higher wage. However, the negotiated wage will not rise by as much as the reservation wage (otherwise the union would escape all the costs), so the union needs to offer its members less insurance against the risk of not being employed by the firm, so employment falls.

(c) An increase in p will increase employment, but its effect on the wage rate could go either way, and, as we have seen, in the case of Cobb–Douglas production functions, there will be no effect.

Thus the comparative static properties of the two models are broadly similar, the main difference lying in the predicted effects of a change in union bargaining power on employment. Given the recent legislative changes in the UK designed to alter the power of the unions, this difference could be very important in predicting their employment consequences, though of course, one must be wary about interpreting such changes as operating solely through the stylised variable s in these models.

Finally notice that the testable prediction of this model is that variables which influence bargaining power should jointly affect wages and employment in a way that depends solely on the slope of the contract curve. Thus if, for example, two variables z_1 and z_2 were thought to influence bargaining power, then the restriction is

$$\frac{\partial w/\partial z_1}{\partial w/\partial z_2} = \frac{\partial n/\partial z_1}{\partial n/\partial z_2} \tag{5.14}$$

This is quite a difficult restriction to implement as a test, since it requires that we be able to identify two separate factors that would influence bargaining strength,[8] and, as pointed out above, economists have not had much to say about what factors affect this.

Empirical tests of the theories

Although there have been a large number of studies of union behaviour in which one or other of the two theories has simply been assumed, it is only very recently that attempts have been made explicitly to test the theories.

Ashenfelter and Brown (1986), Bean and Turnbull (1987), Carruth, Findlay and Oswald (1986), MaCurdy and Pencavel (1986), Nickell and Wadhwani (1987a and b) have all carried out tests, looking at time-series data on wages and employment in industries which are heavily unionised, and approximate the single-union/single-employer framework of the theory. They have particularly concentrated on testing the right-to-manage model, focusing on the test that, conditional on the wage negotiated in the contract, there should be no independent effect on employment of wages in the alternative sector. The data fairly consistently reject this.

Attempts to test the efficient-bargain model have been less convincing. Ashenfelter and Brown test two separate versions. The first – which they call the strong efficiency version – takes it that full efficiency requires that unions operate an income-sharing scheme, and hence, as we showed, employment should be determined by the reservation wage alone, and not by the wage negotiated in the contract. This is rejected by the data. The second version is the more general model which we considered in which employment could be influenced by both the wage negotiated in the contract, and the reservation wage. This is a very indirect test of the model, and what support there is for it is very weak, and some of the signs of the effects are wrong – e.g. an increase in the reservation wage sometimes has the effect of increasing employment.

The only work we know which attempts to test the two models directly using the testable hypotheses discussed above is that by Alogoskoufis and Manning (1987). Unfortunately, they carry out the tests on aggregate data, and, as they admit, there are considerable problems in going from a single-union/single-firm model, to an economy-wide relationship. They show that both models are rejected against a more general alternative theory of how the various parameters affect both wages and employment.

On the whole, then, neither theory seems to be able to account satisfactorily for the data on negotiated wages and their associated employment levels.

[handwritten margin note: BUT TESTING IS THE KEY TO KNOWING IF THE MODEL IS ANY GOOD.]

Drawbacks of the Theory

While one should be aware of how rich these models are, and of what an advance has been made by formulating models of negotiated wages in an explicit bargaining framework, there are clearly a considerable number of limitations of the models as they stand. In the first place, as argued forcefully by Oswald (1987), and noted by Ashenfelter and Brown (1986), unions do not appear to negotiate explicitly over employment. Moreover, while the 'over-employment' characteristic of efficient-bargain models has sometimes been interpreted as consistent with evidence of overmanning and feather-bedding, as Nickell and Andrews (1983) note, these latter phenomena really have more to do with the choice of work practices rather than with the overall total number of people employed. While none of these arguments points decisively to a rejection of the efficient-bargain model,[9] they do point to a need to model more closely what aspects of employment unions do definitely try to control. One obvious candidate is *hours of work*, which historically has been of importance to unions. The second is manning levels or capital per man. In the next section we will review some initial work that has been done in these directions.

A striking feature of these models is the absence of any real role for membership. It is not just that there is no theory of membership, it is the fact that membership seems to be irrelevant in determining the outcome of the bargain.[10] Yet membership is often found to be important in empirical work on wage-determination, where the justification for including it is that it captures union power, though, if these models are what underpin the estimates, there is no good theoretical justification for this. Giving a good account of membership is part of the wider role of explaining clearly where unions get their power from. This is critical, for much of the recent discussion in macroeconomics on wage determination has focused on the idea that the unemployed are outsiders who are powerless to influence the wage which is set by the insiders. If we identify the union as the insiders we have to explain where they get their power and, simultaneously, the size of the union. In section 5.4 we take up these issues.

However, explaining membership is not all that is involved in exploring union power. We also need to consider what alternatives the firm and union may have, and these may include bargaining with other firms and unions. This raises interesting questions about what the right size/structure unions should be; what is the right configuration/level of bargaining, etc. This is the subject matter of our fifth section.

5.3 OTHER FACTORS OF PRODUCTION

In the previous section we pointed out that the single-factor production functions employed in the standard models could be justified if all other factors were chosen by the firm after the employment decision had been made. However, there may be other factors, or, more generally, other aspects of employment, about which the union cares directly, and over which it might want to exercise some control. One obvious factor here is hours of work. A second possibility is that there may be factors which have to be chosen prior to the bargaining between the firm and union. The obvious example is capital. The bargain between the firm and union over wages and employment will therefore be conditioned by the choice of capital. This section will also take up this issue.

Hours of work

With the growth of unemployment, there has been considerable discussion of the possibility of increasing work-sharing as a way of spreading the burden of reduced labour demand more evenly – see, for example, Drèze (1987). However, much of the formal analysis of this issue takes hours of work as exogenous, and looks at the effects of reducing this on the level of wages and employment negotiated by the union. Since hours of work have historically been an extremely important element in the union bargain, this is a rather curious approach to take.

Before bringing in hours, it is worth briefly reformulating the models of the previous section. What we want to do is to invert the utility function so as to write wages as a function of utility, and to think of the firm and union as bargaining over employment and the utility of employed members. From now on we can also think of r as being a reservation level of utility. Thus we can rewrite the gains to the union and firm from any bargain (u,n) as:

$$G^u(u,n;r) \equiv n(u-r) \tag{5.15}$$

and

$$G^f(u,n;p) \equiv pf(n) - w(u)n \tag{5.16}$$

where $w(u)$ is the inverse utility function.

Since nothing of substance has changed all the comparative static predictions of the models of the previous section are entirely unaltered.

Now let us bring hours of work into the picture. They will effect the model in two ways. In the first place we now want to think of consumer utility being a function of consumption, c, and of hours of work, h, which we can write as, say, $u = v(c,h)$. Second, we can rewrite the production function as $F(n,h)$, to allow the possibility that output might not depend simply on total man-hours, but might be quite a complex function of men and hours independently – see Hart (1984).

Now given the huge variety of overtime and other payment schemes that exist – see Brown, Levin, Rosa, Ruffell and Ulph (1986) – we certainly do not want to limit remuneration schemes to that of a uniform wage per hour, but allow the possibility that total pay could be quite a complex function of the number of hours of work. This has two dramatic implications.

In the first place it does not matter whether we think of the bargain as fixing the total hours and total consumption of employed members, or as specifying the parameters of the payment scheme and allowing the employed members to choose their hours/consumption combination freely. As long as there is sufficient freedom in the choice of payment scheme, any given hours/combination can be utility-maximising for some payment scheme.

Second, since all the union really cares about is the utility of its members, it should be indifferent as to how long they actually work, provided they are given sufficient remuneration to maintain their utility. If we invert the $v(.)$ function, we can write $c = \varphi(h,u)$ as the total amount of compensation a worker would need to work h hours if their utility is to be u. For given u, the union is indifferent about hours of work. However the firm is not, for its profits are now:

$$\pi(u,n,h;p) \equiv pF(n,h) - n\varphi(h,u) \tag{5.17}$$

and in general these will vary with hours of work. Since, conditional on u, the union is indifferent about h, *we can always think of h being chosen by the firm alone so as to maximise profits as specified by (5.17)*. Thus define:

$$G^f(u,n;p) \equiv \max_{h \geqslant 0} \pi(u,n,h;p) \tag{5.18}$$

then all the theory of bargaining over u and n takes place as before by simply replacing the definition of G^f in (5.16) with that in (5.18).[11] Moreover, provided the gain function defined by (5.18) has the same qualitative properties as that given by (5.16), all the qualitative comparative static properties go through as well, and, in particular, in terms of understanding employment, nothing new seems to emerge from the introduction of these additional factors into production.

Now it is important to stress that the 'profit-maximisation' that is being conducted in (5.18) is not the standard kind where there is some fixed and exogenous price for the input being chosen. To see this, note that the first-order condition for optimisation is:

$$pF_h(n,h) = n\varphi_h(h,u)$$

or

$$pF_h(n,h)/n = \varphi_h(h,u) \tag{5.19}$$

The left-hand side of (5.19) is just the per capita marginal revenue product of an additional hour's work, while the right-hand side is just the individual marginal rate of substitution between work and consumption. So (5.19) is just the familiar condition for a Pareto-efficient allocation of resources.

Equation (5.19) can be solved to give hours as a function of u,n and p, which we will write as:

$$h = H(u,n,p) \tag{5.20}$$

which, it can be easily shown, has the following three properties:

1. provided consumption and leisure are normal goods, then $H_u < 0$, since an increase in u decreases the MRS, so h has to fall to produce a corresponding increase in the marginal revenue product;

2. sign $(H_u) =$ sign (F_{nh}), so if an increase in n raises the marginal product of an hour's work, a profit-maximising firm will demand more hours, and will demand less if the marginal product of h falls with an increase in n – this latter being the case if output is a function of man-hours alone;

3. $H_p > 0$, for the standard reasons.

Equation (5.20) implies the testable restriction that variables such as r and s should influence hours only through their effects on n and u. We can also use (5.20) to get comparative statics results. Thus from our previous work we know that if u and n are determined in an efficient bargain then an increase in s will raise them both and, if $F_{nh} < 0$, this will unambiguously reduce h.

We can therefore conclude this subsection by saying that provided there are sufficiently rich schemes for compensating workers for all other aspects of employment which directly impinge on their utility, then, even though workers may well wish to control these aspects in the bargain, *in terms of understanding the outcomes of the bargaining process*, there is no loss of generality in assuming these other aspects to be chosen by the employer alone. This applies *a fortiori* to other factors that do not enter directly into the union's ability function. Provided they do not have to be chosen before the bargain is struck, there is nothing to be gained from formally allowing them to be part of the bargain, for a rational union would always want them to be chosen so as to maximise profits, conditional on employment and utility. We therefore turn to the possible implications of there being some factors that have to be chosen before the bargaining over employment and utility takes place.

Bargaining over capital

Suppose that the firm has production function $f(n,K)$, where, as before n is the number of workers and K is the capital stock. Again we assume that both factors are essential, so that, for all $K \geqslant 0$, $f(0, k) \equiv 0$, while for all $n \geqslant 0$, $f(n,0) \equiv 0$.

As before, the firm sells its output in a perfectly competitive market at the price p. It also faces a perfectly competitive capital market, and can hire as much capital as it wants at the rental rate ρ. Finally, in order to focus on the issues of concern, we assume that workers are risk-neutral, so that essentially all the union cares about is:

$$W \equiv n(w - r) \tag{5.21}$$

the excess of the wage-bill paid to workers employed by the firm over what they would have received in competitive labour markets. As we saw in section 5.2, in any efficient bargain employment will be set at the competitive level; the firm just receives a share $(1 - s)$ of the profits it would have made had it faced competitive labour markets (where s denotes the relative union strength), and the wage surplus, W, is just the remaining proportion s of these competitive profits.

The critical question now is what determines these competitive profits and the answer to this depends on what we assume can be bargained over by the firm and union.

In what follows it will be essential to distinguish between the firm's *capital revenue function*, $\varphi(K,p,r)$, defined by

$$\varphi(K,p,r) = \max \; [pf(n,K) - rn] \tag{5.22}$$

$$h \geqslant 0$$

and its *capital profit function*, $\pi(K,p,r,p)$, defined by

$$\pi(K,p,r,\rho) = \varphi(K,p,r) - \rho K \tag{5.23}$$

Thus $\varphi(K,p,r)$ gives the total revenue accruing to the firm from choice of K, if labour markets were perfectly competitive, but ignores the cost of capital, while $\pi(K,p,r,\rho)$ simply deducts the cost of capital from this revenue.

To return to the question of what are the appropriate competitive profits being shared between the firm and union, let us suppose, first, that the firm and union can bargain over wages, employment and capital. This can only happen if the bargain takes place before any capital has been installed. In this case, in the absence of any agreement, the firm hires no labour or capital, so its disagreement profits are zero, and the relevant pay-off for the firm in the Nash bargaining solution is given by its capital-profit function, less what it pays to the union, W. Now note that the union does not care directly about the level of capital. This implies that *whatever level of wage surplus* the two parties agree to be optimal, they *both* agree that the level of capital should be such as to *maximise the capital-profit function*. It is easy to see that this implies that the level of capital chosen will be such that the marginal revenue product of capital equals the rental rate of capital. So in this case the levels of both capital and labour employed by the firm will correspond to those that would prevail under perfect competition. It is clear why the firm wants this but why does the union also want it? This is just an application of the result we saw earlier in section 5.3 – that since all the union cares about is utility, then if there is some other factor that can be bargained over which does not directly affect union utility, this will be chosen by the standard principles of profit-maximisation. So let:

$$\hat{\pi}(p,r,\rho) \equiv \max_{K \geqslant 0} [\pi(K,p,r,\rho)] \qquad (5.24)$$

then $\hat{\pi}(.)$ gives us, for this case, the competitive profits that will be split between the firm and the union in the proportions $(1 - s)$ and s.

Notice that this implies that the union implicitly shares with the firm in paying for the cost of the capital investment – in return though for an equivalent share in the return from capital. Of course, the union does not literally pay for its share of capital; it simply takes rather lower wages; it is the firm that actually pays for the capital. But once the capital has been sunk, the firm has lost this bargaining threat. How does this affect the situation? It implies that if a bargain over wages and employment took place after the firm had sunk the capital then the relevant 'pie' would now be the *capital revenue function*. To see why, consider the firm's pay-off. If agreement is reached to pay the union W then the firm gets $\pi(K,p,r,\rho) - W$; but if no agreement is reached the firm still has to pay for the capital so its disagreement pay-off is $- \rho K$. The firm's gain from agreeing to the bargain W is the difference between its profits with agreement and its profit without agreement, and, given our definitions, this is clearly $\varphi(K,p,r) - W$. So for any given K chosen by the firm, the firm and union share $\varphi(K,p,r)$ in the proportions $(1 - s)$ and s, and the union no longer has to pay a share of the costs of the capital. For any given K, the union is clearly better-off in the bargain that takes place after the investment has been sunk than in the one that takes place before it is sunk. This makes precise the notion that the union is in a stronger bargaining position once the firm is locked-in to the project. So if the union is not committed (e.g. through a legally-binding contract) to a bargain it struck before the investment project started, it will always wish to renege once such a project has started.

But this is not the end of the story, for there is still the level of investment to be determined. It is simplest to assume that if the union and firm cannot sign long-term contracts, then the firm chooses the level of capital unilaterally. In making its decision the firm has to anticipate the outcome of the subsequent bargain that will be struck with the union over wages and employment. Since the firm now just gets a share $(1 - s)$ of any revenue accruing from capital, its pay-off when it selects investment level K is $(1 - s).\varphi(K,p,r) - \rho K$, and so the first order condition for choice of K is:

$$\partial\varphi/\partial K = \rho/(1 - s). \tag{5.25}$$

Thus the firm acts as if it faced the higher rental rate $\rho/(1 - s)$ not ρ, and this will lead it to select a lower level of capital. This simply reflects the fact that the firm wishes to offset the lock-in effect associated with capital, by choosing less capital into which to be locked.

Thus there are going to be two effects on the union's pay-off. First, the union is better-off because it no longer contributes to paying for capital; but because the level of investment is inefficient, the revenue it is sharing is below its optimal level and this will tend to make the union worse-off. Of course for both reasons, the firm is unambiguously worse-off. To see how the two effects work out for the union, note that as s tends to 1 (the union gets stronger) the shadow cost of capital tends to infinity so that capital tends to zero; the union will be worse-off without binding contracts than with them. On the other hand, as s tends to zero (the union is very weak), the shadow cost of capital tends to ρ, so the loss of profits will be negligible and the union will be better-off without binding contracts than with them. For intermediate values of s, however, Grout (1984) shows that the relative pay-offs to the union can vary in complex ways. The implication is thus that weak unions gain, and strong unions lose from an inability to sign long-term binding contracts.

5.4 MEMBERSHIP

There is a well-established literature of econometric models of union wage-determination, in which wages and union membership are modelled as being simultaneously determined – see, for example, Schmidt and Strauss (1976) and Lee (1978) – though these models often have no explicit theoretical underpinnings. This two-way linkage between wages and membership also accords with much of the discussion on unions by academics and others. In contrast the models we have been discussing so far neither give membership any role in influencing wages, nor, as they stand, do they offer any explanation of membership.

The first weakness is, in part, a reflection of the assumption that membership is so large that employment is never constrained by it. The second weakness is that any theory of membership we might try to draw out of the current models would be distinctly odd. To see this, consider the case where a closed shop operates, and wages are negotiated as part of an efficient contract. Suppose initially membership is so large that it is above the level of employment determined in the bargain in section 5.3. Because of the closed shop, workers outside the union will have to work in the alternative sector at the reservation wage, r. Assuming the firm draws workers at random from the pool of members, each union member will have a higher expected utility than non-union members who will therefore be keen to join. But existing members will want to keep them out, because although admitting them has no effect on wages and employment, a larger pool size will reduce the probability of a worker getting employment with the firm. If there were to be any natural wastage, membership will therefore contract. If it contracts to the point where it is a binding constraint on employment, then all union workers will certainly obtain employment, and, if there is diminishing average productivity, the wage at which they are employed is a decreasing function of membership (since higher membership lowers the per capita surplus to be split with the firm). Once again, the incentive is to contract the union. The theory seems to imply unions of infinitesimal size.

The failure to account for the way membership affects the bargaining outcome (perhaps by affecting union power) is the crucial lack in the models discussed so far. Thus any fully satisfactory account of membership and its impact on wages and employment, must simultaneously give some explanation of where the union gets its power to appropriate some of the surplus. In doing so, the theory would link in closely with another strand of current labour economics, and bring the focus of concern on explaining unemployment into greater prominence. For the central concern of much of the recent analysis of involuntary unemployment is to explain the power of employed workers to command a wage above the competitive level while there are identical workers who would be willing to work at that wage, or even below it, but are unable to do so.

There are now a variety of different accounts of union membership, and, more widely, of involuntary unemployment. We begin with a rather simple notion drawing on the work of Kidd and Oswald (1987). Suppose that unions retain the closed-shop arrangement so that firms must hire union workers, but now suppose that when employment is below membership, then some of those unemployed workers will quit the union; so membership in one period is related to employment in the previous period. To see the implications of this we assume that we have a simple monopoly union model, in which if the union determines a wage w, employment will be chosen by the firm's labour demand curve $D(w) \equiv \hat{n}(w/p)$, where this latter function is defined in Section 5.2.

Suppose first that there is a single period, union membership is m, and the union chooses the wage to maximise its gain:

$$G^u(w) \equiv D(w)[u(w) - u(r)] \tag{5.26}$$

Notice that since, in determining w, m is treated as fixed, this is equivalent to maximising the *utilitarian* objective function:

$$V(w) \equiv [D(w)u(w)] + [(m - D(w))u(r)] \tag{5.27}$$

Further,with m fixed nothing would change if we used instead the *average utility* objective function:

$$\bar{V}(w) \equiv V(w)/m \tag{5.28}$$

Now suppose there are two periods and that membership in period 2 is given in obvious notation, by

$$m_2 = m_1 + \lambda(n_1 - m_1) \qquad n_1 \leqslant m_1$$

where λ is a parameter lying between 0 and 1 which measures the rate at which membership decays. Let δ be the union's discount factor. With the utilitarian objective, the union will now choose wage rates w_1, w_2 to

$$\max \; V(w_1,w_2) \equiv \{D(w_1)u(w_1) + [m_1 - D(w_1)]u(r)\}$$

$$+ \delta\{D(w_2)u(w_2) + [m_1 + \lambda(D(w_1) - m_1) - D(w_2)]u(r)\} \tag{5.29}$$

where we assume that the solution will always involve employment in period 1 below membership in period 1. Note first that as far as w_2 is concerned, the objective function is analogous to (5.27) so, not surprisingly, the wage in the second period will be just the static monopoly union wage. Eliminating terms in w_2 and m_1 then the components of (5.29) that concern w_1 are just:

$$D(w_1) [u(w_1) - (1 - \delta\lambda)u(r)]$$

so that in setting the first-period wage the union effectively acts like a static monopoly union with a lower reservation wage. This leads the union to set a first-period wage below the static monopoly union wage, and hence raise the level of employment. This is not surprising; the utilitarian objective implies that the union values members *per se*, so if next period's membership is positively related to this period's employment the union will seek to boost current employment. Introducing the dynamic analysis may thus reduce the employment implications of the monopoly union model without resorting to efficient bargains.

However, this conclusion is reversed if we assume that the union cares only about the average utility of its members. (It is straightforward to show this using the above line of analysis.) Again this is not surprising: reducing membership reduces the risk that any one member will find himself unemployed and so raises average utility, and so the union will take steps to reduce its membership by raising wages in the first period.

So far we have just described the short-run equilibrium of the model in which employment is below the membership level. Clearly the only long-run solution is that in which employment equals membership, which will occur, in the utilitarian case, at a level of employment above that predicted by the one-period model.

The utility function employed in (5.29) rests on two assumptions: first, the union does not care about the utility achieved in the second period by those first-period members who leave the union; second, those who are employed in the second period are again randomly drawn with equal probability from the membership pool, so employment status in the first period does not affect employment opportunities in the second. To deal with the first point, if we assume that the members who leave at the end of period 1 just earn the reservation wage in period 2, then if the union cared about these people we should add $(m_1 - m_2)u(r)$ to second-period utility. But then the union's utility function becomes just:

$$V(w_1,w_2) = \{D(w_1)u(w_1) + [m_1 - D(w_1)]u(r)\} +$$

$$\delta\{D(w_2)u(w_2) + [m_1 - D(w_2)]u(r)\} \qquad (5.30)$$

Now with m_1 given the outcome of using the objective function (5.30) will be to set the standard one-period monopoly union wage in each period (Carruth and Oswald, 1985). While membership will simply shrink until it equals employment at that wage, this dynamic movement in membership will have no effect on wages or employment.

To deal with the second point, we consider some models in which employment-probability in one period is related to employment status in the previous one. This arises in its starkest form when firms operate seniority rules for laying-off workers; that is, the firm will lay off workers in the inverse order of the length of time they have been employed by the firm. This immediately raises the problem that workers are now no longer identical, and so would not be unanimous in their views about any particular wage and employment package.[12] To resolve these differences, we suppose the union's policy is determined by majority voting, in which case it is a well-known result (Mueller, 1980) that the policy chosen by the union will be that which maximises the utility of the median voter, i.e. the member with median seniority status.

To see the implication of this consider a simple one-period model in which there is no uncertainty, so the median voter can choose a sure level of wages and employment. The median voter will clearly never want to choose an overall level of employment that would make him unemployed, but, as long as employment is sufficiently great to avoid this, he will be indifferent as to the actual level of employment. Hence, the union's indifference curves which we drew in Figure 5.2 will now become horizontal straight lines defined over values of employment greater than or equal to that which just keeps the median voter employed. Recalling once again the principle we established earlier that where a factor does not impinge directly on union utility then, in an efficient bargain, it will be chosen to maximise profits, we get the immediate result that for this case all efficient bargains lie on the labour demand curve (Oswald, 1987) so that the distinction between efficient contracts and the right-to-manage model disappears.

To see how the introduction of seniority can address the issue of membership, let us consider the implications of the above model of wage-determination for members not employed. We now assume that workers who remain union members but are laid-off receive only unemployment pay, while if they quit the union and work permanently in the competitive sector they will receive the competitive wage, and this yields greater utility than being unemployed. Now notice that if demand is static and known with certainty then if employment is chosen by seniority a union member who is laid-off will never be employed, so it is reasonable to assume that they will quit the union and membership will shrink. Assuming, as we did above, that when the median member decides on the wage he takes membership as given, then we again obtain a rather odd story of membership. Starting with some arbitrary initial membership, the median member will bargain for a particular wage, and suppose this results in some members being unemployed. They quit, so that membership now shrinks to employment. But this will change the identity of the median worker, and it must now pay him to raise wages. But this process will continue until membership becomes negligible.

To circumvent this, we follow Grossman (1983) and Booth (1985) and suppose now that demand is uncertain, and that given a bargained wage, the firm will choose employment once it learns the actual level of demand, though, given a closed shop, employed workers can only be drawn from the pool of union members. The introduction of uncertainty has two implications: first, in general, the median voter will now face some positive probability of being laid-off; while, second, a union member laid-off when demand is low can still have some probability of being re-employed by the firm at a wage above the competitive wage when demand is high. Wages and membership are now determined by two conditions. Given the current membership, the median voter will bargain for a wage taking account of the effect of wages on his probability of employment. Given the bargained wage, membership is determined by the condition that for the marginal member of the union (i.e. the most junior) the expected utility of staying in the union is equal to the utility he would get for certain in the competitive sector. The previous argument about the membership shrinking to zero no longer works; for with a very small membership, the marginal worker will either have a reasonably high probability of employment or a very high wage when employed, and in either case will have expected utility above that in the competitive sector, so that membership would actually rise.

In a similar model Gottfries and Horn (1987) look at the wage-path which will emerge over time. Suppose that a low level of demand occurred last period, leading to a low level of employment, and, as in the Kidd and Oswald model, this leads to a low membership in the current period. Faced with the same random pattern of demand, the existing union-members now face a low probability of unemployment, and so can afford to raise wages leading to a persistent low level of employment. So even without any autocorrelation in demand shocks, there will be a cyclical pattern to wages and employment. This phenomenon – that high levels of unemployment in one perod can generate effects leading to high unemployment persisting into subsequent periods – is known as *hysteresis*, and this model gives one account of how this phenomenon can arise. For another account see, for example, Blanchard and Summers (1986, 1987).

While these models provide some interesting insights into the dynamics of union membership, they seem to carry the rather odd implication that as membership rises, the wage which the union can negotiate falls. Essentially this reflects the fact that these models assume that union-members have priority in employment, so that the firm cannot threaten to employ entirely non-union workers at a wage below that fixed by the union. Of course if there was an infinitely elastic supply of workers available to work for the firm at a reservation wage, and union members had no priority in employment, the union would be powerless to raise wages above the reservation level. But, on the more plausible assumption that there is only a finite number of workers of a particular type available to the economy, then one might look for an explanation of union-membership by analysing how union power is related to union size.

A model which focuses on this issue, and which is directly related to the bargaining models of section 5.2, is that of Booth and Ulph (1988a). Here there is an exogenously given pool of workers who have some skill that the firm wishes to hire. The size of this pool is large, but finite. Suppose m of these workers are in a union; that a closed shop is in operation; and that efficient bargaining takes place over wages and employment as in the standard bargaining model described in section 5.2, subject to the constraint that employment does not exceed union size.

Although the union operates a closed shop, which means that if the firm continues to deal with the union it must employ only union-members, the critical difference is that it is now assumed that the firm has the alternative option of breaking off all negotiations with the union and hiring non-union workers at the reservation wage. The way the presence of this outside option affects the bargain is as follows. If the profits to be made in the outside option do not exceed those in the bargain described above, then this standard bargaining solution prevails. If the profits in the outside option are greater than those in the standard bargain, then the standard bargain is abandoned, and wages and employment are set at the point on the contract curve corresponding to the profits in the outside option. The implications of this are immediate:

1. To have any power at all to extract a wage above the reservation wage, the union must be sufficiently large for the number of non-union workers to be below the competitive number the firm

would like to employ. Hence there is a minimum critical size of union.

2. As membership increases above this level, the profits in the outside option fall, raising wages, employment and total utility of the union.

3. Once profits in the outside option have fallen to those in the standard bargain, then further increases in membership have no effect on the contract, and hence utility. So there is also a maximum effective size of union. If membership is at this maximum level, then wages and employment are as described in the standard bargain, and the introduction of membership has not affected the predictive power of that theory.

4. Union members are better-off than non-union members who, because of the closed shop, can only work in the alternative sector. Therefore they will wish to join. Existing members will let them if this raises *average* utility. This certainly happens in the neighbourhood of the minimum union size, so membership will be above the minimum. There will be no incentive to let it go above the maximum, for beyond this total utility is fixed, and so average utility must fall. *Thus there will always be some outsiders, who are worse-off than those inside the union.* While it is certainly possible for equilibrium membership to be at the maximum, whether or not this is so depends on the nature of returns to scale, and the size of the bargaining strength.

Similar ideas to those of the Booth and Ulph model are contained both in Osborne (1984) where it is the firm that picks the union size, and does so in order to maintain a 'reserve' army with which to discipline the union, and in Sabourian (1988) where there is no explicit union, but a wage norm emerges as a perfect equilibrium of a bargaining game.

The essence of these models is that, while there are outside workers who are perfect substitutes for the insiders, and who would be willing to work for a lower wage, the firm cannot in fact make greater profits by employing them. There are a number of other insider/outsider models in the literature, which appeal to various costs of replacing the insiders to underpin their power. Thus Lindbeck and Snower (1984, 1986) explicitly consider hiring and firing costs. Shaked and Sutton (1984) appeal to a delay in replacing the workforce. In Solow (1985) insiders have firm specific human capital and there are costs of training outsiders to the same level of skill. Frank (1985) simply assumes that new workers have to be members of the union and that the wages of new workers are negotiated by existing old workers, who are thus able to extract all the surplus that accrues from hiring new workers. One feature of all these models is that there are now genuine economic differences between insiders and outsiders, and even in a Walrasian economy one would expect them to be treated differently. It is far from clear therefore that these models give a good account of involuntary unemployment.

It should be clear that this is an area where a great deal more work remains to be done. With the exception of Sabourian (1988) one drawback that is common to them all is that they are grounded in the single-firm/single-union framework. This is particularly worrying in the Booth–Ulph model, where the firm might reasonably consider the possibility that non-union members might unionise if it starts to deal with them. Equally, it is not clear why new firms do not emerge to employ the non-union workers and hence undercut the unionised firms. It is to some preliminary analyses of these issues that we now turn.

5.5 THE STRUCTURE OF BARGAINING

Both within a country like the UK and more especially in making international comparisons (see Bamber and Lansbury, 1987) we observe a wide range of bargaining structures – e.g. a nation-wide association of employers bargaining with a consortium of unions; a single firm bargaining with a number of separate unions; a single union bargaining with a number of independent employers. We need to ask not only how these different bargaining structures affect the resulting wage or employment levels but more importantly why particular institutional structures have emerged. At first sight it might be thought that it would pay each side to try to bargain in as large a unit as possible with as fragmented a set of opponents as possible; one application of this logic is the argument that an important reason for the emergence of multinational companies is that it allows them to bargain with a workforce organised into separate national unions (Horn and Wolinsky, 1985). Attempts to provide formal analyses of these issues are very recent (Horn and Wolinsky (1988), Davidson (1986), Fung (1986), Ulph (1989), and Bennett and Ulph (1988) and we shall see that they cast doubt on the proposition that 'bigger is always better' in bargaining, and thus provide some rationale for expecting a diversity of bargaining structures.

To illustrate the way in which our earlier analyses of bargaining need to be modified we shall begin with the case where there is a single firm, and analyse the outcome of bargaining when the workforce is organised in a single union and when it is organised in several unions. We shall deal with the simplest possible model, so suppose that the workforce can be considered to consist of two groups of workers, whose employment levels, wages and reservation wages are denoted by L_i, w_i, r_i, $i = 1,2$ respectively. Each group of workers cares only about the surplus wage bill $B_i \equiv L_i(w_i - r_i)$, and so is happy for the firm to choose employment levels that would maximise profits if the firm just had to pay reservation wages r_1, r_2, with these profits being divided according to the bargaining strengths of the two sides, which we shall assume to be equal.

We begin with the case where the two groups of workers form a single union (which aims to maximise the total surplus wage bill $B_1 + B_2$). Let Π^* denote the maximum profits when both groups of workers are hired at their reservation wages. Then from our assumptions the firm will receive a pay-off, $\frac{1}{2}\Pi^*$, and the unions a pay-off, $B_1 + B_2 = \frac{1}{2}\Pi^*$. This is standard, and the interest is in the case where each group of workers forms a separate union which bargains independently with the firm. The bargain between the firm and any union needs to specify the pay-off to that union if it reaches agreement with the firm and the other union has also reached agreement, and the pay-off to that union if it reaches agreement with the firm and the other union does not. Let π_i^* denote the maximum profits the firm could earn if it could only hire workers from union i, $i = 1,2$. We suppose that in the event that only union i has reached agreement with the firm, the firm and union i each receive $\frac{1}{2}\pi_i^*$, the pay-offs in a single union/firm bargain. Now consider the determination of the pay-offs, B_i, when both unions have reached agreement and consider the position of union 1 assuming that union 2 and the firm have already agreed a pay-off, B_2, to union 2. In the event of agreement, union 1 gets B_1, the firm gets $\Pi^* - B_1 - B_2$; in the event of disagreement, union 1 gets nothing, the firm gets $\frac{1}{2}\pi_2^*$; so the surplus available for bargaining over between the firm and union 1 is just $\Pi^* - B_2 - \frac{1}{2}\pi_2^*$, and so union 1 gets a pay-off;

$$B_1 = \frac{1}{2}[\Pi^* - B_2 - \frac{1}{2}\pi_2^*] \tag{5.31}$$

A similar expression applies to union 2. Solving we get

$$B_1 = \frac{1}{3}[\Pi^* - \pi_2^* + \frac{1}{2}\pi_1^*] \tag{5.32}$$

with a similar expression for B_2. Adding, we obtain the total pay-off to the unions under separate bargaining:

$$B_1 + B_2 = \frac{1}{3}[2\Pi^* - \frac{1}{2}\pi_1^* - \frac{1}{2}\pi_2^*] \tag{5.33}$$

In comparing this with the pay-off to the unions under joint bargaining, $\frac{1}{2}\Pi^*$, we can see there are two factors at work; the term $2\Pi^*$ arises from the fact that when the unions bargain separately they get 'two bites at the cherry', and this acts to raise the unions' pay-off; on the other hand the terms $-\frac{1}{2}\pi_i^*$ arise from the fact that the firm now has a fallback position if it is unsuccessful in its bargain with one union (it can use workers from the other union), and this allows the firm to play off one union against the other, reducing the pay-off to the unions. How these two forces interact depends on the relationship between the three profit terms, and we consider two extreme cases. Suppose the two sets of workers are *perfect complements* in the sense that both groups are essential to production; then $\pi_i^* = 0$, $i = 1,2$, and from (5.33) we see that

$$B_1 + B_2 = \frac{2}{3}\Pi^*$$

so that the unions are better off bargaining separately. If we suppose that the two sets of workers are *perfect substitutes* in the sense that the firm can hire all its workforce from one union if need be, then $i = \Pi^*$, $i = 1,2$, and from (5.33)

$$B_1 + B_2 = \frac{1}{3}\Pi^*$$

so that unions are worse off if they bargain separately.

The above results generalise very naturally to the case of many, say *n*, groups of workers. With perfect complementarity the workers would get a share of profits equal to $n/(n+1)$, while with perfect substitutability they would get a share equal to $1/(n+1)$, so with *n* large the workers will get almost all the surplus if they are complementary, and almost nothing if they are substitutes. The results also generalise to somewhat different assumptions about the nature of the bargaining process (with respect to the outcome when only one union reaches agreement) and union utility functions (see the papers cited earlier). The intuition behind these results is clear. If individual groups of workers have the power to halt production by themselves, then they do better to apply this power in repeated bargains; if the firm can just go elsewhere for its workers then any individual group of workers is relatively powerless, and the workers do better bargaining jointly, where they can threaten jointly to stop production.

We have established one set of circumstances under which it may pay unions to bargain separately. There is another, though one that is less intuitively obvious. Suppose that workers are perfect substitutes, and that we now introduce capital into the model. If the workers and firm can sign long-term binding contracts, then as we saw in section 5.2, this makes little difference to our earlier analysis, and workers would be better-off bargaining jointly. But now suppose that they cannot sign binding contracts; then as we saw in section 5.2 the firm will now under-invest in capital, and if the (joint) union is fairly strong the workers can be hurt by this under-investment. Now by bargaining separately the workers will weaken their bargaining position, and this will lead the firm to increase its investment, and the gains the workers get from this may more than offset any loss of bargaining strength. Ulph (1989) shows that when there are no binding contracts, unions can indeed be better-off bargaining separately (and indeed may be better-off than they would be if there were binding contracts and joint bargaining); moreover the firm will now be induced to *over-invest* in capital, essentially because if the bargain with the unions takes place *after* capital has been installed and the firm wants to be able to play off one union against another it needs a reasonable amount of production capacity installed with each union to make its threats to produce with only one union credible.

So far we have dealt with the case where there is a single firm but the workforce may be organised into one or more unions. Some of the results presented carry over to the case of more than one firm. Davidson (1986) considers a model where there are two firms, each with its own workforce of identical workers, producing a homogeneous product. There is bargaining over wages only, and Davidson shows that again the unions are better-off if they cooperate in their bargaining than if they bargain independently. However the rationale is slightly different from the Horn and Wolinsky (1988) case, for the firms cannot directly replace their workforce by members of another union, and so cannot play off one union against another. Nevertheless unions are indirectly competing with each other through the product market, for if one union tries to cut its wage to attract more employment (by lowering its firm's costs) this will hurt the other union's employment prospects, and it is better for the unions if they can take account of these external effects on each other. There is another factor at work. If the unions bargain individually, then, when they threaten their firm with a strike, the union also loses its only source of employment. But when the unions bargain cooperatively, then, when they confront one firm, they always have the threat that if they were to close that firm down (through a strike), the other firm would be able to expand its output (since it has the market to itself) and so the union's losses from the strike would be partially offset. So strikes are less costly for the unions, and this will raise their utility from the bargain.

Related issues have been considered by Booth and Ulph (1988b), who allow unions to bargain over wages and employment. The crucial difference now is that when unions combine, this effectively merges the firms as well, thus conferring additional monopoly power which the union can exploit to raise wages. However this can only be exploited by lowering output and employment, and, if workers are sufficiently risk-averse, this cooperation between unions may be disadvantageous.

The final comparison we shall consider is where there is a single union of identical workers which faces two firms producing a homogeneous product, and we ask what happens to the union if the firms bargain independently or cooperatively. It might be thought that the situation would be symmetrical to that of Horn and Wolinsky, with the union always preferring to bargain against the firms acting independently. But as Bennett and Ulph (1988) show this need not always be the case. If we consider first the case of efficient bargains, then when the two firms can collude in their bargains, they are also effectively colluding in the output market, and so will wish to raise profits by cutting output. Despite the fact that the union can raise its reservation pay-off when it deals with the firms independently, the firms are more profitable when they collude, and if the union's preferences give a high weight to wages rather than employment, then the union will do better when the firms collude. When there is wage-only bargaining, then collusion by the firms no longer implies that they can earn monopoly profits. Nevertheless, despite Davidson's argument that the union can raise its reservation pay-off against an individual firm by threatening that in the event of a strike the rival firm will expand its output, the other argument of Davidson now works in favour of the firms colluding – i.e. when the firms bargain independently they are better able to resist wage increases because of the consequences for lost employment if one firm's costs are raised relative to those of its rival. It turns out that the union always does better when bargaining against firms that collude than against firms who bargain non-cooperatively, and correspondingly, the profits of the firms are lower when they collude.

The work reported in this section has shown that the question of how different groupings of the two parties to a bargain affects the bargaining outcome is not as straightforward as one might have imagined; in particular, the intuitive notion that it always pays one side to bargain in a coordinated way against a fragmented opposition is unfounded in a number of important cases. Features such as the degree of complementarity between workers, the extent to which long-term contracts can be negotiated, and workers' preferences for wages rather than employment will all affect the gains to the various parties from different bargaining structures. Of course, identifying the relative gains to different parties does not itself explain which bargaining structure will emerge. But as long as the interests of the two parties concerned has some bearing on which institutional structure will arise, then variations in the factors listed above will help to explain why we observe a wide variety of bargaining structures. The rather simple nature of the models employed so far, however, provides ample scope for future research in this field.

5.6   CONCLUSIONS

Two broad themes have emerged from this survey. One is the importance of specifying what is to be included in the bargain; in general both parties stand to gain from having anything that might affect their welfare included in the bargain. Yet empirical evidence suggests that relatively few items are bargained over, and it is an unresolved problem to find convincing models of why this should be the case. Obviously transactions costs, in particular the costs of monitoring and enforcing complex contracts, will be a large part of the story, but such factors need to be explicitly modelled. Malcomson (1983) has argued that enforcement of such contracts is indeed an important rationale for the existence of unions.

The second theme has been to embed the bargain between a union and firm in a more general context where there are other alternatives open to the two sides. Work in this field is still rather rudimentary, with results depending a lot on exogenously imposed constraints on what firms can do. What is required is a theory where all agents, firms, union-members, non-union-members, employed and unemployed are acting rationally, but some surplus still emerges for union-members.

One issue on which we have touched only briefly in discussing this latter work is that of carefully modelling the structure of the product market, and the interlinkages between it and the labour market. The idea that imperfections in the labour market go hand in hand with those in the product market is not a new one, and some models exist along these lines – see for example Hart (1982), Snower (1983), Benassy (1976) – but much still remains to be done.

Finally, there is one weakness of all the work discussed here. This is that we have simply adopted particular solution concepts. Recently bargaining theory has emphasised that the outcomes of bargains will depend on the precise sequence of threat and counter-threat made in the process of reaching a settlement. Some work on these lines appears in some recent analyses of strikes, but this is another area where much fruitful work remains to be done.

6 Strikes: Models and Evidence*

DAVID SAPSFORD

6.1 INTRODUCTION

Why do strikes occur? This is a question which has attracted the attention of labour economists fairly intensively for at least the past six decades. This chapter provides a review of the economists' analysis of strike activity, covering both the main theoretical models and the empirical evidence. The chapter begins with a brief review of the early (i.e. pre-1967) literature which, as we will see, focused its principal attention on questions regarding the existence and strength of cyclical fluctuations in strike activity. In section 6.3 we consider in some detail the more recent – primarily econometric – studies which first appeared in the US literature in the late 1960s. This approach spread fairly rapidly throughout the international literature as researchers in a wide range of countries adapted the basic model to suit their local institutional and other circumstances and fitted it, with varying degrees of success, to local data at various levels of aggregation. In section 6.4 we consider some of the important recent developments which have occurred in the economic analysis of strike activity, while the final section provides some concluding remarks.

6.2 EARLY LITERATURE: CYCLES OF STRIKES

As already noted, much of the early literature concentrated on the relationship between some measure of strike activity, most commonly strike frequency (i.e. the number of strikes beginning in each time-period) and the business cycle. As long ago as 1921, Hansen noted the existence of a *positive* relationship between aggregate strike frequency in the USA and the level of wholesale prices, as a proxy for the level of business or economic activity, over the period 1889–1919: a relationship subsequently found to hold up to 1937 by Griffin (1939). Despite differences in statistical methods and cyclical indicators used, numerous studies of different countries and time-periods reached essentially the same conclusion regarding the pro-cyclical behaviour of strike frequency (e.g. Douglas, 1923; Douty, 1932; Gomberg, 1944; Jurkat and Jurkat, 1949; Hopkins, 1953; Levitt, 1953).

One of the most notable contributions within this literature was Rees's (1952) investigation into the relationship between strike activity and business fluctuations in the US over the period 1915 to 1949. Using the then relatively modern National Bureau of Economic Research (NBER) techniques of reference cycle analysis (Burns and Mitchell, 1946) Rees, analysing monthly data, found evidence of a strong positive correlation between strike frequency and the business cycle and noted the existence of a tendency for strikes to lead at the upper turning-point of the cycle (by an average of 4 months) and to lag (by an average of 6 months) at the lower turning-point. One of the interesting features of Rees's analysis is the fact that he went somewhat further than most previous investigators in seeking to explain, as opposed to merely documenting, the observed pro-cyclical behaviour of strike frequency. Rees attributed the observed cyclical fluctuations in strike frequency to variations over the cycle in the propensity to strike of workers in a given unit (be it a department, a plant or a company) as opposed to variations over the cycle in either the number of such units organised by unions or in the 'scope' of strikes.[1] Rees offered an explanation of the observed cyclical behaviour of strike frequency in terms of various *strategic advantages* offered to workers in a given unit by rising employment and business conditions during the upswing (including improvements in employment opportunities on a temporary basis should a strike occur, or on a more permanent basis should the employer succeed in replacing striking workers; the employer's reluctance to lose his share of an expanding market and so forth).[2] Rees's analysis, however, was subsequently criticised by O'Brien (1965, p. 654) as inadequate on the grounds that it overstated the active role of labour in the strike process and understated that of the employer: being a valid explanation of fluctuations in strike frequency if, and only if, the response or resistance behaviour of employers to workers' strike threats remains itself invariant with respect to the level of economic activity – clearly an unlikely state of affairs.

As discussed more fully in Sapsford (1982) this sort of analytical over-emphasis on the active role of workers at the expense of that of the employer is an unsatisfactory feature of much of the early literature and gives rise to its general failure to take proper account of the *simultaneous* influence of cyclical forces on employers' behaviour. This type of problem, as we shall see in section 6.3, has however also found its way into much of the more recent econometric literature within which many models typically include amongst their vector of explanatory variables a variable specified to represent the level of business or cyclical activity (Sapsford, 1978).

Hicks's theory of strikes

As is clear from the above, much of the early literature was essentially empirical in nature, concentrating more or less exclusively upon the cyclical behaviour of strike activity. An important exception however, was Hicks's model of industrial disputes which first appeared in his *Theory of Wages* in 1932 (see Hicks, 1963, pp. 136–58) and which, as we shall see below, has proved quite influential in the context of the more recent literature. Hicks's model emphasises the role of the strike threat as a weapon by which pressure can be put upon the employer in collective bargaining to pay a higher wage than he would otherwise do. Hicks saw the union's ability to obtain such improvements in wages and other conditions as being derived from the threat of imposing on the employer a cost even greater than that associated with such a settlement and viewed this as providing the compulsion towards agreement. The essence of Hicks's theory is that both the employer's tendency to concede and the union's tendency to resist are functions of the *expected* length of the threatened strike.

According to Hicks, the employer chooses between the two alternatives confronting him (i.e. pay the higher wage or take the strike) in the light of his assessment of the costs involved in each. Accordingly, Hicks constructed the 'employer's concession curve' shown in Figure 6.1 which relates the highest wage that the employer will be willing to pay in order to avoid a strike, to the expected length of the threatened strike. At points on this curve, the expected cost of the strike and the expected cost of concession, suitably discounted, are equal, so that at any lower wage demand the employer will prefer to settle and avoid a strike, while at any higher wage he will prefer a strike to take place.

The intercept of this curve on the vertical axis (OZ) is the wage which the employer would pay in the absence of union pressure, and the curve is assumed to have a positive slope, because the expected cost of the threatened strike is positively related to its expected length, and the expected cost of concession is positively related to the wage demanded. In addition, Hicks argued that the employer's concession curve cannot rise above some upper limit dictated by the wage at which the employer will prefer to shut down, so that the slope of the employer's curve must eventually become a decreasing function of expected strike length.

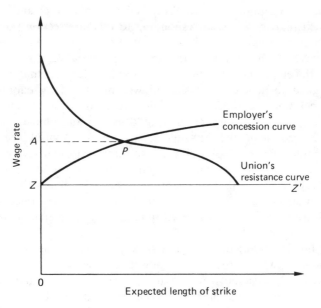

FIGURE 6.1 Hicks's theory of strikes

Similarly, Hicks constructed the 'union's resistance curve', which shows the minimum wage which the union will accept rather than undergo a strike as a function of the expected length of the strike. Since this curve shows the length of time for which the union members will be willing to stand out rather than allow their wage rate to fall below any particular level, Hicks argued that it will have a negative slope, because the 'temporary privations' (Hicks, 1963, p. 142) that they will be willing to endure to prevent the wage rate falling below a particular level are a decreasing function of the wage level in question. Finally, Hicks argued that the resistance curve must cut ZZ' at some finite distance along it, indicating the maximum time for which the union can organise a stoppage, whatever the offered wage, and that it generally intersects the vertical axis, indicating a wage sufficiently high for the union not to seek to go beyond it. Hicks also argued that the resistance curve will typically be almost horizontal over a considerable part of its length, indicating that there is some particular wage level to which the workers consider themselves entitled and in order to secure which they will 'stand out for a long time' (1963, p. 143).

Given that these two functions have opposite slopes, there will be a unique point of intersection (P in Figure 6.1) and Hicks argued that the wage corresponding to this intersection point 'is the highest wage which skilful negotiations can extract from the employer' (1963, p. 144). If the union demands a wage in excess of OA, the employer will refuse it, because he calculates that a strike designed to achieve this demand will not last long enough to compel him to concede. If the union demands a wage below OA, the employer will concede, offering little resistance, but the union will have done badly for its members, since more 'skilful' negotiating could have resulted in a more favourable settlement. Hicks then argued that the union, given imperfect knowledge of the employer's curve will typically prefer to begin bargaining by setting its initial claims high, to be subsequently modified once some indication of the employer's attitude has begun to emerge during bargaining.

While Hicks accepts that some strikes are more or less inevitable because 'weapons grow rusty if unused . . . (so that unions) embark on strikes occasionally, not so much to secure greater gains upon that occasion . . . but in order to keep their weapon burnished for future use, and to keep employers thoroughly conscious of the union's power' he nevertheless argues that 'the majority of actual strikes are doubtless the result of faulty negotiation' (1963, p. 146).

According to Hicks, strikes arise because of incomplete information, which results in a miscalculation on the part of one or both parties as to the shape and location of the other's curve. As already noted, a union demand in excess of OA (for example) will be refused by the employer because he estimates that a strike undertaken to obtain such a wage will not last long enough to compel him to concede, so that a strike is the lesser (i.e. least costly) evil. If, however, the union and employer differ in their estimate of each other's curve, the union, according to Hicks, may hold out for its demand in the belief that it can induce the employer to accept it, while at the same time the employer refuses to concede, believing that the union cannot hold out for a sufficient time for a concession to be worth his while. Under these circumstances Hicks sees a strike as inevitable but stresses that it 'arises from the divergence of estimates and from no other cause' (1963, p. 147).

In short, Hicks sees the majority of strikes as resulting from imperfect information and a resulting divergence of estimates since 'adequate knowledge will always make a settlement possible' (1963, p. 147). Hicks's model points to the importance of imperfect and asymmetric information and as we will see in section 6.4 these issues are explored and developed further in a number of more recent models.

6.3   ECONOMETRIC MODELS OF STRIKE ACTIVITY

Ashenfelter and Johnson (1969) represents an important methodological watershed in the analysis of strike activity. Prior to its appearance, economists concentrated more or less exclusively on the *cyclical* behaviour of strike activity, whereas after its publication emphasis was quickly shifted towards the use of econometric modelling techniques in an attempt to unravel the behavioural mechanisms involved in union–employer conflict. In view of the importance of this paper, the Ashenfelter and Johnson (A–J) model is described below, together with some of the most important of the various extensions to their approach which appeared in the 1970s'.

The Ashenfelter and Johnson model

The analytical framework within which A–J construct their model, may be described as 'political' in the sense of Ross (1948) i.e. it sees the union as an institution and stresses the distinction between the union leadership, on the one hand, and the rank-and-file membership, on the other. This approach sees the objectives of the union leadership as not only the survival and growth of the union as an institution but also their own political survival, and puts emphasis on the interactions which take place between the leadership and their members during wage negotiations. The model is a fairly straightforward optimisation one in which the employer-firm, faced with the union's 'last' demand (defined by A–J as the wage increase which is acceptable to the rank and file at the date of contract expiration), compares and selects the least costly of the two alternative choices open to it: either concede the union's demand, and thereby avoid a strike, or resist and take a strike (with its associated costs in terms of foregone production and so on) in the expectation of achieving lower wage costs over the duration of the ensuing contract period. In essence, the employer in this model faces a trade-off between foregone profits over the duration of the strike and the prospect of increased future profits as a consequence of decreased future wage costs secured via the strike. Denoting the negotiated wage increase which is acceptable to the union rank and file by y_A we have

$$y_A \equiv \frac{\Delta W}{\hat{W}} \tag{6.1}$$

where $\hat{W}$ is the previous contract wage rate and ΔW is the absolute wage increase. A–J assume the existence of a Hicksian type decay function, or consessions schedule, of the form:

$$y_A = v(s), \ y_A' < 0 \tag{6.2}$$

which specifies y_A as a declining function of strike length, s. Specifically they assume that equation (6.2) takes the form:

$$y_A = y^* + (y_0 - y^*)e^{-\tau s} \quad * \tag{6.3}$$

the form of which is shown diagrammatically in Figure 6.2, where $y_0 = v(0)$ is the acceptable wage increase at the time of contract expiration, τ denotes the speed at which the acceptable wage increase declines during the strike and $y^* = v(\infty)$ denotes some wage increase which the union would not accept even with an indefinitely long strike. On the assumption that the firm *knows* (6.3) and that it expects to produce a fixed output (Q) with the same technology to sell at the same price (P) into the indefinite future its profit level in each period may be written as

$$\pi = PQ - LW - H \tag{6.4}$$

where L denotes labour input (in hours), H the level of fixed costs and W the negotiated wage rate. From (6.1) we have

$$W = \hat{W}(1 + y_A) \tag{6.5}$$

and the present value of the future profit stream V is

$$V = \int_0^\infty \pi e^{-rt}\, dt \tag{6.6}$$

where r denotes the employer's discount rate. Substituting (6.3), (6.4) and (6.5) into (6.6) we obtain

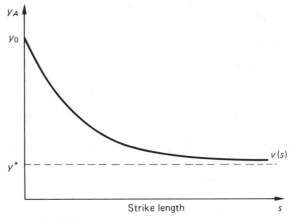

FIGURE 6.2   Union concession schedule

$$V = \int_0^\infty \{PQ - L\hat{W}[1 + y^* + (y_0 - y^*)e^{-\tau s}]\}e^{-rt}\,dt -$$
$$\int_0^\infty H \cdot e^{-rt}\,dt \qquad (6.7)$$

which, upon integration, gives

$$V = \{PQ - L\hat{W}[1 + y^* + (y_0 - y^*)e^{-\tau s}]\} \cdot \frac{e^{-rs}}{r} - \frac{H}{r} \qquad (6.8)$$

which is immediately seen to depend *solely* on the length of the strike, s. Assuming that the firm's objective is the maximisation of V, it has the choice of either agreeing on y_0, and thereby avoiding a strike, or of rejecting y_0 and incurring a strike which eventually results in a lower wage increase. The employer's optimal solution is obtained by differentiating (6.8) and setting $\dfrac{dV}{ds} = 0$ as :

$$s' = -\frac{1}{\tau} \ln \left[\frac{PQ - L\hat{W}(1 + y^*)}{L\hat{W}(1 + \frac{\tau}{r})(y_0 - y^*)} \right] \qquad (6.9)$$

where s' denotes the optimal (i.e. V maximising) strike length, noting that the second-order condition $d^2V/ds^2 < 0$ is satisfied for $y_0 > y^*$, which is true by assumption. If s' is greater than zero the employer maximises discounted profit by not agreeing to y_0 and taking a strike: otherwise he maximises V by agreeing to y_0 and avoiding a strike. Thus for a strike to occur $s' > 0$, which from (6.9) requires that:

$$y_0 > \frac{PQ - L\hat{W}(1 - \frac{\tau}{r} y^*)}{L\hat{W}(1 + \frac{\tau}{r})} \qquad (6.10)$$

Other things being equal, condition (6.10) is more likely to be satisifed, and hence a strike is more likely to occur, the *higher* are y_0 (the union's pre-strike demand) and τ (the rate at which workers' resistance decays during the strike) and the *lower* are P, Q/L (the average product of labour: which as A–J point out, in this model, is inversely related to the ratio of the wage bill to total cost) r and y^*. Rewriting (6.10) using (6.4), as

$$y_0 > \frac{\hat{\pi} + H + \frac{\tau}{r} L\hat{W}y^*}{L\hat{W}(1 + \frac{\tau}{r})} \qquad (6.11)$$

indicates that a strike is less likely to occur in a given firm, the greater is the previous profit-level ($\hat{\pi}$) relative to the previous wage bill.

In summary then, this model predicts that *ceteris paribus* the probability of a strike occurring in a given period is *positively* related to the size of both the minimum wage-increase acceptable to the union rank and file at the commencement of the strike (y_0) and τ, (the employer's estimate of) the rate at which workers' resistance decays during the strike and *negatively* related to the price of output (P), the average product of labour, the employer's rate of discount (r) and y^*, the horizontal asymptote of the union's concession schedule, i.e. that wage-increase they regard as wholly unacceptable.

Empirical evidence

In order to obtain a testable version of the above model A–J make a number of simplifying assumptions and put forward some fairly *ad hoc* hypotheses regarding the determinants of y_0: namely that y_0 can be expected to be negatively related to the unemployment rate negatively related to a moving average of previous real wage changes and positively related to the firm's profit level. On the basis of these assumptions A–J find what they claim to be a reasonable degree of empirical support for their model from aggregate US data covering the period 1952 (first quarter) to 1967 (second quarter).

The A–J model was considerably more sophisticated than its predecessors and became especially important because it appeared to offer a testable set of hypotheses, reasonably grounded in microeconomic theory, regarding the influence of a range of economic variables upon strike activity. Researchers in a number of countries quickly set about adapting (though sometimes only very superficially) the A–J model to suit their own local institutional and other characteristics, and throughout the 1970s, studies applying A–J type models to different countries and time-periods appeared in the literature. For example, Pencavel (1970) against post-war British data; against Australian data by Phipps (1977); Canadian data by Walsh (1975) and New Zealand data by Turkington (1975) and Hazledine *et al.* (1977).

Criticisms

The A–J model has been criticised on a variety of grounds, both theoretical and empirical. On the theoretical level, the model's major deficiency is the 'one-sidedness' of its approach in the sense that it assumes that the union comes to the negotiations with the predetermined claim y_0, which it then communicates to the employer. The bargaining process then reduces simply to a situation where the employer, knowing the union concession function (6.3), maximises its objective function subject to the *given* union demand y_0. The model therefore simply ignores the bargaining which typically occurs between the union and the employer before the point where one party (perhaps, but by no means necessarily, the union) presents the other party with the sort of either/or choice analysed by the A–J model. This is a serious deficiency since it may be argued that such bargaining may be precisely the mechanism by which either the size of y_0 (the union's threat-accompanied wage-demand) is actually determined (Rabinovitch and Swary, 1976) or by which the union (say) seeks to hide from the employer the magnitude of its true y_0 in order to lead the employer into overestimating its value (Hamermesh, 1973). This weakness of the model was neatly summarised by Rabinovitch and Swary who pointed out that according to A–J 'the union acts as the sole cause for the strike ... [because the model] ignores the simultaneous effects of these same [economic and political] factors on management as well as the interactive effects of each side's position on the other' (Rabinovitch and Swary, 1976, p. 683) (parentheses added). Indeed in some recent work (Siebert, Bertrand and Addison, 1985) it has been argued that the logic of the A–J type of approach might equally plausibly be reversed in order to provide a model where the union maximises, subject to the given demand of the employer. (For attempts to construct models where the union, like the employer, follows a maximising strategy and where interdependency exists between the consessions of one bargainer and the demands of the other see Rabinovich and Swary, 1976, and Kaufman, 1981.)

On the empirical side, and no doubt related to the theoretical deficiencies noted above, the A–J-type models have proved disappointing. While they initially yielded what appeared to be reasonable empirical results they have generally performed poorly outside specific sample periods. This is particularly evident in the case of the British experience. As noted above, Pencavel (1970) applied the model to UK data, on a quarterly basis for the 1950 to mid-1967 period. However, it soon became clear (Hunter, 1973) that the predictive power of the model broke down when the sample period was extended to the end of 1972. Likewise, the related model due to Shorey (1977), which like Pencavel's was originally estimated against data covering the period 1950 (first quarter) through to 1967 (second quarter) proved unable to track post-sample events, showing a consistent tendency to under-predict when observations covering the period up to 1972 were added to the data set. (For a more detailed discussion of the question of structural stability in the context of British strike equations, see Cameron, 1984, and for similar evidence regarding the inability of the A–J model to explain the pattern of strike activity in the USA between 1967 and 1977 see Moore and Pearce, 1982.)

Some extensions

In view of the above deficiencies, the A–J-type model has been extended in a variety of directions (with varying degrees of success) in attempts to improve both its theoretical adequacy and empirical performance. For example, Kaufman (1981) explored in some detail the role of price expectations, while Sapsford (1982) used the bargaining model proposed by both Zeuthen (1930) and Harsanyi (1956) in analysing the determination by the union of its threat accompanied money wage demand, y_0 (for further discussion of the bargaining approach see Nash, 1950; Cross, 1969). Rabinovitch and Swary (1976) built a two-sided version of the A–J model which emphasised the search by each side for optimal decisions based on assumptions regarding the other's unknown real intentions; Phipps (1977) showed how the basic model could be extended to allow for expected output-price variations, while Davies (1979) investigated the role of incomes policies. The foregoing lists of extensions is by no means exhaustive but one particularly important extension is that provided by Farber (1978).

The Farber model

Although A–J present their model as one of strike activity it does

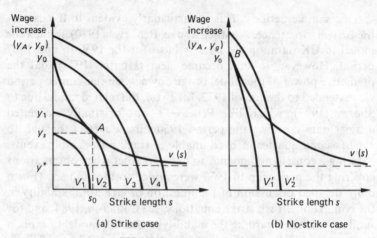

FIGURE 6.3   Farber's model

have a number of direct implications for wage determination and it
is this aspect of the model which is developed in Farber (1978).
This analysis, which amounts to an extension of the A–J approach
to provide a model in which the wage outcome and the occurrence
of strikes are *jointly* determined, can be conveniently seen from
Figure 6.3(a).

The vertical and horizontal axes in this diagram refer respectively to the minimum proportionate wage increase which is acceptable to the union (y_A) and to the strike length (s). The curve $v(s)$ is
the union concession schedule (6.2 above as already plotted in
Figure 6.2). The curves marked V in Figure 6.3 are the firm's iso-
present value curves, each of which is the locus of wage-increase/
strike-length combinations which give rise to a given present value
of the firm's future profit stream V, as set out in equation (6.6).
Letting y_g denote the wage-increase actually granted we have, from
equation (6.8) that, *ceteris paribus*,

$$V = f(y_g, s) \tag{6.12}$$

where $\delta V/\delta y_g < 0$ and $\delta V/\delta s < 0$. Totally differentiating (6.12) and
setting $dV = 0$ yields the following expression for the slope of the
firm's iso-present value curves:

$$\frac{dy_g}{ds} = -\frac{\delta V}{\delta s} \Big/ \frac{\delta V}{\delta y_g} < 0$$

Figure 6.3(a) shows a family of such curves where, clearly, $V_1 > V_2 > V_3 > V_4$. The firm's objective in this model is the maximisation of the present value of its future profit stream V (i.e. to get as close to the origin in Figure 6.3(a) as possible), and treating the union's concession-schedule as a constraint we see that its objective is achieved at the point of tangency between the union's concession-schedule and an iso-present value curve. This solution results in a proportionate wage increase of y_s and a strike of duration s_0 as shown by point A in Figure 6.3(a). If the iso-present value curves, however, are everywhere steeper than the union's concession-schedule, the firm's optimal decision corresponds to a corner solution. Such a solution is shown by point B in Figure 6.3(b) indicating that in this case V is maximised by paying a wage increase of y_0 in order to achieve a settlement without a strike.

It is important to notice from Figure 6.3(a) that the final outcome predicted is *not* Pareto-optimal. The final settlement is represented by the interior solution A, which gives rise to a wage increase of y_s. But this increase only occurs after a strike of length s_0 takes place and involves both lost income to the union members and a reduction in present value to the firm. If the firm had settled for any wage increases up to y_1 both parties would have benefited since the firm would have been on a higher iso-present value curve, while the union membership would have achieved at least the same wage increase without any foregone income.

Farber tested the preceding model against a *micro* data set composed of the negotiated wage settlements of ten large US manufacturing firms, each of which was located in a different 2-digit Standard Industrial Classification (SIC) industry, over the period 1954–70. The sample covered a total of eighty settlements, in twenty-one of which strikes occurred. For estimation purposes Farber modelled the union's concession rate (τ in equation (6.3) above) as being negatively related to both strike benefits and the membership's ability to replace income lost during a strike through such sources as temporary alternative employment opportunities (the availability of which, he argued, is likely to depend on the unemployment rate). In addition, he argued that the union's concession rate is likely to be a decreasing function of the mood of militancy of the rank and file, as determined by such factors as previous real-wage changes and the magnitude of the costs which they anticipate a strike will impose upon the employer. Farber also suggested that the horizontal asymptote of the union's concession schedule, y^*, will depend positively upon the best alternative wage elsewhere available to union members and, seeing the latter as being dependent on the strength of demand in the labour market, he argued that y^* will be inversely related to the unemployment rate.

In essence, Farber's model predicts that factors which imply a lower union-concession-rate decrease the likelihood of a strike occurring (because as shown in Figure 6.3 they result in a flatter $v(s)$ curve, which, *ceteris paribus*, increases the chances of the optimal solution being a corner/no-strike one as opposed to an interior/strike one) and indeed Farber's maximum likelihood estimation provides a degree of empirical support for the model. However, it should be noted that while most of the estimated coefficients have signs which are in accordance with Farber's hypotheses, a disturbingly large proportion of them failed to achieve statistical significance (Farber, 1978, p. 269). On a more positive note, however, the results did suggest that the union's rate of concession – and hence the probability of a strike occurring – was significantly and positively influenced by the operation of the US voluntary wage-guidelines which were in effect between 1962 and 1966 (which he argued brought outside pressure to bear upon the union to concede) and negatively and significantly related to the potential effectiveness of a strike, as proxied by labour's share of total sales.

Finally it is important to remember that Farber's model suffers from the same basic deficiencies as the A–J model from which it emanates and it may well be that it is these deficiencies which lay behind its disappointing empirical performance. In particular, while Farber's formulation makes clear the central role played by the union's concession-rate – or more correctly the employer's estimate of this – in determining whether or not a wage-negotiation results in a strike, it totally ignores the possibility which has long been recognised in the literature (e.g. Chamberlain, 1951; Cartter, 1959) that it may be in the union's interest to conceal from the employer the true value of its concession rate. By embarking on a variety of tactical bargaining manoeuvres designed to coax the employer into under-estimating the value of τ, the union may lead the employer into overestimating the optimality of settling at a corner solution by conceding y_0 without a strike and, therefore, without the imposition of any foregone income upon the union.

However, like A–J before him, Farber ignores this possibility by assuming bargaining away completely.

6.4 SOME RECENT DEVELOPMENTS

While the empirical literature on strikes continues to grow, with numerous writers extending or seeking to improve upon the basic A–J-type of approach and to test it against alternative data sets and aggregation levels,[3] there have been a number of interesting theoretical developments over recent years concerning the role of information, costs and asymmetries in information and it is to these studies which we now turn our attention.

Information and strikes

As we have already seen, one of the major deficiencies of the A–J model, and its various extensions including that due to Farber (1978), is that it assumes away maximisation behaviour on the part of the union in the determination of its optimal threat-accompanied money-wage-demand (to use game-theoretic terminology) as denoted by y_0 above. Instead, it effectively assumes that the union communicates y_0 to the employer who then, armed with *perfect knowledge* of both this and the union's concession-schedule, merely decides whether to take a strike or concede the union's claim y_0 according to whichever choice maximises the present value of his future profit-stream.

As noted above, Hicks drew attention to the importance of information in bargaining by arguing that 'adequate knowledge will always make a settlement possible' (Hicks, 1963, p. 147) and a number of recent investigators, dissatisfied with the A–J approach, have taken this as their starting point. One can discern two main, but related, approaches in the recent literature to the role of information in the bargaining–strike process and these relate to (a) the possibility that strikes may occur because of miscalculations which result from imperfections in the knowledge of each bargainer regarding the other's position, and (b) the role of *asymmetries* in information between the union on the one hand and the employer on the other.

Strikes as a consequence of imperfect information

In a recent paper Mauro (1982) develops Hicks's argument regarding the importance of imperfect information by constructing a model in which strikes occur as a consequence of misperceptions which arise because each party to the bargaining process uses variables different from the other's to form its concessions schedule and because each is not fully aware of the opponent's position.[4] Specifically Mauro constructs a model in which a strike can occur if one bargainer bases its estimate of the opponent's position on the *same* variables employed to form its own position when the opponent's position is actually based on different variables.

The model is easily understood diagramatically by merely re-plotting Hicks's diagram (Figure 6.1) to show both the actual employer-concession and union resistance-curves (denoted by *ECC* and *URC* respectively as in Figure 6.4) together with both the union's perception of the employer's curve (ECC_u) and the employer's perception of the union's curve (URC_E).[5] According to Mauro (1982, pp. 524–5) the misperceptions depicted in Figure 6.4 may arise if, for example, the employer were to us his product price (via its influence on his demand for labour) as one of the arguments

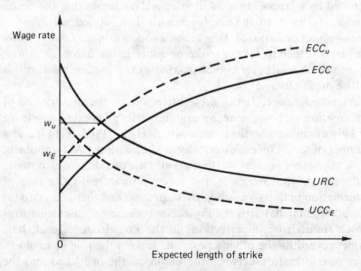

FIGURE 6.4   Mauro's model

of his concession function, while the union includes the level of consumer prices in its resistance function (via its influence on the real wage and on labour-supply decisions) under conditions where consumer prices grow more rapidly than the firm's product price and where each party forms its perception of the other's schedule by using the price variable used in the derivation of its own schedule.[6]

From Figure 6.4 it is clear that while the union expects the outcome of negotiations to be the wage w_u, the employer expects the lower settlement w_E, thus creating a divergence equal to $(w_u - w_E)$. Mauro assumes that the probability of a strike occurring is positively related to the magnitude of this divergence.

On the basis of some simplifying assumptions, Mauro finds a measure of empirical support for his imperfect-information model from maximum-likelihood-logit estimation against a micro data set relating to the course of negotiations in a sample of fourteen particular US firms over a period of about thirty years, covering 149 contract-expirations, approximately one quarter of which resulted in strikes. While Mauro's model is useful because of the importance it attaches to the role of less-than-perfect information, and the consequent possibility of miscalculations as a source of strikes, it does suffer from something of a problem in that it is by no means obvious why one party should use, and *continue* to use, different information in estimating the slope and position of its opponent's curve from that actually used by the opponent himself.

Asymmetric information models of strikes

In recent years a number of models which see strikes arising as a consequence of asymmetries in the amount of information available to bargainers have appeared in the literature (e.g. Hayes, 1984; Turk, 1984; Tracy, 1987; Booth and Cressy, 1987). Although precise details vary from one model to another, the basic idea is that one bargainer (typically the employer) possesses a larger information set than the other, and that the bargaining process serves as a learning mechanism, in which the less well-informed party infers information regarding the other's position by observing his or her behaviour during the negotiations. Representative of this literature is the model due to Tracy (1987) which assumes that uncertainty exists regarding the size of the rents (or the 'cake') to be divided between the union and the employer. Such rents, according to Tracy, consist of both *quasi*-rents, arising through specificity in the employer–worker match and occurring because the productivity of union labour is higher within than outside the firm, and *monopoly* rents generated by output restrictions. Within this framework, Tracy assumes for simplicity that the employer enters negotiations with full information regarding the size of the rents to be divided but that the union negotiates from a position of incomplete information regarding this magnitude. Under this setup, Tracy sees bargaining as a learning process in which the union makes a contract offer (consisting of a wage rate) at each round of the bargaining process, and infers information about the employer's private information by observing his behaviour in response to such offers.

Bargaining is assumed to continue as long as the value of the information which is expected to be gleaned from a further round of negotiations outweighs the additional bargaining costs. A strike is assumed to take place whenever the process continues beyond the expiration date of the current contract and by raising the costs of continuing the bargaining/learning process, strikes are seen in this model as the mechanism which brings about eventual settlement.

To illustrate the model let P denote the present value of the firm's profits over the next contract period, net of non-labour costs, calculated on the basis that the firm accepts the union's first contract offer so that no strike occurs. At the commencement of negotiations the firm is assumed to know P while Tracy assumes that the union believes that P is *uniformly distributed* over the interval $(\underline{P}, \ \bar{P})$. The pay-offs to the union and the firm from agreeing to a wage, w, after t rounds of negotiations are:

$$\pi_u(w;t) = w\delta_u^{t-1}$$

$$\pi_F(w;P;t) = (P - w)\delta_F^{t-1}$$

where δ_u and δ_F denote discount factors for the union and the employer/firm respectively. If the union's initial-contract/wage-offer is accepted then no strike occurs and $t = 1$; otherwise a strike begins and each side's pay-off from a settlement is discounted in light of its respective strike costs. In other words, in this model there are only two possible outcomes of the first round of negotiations: either a strike occurs or a settlement is achieved on the basis of the union's first-offered wage-contract. In the former case, the union is assumed to continue to make offers, and thereby to gain improved information regarding the employer's position, until a settlement may eventually be achieved. Tracy works with a model with a fixed number of rounds and assumes that if no agreement is reached after (say) N rounds, the bargaining pair will split up and go their separate ways, with the union members receiving competitive wages elsewhere in the local labour market, while the firm earns only normal profits in the next-best alternative use of its resources.

At each round of the bargaining process, the union is assumed to select the wage demand which maximizes its expected return, conditional on the information which it has at its disposal. To see how bargaining can serve as a learning mechanism for the union, consider what it can learn by observing whether the firm accepts or rejects its wage demand in round $N-1$. Letting I_{N-1} denote the firm's information set at the commencement of the Nth round of negotiations and $E(w_N/I_{N-1})$ denote the firm's conditional expectation of the union's Nth round wage demand we obtain $\hat{P}(w_{N-1})$, the level of profitability for the firm if it is indifferent between accepting w_{N-1} or continuing the strike one round and accepting the next union-wage-demand, by solving the following equation:

$$\hat{P}(w_{N-1}) - w_{N-1} = [\hat{P}(w_{N-1}) - E(w_N/I_{N-1})]\delta_F$$

from which

$$\hat{P}(w_{N-1}) = \frac{w_{N-1} - E(w_N/L_{N-1})\delta_F}{(1-\delta_F)} \tag{6.13}$$

Accordingly by simply observing whether the firm accepts its wage demand w_{N-1}, the union learns whether the firm's profitability is greater or less than $\hat{P}(w_{N-1})$ defined in (6.13) above. If the firm rejects the union's demand then the union has learned that the firm's profitability is less than or equal to $\hat{P}(w_{N-1})$ and it therefore updates its beliefs by assigning a zero probability to P lying in the interval $[P(w_{N-1}), P(w_{N-2})]$ and in consequence, it enters the Nth round of negotiations with the posterior belief that P is still uniformly distributed but over the restricted interval $[\underline{P}, \hat{P}(w_{N-1})]$.

On the assumption that the union selects its wage demand so as to maximise its expected pay-off, Tracy derives, by induction, the following expression for the union's optimal wage demand in round $j+1$, in the case where $\hat{P}(w_{N-1}) > \underline{\hat{P}}$, for $j \leqslant N-2$ as:

$$w_{j+1}^{*} = R + C_{j+1}[\hat{P}(w_j) - R] \tag{6.14}$$

where

$$C_{j+1} = \frac{(1 - \delta_F + \delta_F C_{j+2})^2}{2(1 - \delta_F + \delta_F C_{j+2}) - \delta_u C_{j+2}} \tag{6.15}$$

and where R denotes the present value of the flow of competitive wages in the local labour market. Expression (6.14) is described as the *union's optimal concession function*.

It should be recalled that in this model a strike occurs if the firm rejects the union's first-round wage-demand and Tracy writes the probability of a strike occurring as:[7]

$$P(s) = \frac{\hat{P}(w_1^*) - \underline{P}}{\bar{P} - \underline{P}} \tag{6.16}$$

from which it follows that, other things being equal, the probability of a strike occurring is *positively* related to both the extent of the union's uncertainty over the firm's profitability and the value of the union members' outside opportunities (R).[8] Strike probability in this model is also shown to be *negatively* related to the size of total expected rents. The foregoing model also has implications for the duration of strikes and Tracy (1987, pp. 159–60) demonstrates that the model predicts that the expected duration of a strike *increases* with the union's uncertainty about the firm's profitability and with the value of union-workers' outside opportunities but *decreases* as the size of total rents increases.

In summary, the asymmetric information approach predicts from its analysis of an N-round bargaining model incorporating optimal behaviour by both union and employer at each round of negotiations, that both the probability of a strike and its expected duration will be positively related to the degree of uncertainty facing the union and the value of its outside opportunities and negatively related to the total expected size of the 'cake' to be shared between the union and the firm.

Empirical evidence

For estimation purposes Tracy proxied quasi-rents by both the industry's average period of job tenure and years of labour-market experience of union workers; while monopoly rents were proxied by a four-firm concentration ratio in the four-digit industry classification. Union uncertainty was proxied by measures of investor uncertainty over the firm's future profitability, with the measure being subdivided into separate components resulting from economy and firm-specific events. The union-membership's outside opportunities will be influenced by the likelihood of members finding part-time jobs to help offset strike costs and were therefore seen as being determined by local labour market conditions and were accordingly proxied by forecast residuals about local employment equations.

Using logit analysis, Tracy obtains results from analysis of a micro data set covering major contract negotiations in US manufacturing industry between 1973 and 1977 which lend some degree of support to each of the model's three main predictions. More specifically, while Tracy's evidence seems to suggest that both economy-wide and firm-specific measures of union uncertainty are positively related to strike activity they do indicate that firm-specific uncertainty exerts the largest and most significant influence. The hypothesis that larger rents discourage strikes fares less well since both of the quasi-rent proxies fail to achieve significance, while the concentration ratio variable is both incorrectly signed and significant. Finally, the evidence offers support for the predicted positive influence of the membership's outside opportunities on strike probability, although it should be noted that the local employment residual term was found to be both incorrectly signed and significant.

While these results are quite encouraging, it remains to be seen, at the time of writing, whether asymmetric information models will prove useful in explaining variability in other samples. However, some tentative results obtained from application of a closely related model to a UK micro data set derived from the 1984

Workplace Industrial Relations Survey (Booth and Cressy, 1987) would seem to suggest that such models may well have a bright future ahead of them.

Joint cost minimisation models

The final recent development to be considered concerns the role of strike costs relative to the costs of alternative ways of reaching agreements under collective bargaining. Reder and Neumann (1980) construct a model which predicts that the incidence of strike activity varies inversely across industries according to the costs associated with such action. Reder and Neumann place particular emphasis on the idea of collective bargaining as a *sequence* of negotiations and analyse a series of bargains in which bargainers learn about each other's pattern of behaviour during the bargaining process and develop what they term conventions or bargaining *protocols*,[9] the purpose of which is to guide subsequent bargaining activity. Their basic notion is that learning is mutual and that the union and the employer (the bargaining pair), both of whom are assumed to be risk-neutral, learn about each other's customary behaviour in bargaining situations through repeated interaction. The consequence of this learning process is that each becomes better able than an inexperienced bargainer to predict the minimum offer that will induce the other to accept a contract. Both strike activity and the implementation of protocols involve costs to both parties. In the former case, this cost is foregone *net* income in the form of wages and profits to the respective parties, while in the latter case, the cost is seen as a lower expected pay-off which arises from the restrictions upon behaviour implied by adherence to the protocol. According to Reder and Neumann each party will, however, accept the restrictions implied by the protocol if it results in a reduction in its expected cost of strike activity over a sequence of contract negotiations which more than outweighs the reduction in expected pay-offs. Reder and Neumann assume that each party shares the same objective: namely the minimisation of the *total* expected costs of strikes to both parties combined and argue that the protocol is the choice variable by which this objective is achieved. According to this model, a bargaining pair chooses amongst the range of alternative possible protocols so as to minimise total *joint* expected cost of strike activity over its lifetime, net of the costs involved in the specification of the protocol which arise from the need to devise and agree upon either formulae or conventions to apply to the large number of states of the world which may apply over the protocol's life.

The essence of Reder and Neumann's model is therefore that bargainers select a protocol in order to balance the reduction in cost from diminished strike activity against the increased cost of specifying a more detailed protocol, in the sense of one covering a larger number of possible states of the world. Clearly this balancing of costs and benefits does not necessarily result in the adoption of a protocol which prevents *all* strikes. Since the costs of strike activity will, in general, vary across different bargaining pairs, such cost-minimising behaviour gives rise to the model's basic prediction: namely that those bargainers who face higher costs per 'unit' of strike activity will, *ceteris paribus*, select more comprehensive protocols characterised by a lower expected quantity of strike activity and a larger protocol specification cost than those selected by bargaining pairs facing lower strike costs.

Evidence

Reder and Neumann recognise that unit strike costs to both parties combined vary inversely with the ease of intertemporal substitution of production and labour input, both pre- and post-strike, for that 'lost' during a strike. Proxying strike costs inversely by a variable measuring inventories of finished goods and directly by a variable measuring shipments of finished goods Reder and Neumann find a not-unreasonable degree of empirical support from their analysis of a pooled series of cross-sections relating to fourteen US manufacturing industries for their basic prediction that the incidence of strike activity (as proxied by (a) the number of strikes (b) their mean duration and (c) man days of strikes per employed worker) decreases as its *joint* cost increases.

6.5 CONCLUDING REMARKS

This chapter has taken as its subject matter the economists' approach to the analysis of strike activity. In it we have seen how the early literature was content to explore the relationship between strikes and the business cycle and how this approach was largely superseded in the late 1960s and early 1970s by a more formal econometric approach. The chapter went on to consider both the strengths and weaknesses of the latter approach and concluded by reviewing a number of more recent models. However, whether these more recent models (with their particular emphasis on such issues as the quantity, quality and cost of information) will stand the empirical and theoretical tests of time any more successfully than their predecessors remains to be seen.

7 Segmented Labour Markets

ROBERT McNABB and PAUL RYAN

7.1 INTRODUCTION

During the past twenty years economists dissatisfied with orthodox theory have proposed different explanations of how labour markets operate. Some of the alternatives simply extend orthodoxy to include the effects of various institutional factors; others have explicitly sought a new paradigm. All reject a predominantly competitive analysis, insisting instead upon the fragmented nature of labour markets and the importance of institutional and social influences upon pay and employment. 'Labour market segmentation' (LMS) provides a common label for these alternative approaches.[1]

The segmentationist approach has both a recent and a distant history. Its recent origins are twofold. First, studies of urban labour and poverty in the USA in the 1960s documented the failure of a manpower policy based upon increasing individuals' human capital to improve their fortunes in the labour market (Piore, 1970). Second, segmentation of work experiences has provided radical economists with a theory of the political fragmentation of the US working class (Gordon, Edwards and Reich, 1982). In a longer perspective, the segmentationist approach may be traced back to John Stuart Mill and Cairnes, who explicitly rejected Adam Smith's essentially competitive conception of the labour market in favour of 'non-competing groups' (Mill, 1885; Cairnes, 1874); and to the American institutionalists of the 1940s and 1950s,

ECCLECTIC

who developed the concepts of balkanised and structured labour markets (Dunlop, 1957; Kerr, 1954).

The contemporary segmentationist literature is highly variegated. Analyses differ in the outcomes of interest (pay or mobility); in the delineation of segments (by job, industry, gender, race or age); and in the methodology of investigation, whether qualitative or econometric. However, straddling these differences is a broad orientation towards a dualist formulation, first advanced by Piore (1970), in which primary and secondary segments are distinguished within the labour market.

In this chapter we consider both dualist and alternative, less restrictive, formulations of the LMS approach. We argue that the dualist variant is both misguided and misleading – misguided in that the evidence generally fails to support dualist propositions, misleading in that it has obscured alternative, less restrictive formulations of segmentation. The segmentation baby need not be discarded along with the bathwater of duality however. Thus this chapter continues with an outline of alternative expositions of segmentation (section 7.2). The postulated causes of segmentation are discussed in section 7.3, followed in section 7.4 by an assessment of the evidence. The conclusions are presented in section 7.5.

7.2   DESCRIPTIONS OF SEGMENTATION

The starting-point must be the 'segment,' an area of employment which is separated or segregated from the wider labour market. Thus John Stuart Mill argued that social, occupational and spatial barriers to mobility often made it difficult or impossible for workers to move from one part of the labour market to another. In particular, unskilled manual labourers and their children were confined to the least-rewarding segment of the labour market as a result of their inability to acquire the skills required for advancement (Mill, 1885). The advantages of workers in favoured segments thus lay outside the reach of the less well-placed.

The modern dualist literature advances similar propositions. In Piore's well known description:

> the primary market offers jobs which possess several of the following traits: high wages, good working conditions, employ-

ment stability and job security, equity and due process in the administration of work rules, and chances for advancement. The ... secondary market has jobs which, relative to those in the primary sector, are decidedly less attractive. They tend to involve low wages, poor working conditions, considerable variability in employment, harsh and often arbitrary discipline, and little opportunity to advance. The poor are confined to the secondary labour market (1970).

Duality is manifested principally in job rewards: in particular, pay is low and job loss is high in the secondary sector. Furthermore, in the secondary segment the acquisition of more education and training fails to improve a person's job rewards – and may not even permit movement into the primary sector.

The LMS approach emphasises demand side and institutional factors, in contrast to the supply side and individual factors which dominate orthodox analysis of the labour market. Thus duality is seen as the result of the characteristics of jobs rather than workers. Nevertheless a parallel duality is found in worker attributes. Secondary jobs are filled largely by groups whose attachment to paid employment is weak, notably non-whites, females and youths. Primary jobs tend to be the preserve of 'prime age' white males.

Jobs in the primary segment tend to be part of internal labour markets, i.e. employment structures where the pricing and alloca- tion of labour is governed by administrative and institutional rules rather than by market processes. Access to such jobs is granted preferentially, even exclusively, to existing members of the organi- sation, be it a firm, a public agency, a professional association or a craft union. Pay structures within internal markets respond not to excess demand or supply in the external market but rather to organisational requirements. Imbalances in supply and demand *vis-à-vis* the external labour market are dealt with through a variety of non-wage adjustments, including recruitment and training, job redesign, subcontracting and output variation (Doeringer and Piore, 1971; Osterman, 1984).

Three issues came to the fore at an early stage in the dualist literature. The first involves the dimension of labour market outcomes to which duality is most relevant. For some, the key dimension is the stability of employment. Although Piore placed high pay first in the above listing of the advantages of primary

employment, he also maintained that the most important distinguishing attribute of primary jobs 'appears to be the behavioural requirements which they impose upon the workforce,
particularly that of employment stability' (Piore, 1970; Berger and
Piore, 1982). Dualism is commonly interpreted in terms of mobility
in the British literature (Mayhew and Rosewell, 1979). Other
writers, on the other hand, have remained closer to Piore's initial
ranking, treating high earnings as the main reason for describing
primary jobs as good jobs (Bluestone, 1970; Wachtel and Betsey,
1972).

(2) The second issue is the comprehensiveness of the dualist *schema*.
Dualism was initially conceived as a partial classification, comparing the experiences of urban minorities to (at most) the remainder
of the manual labour force. Subsequent work has however sought
to develop it into an exhaustive classification of workers and jobs.
The resulting heterogeneity of the enlarged primary segment has
been accommodated by a dilution of the original duality, as
subsidiary dichotomies (upper and lower tiers, independent and
subordinate tiers) are elaborated amongst primary jobs (Edwards,
Reich and Gordon, 1975; Piore, 1975).

(3) The third issue concerns the viability of dualism itself, strictly
interpreted. Duality may be seen as a restrictive formulation (or
special case) of segmentation, notwithstanding the bias of critics
towards treating the two as synonymous. For segmentation to
prove a valid interpretation of outcomes in the labour market, all
that is needed is a substantial dispersion in the distribution of
labour market outcomes across workers (Figure 7.1, panel b).
Strict duality, on the other hand, requires in addition bimodality
(two peaks) in the distribution and a clear frontier between the two
segments (α in Figure 7.1, panel c).

Although dualism has dominated the LMS literature, some have
viewed the labour market in terms either of multiple segments
(Freedman, 1976; Buchele, 1976) or of a continuous 'job queue' in
which job rewards are highly differentiated but no clear segments
are distinguished (Thurow, 1975). In the latter interpretation,
dualist terminology may still be employed, as when all jobs above
an arbitrary frontier such as λ in Figure 7.1 (panel b) are defined as
primary and the remainder as secondary. In this case duality is
simply a heuristic convenience, a vivid but essentially arbitrary way
of conveying the wider concept of segmentation.

155

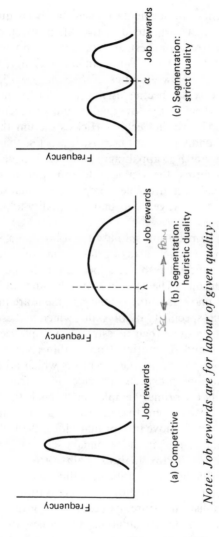

Note: Job rewards are for labour of given quality.

FIGURE 7.1   Duality and segmentation

The orthodox critique

The distinctiveness of segmentationism has been questioned by orthodox economists, who tend to treat its propositions as either empirically incorrect or best interpreted in competitive terms (Wachter, 1974; Cain, 1976; Taubman and Wachter, 1986). Thus, taking pay first, the low earnings of secondary workers are seen from the orthodox perspective as the result of the implication in competitive markets of the low quality and productivity of their labour power. The verdict echoes Hicks's dictum that unskilled labour is 'often badly paid, not because it gets less than it is worth, but because it is worth so appallingly little' (Hicks, 1963, p. 82). Put in Marshallian terms, the visible differentiation of wages across segments conceals an invisible competitive equalisation of efficiency wages (i.e. wages per unit of quality-adjusted labour input).

Similarly, in terms of job stability the job ladders, employment security and low turnover rates of primary employment are seen as consistent with efficient resource allocation under particular technological conditions. The stability of jobs and workers in the internal labour markets of the primary segment are interpreted as the result of firm-specificity in job skills, which makes it profitable for employers to protect their investment in employees by providing job security and promoting from within (Becker, 1975). Efficiency is also improved by the incentives which job-ladders and internal promotion prospects provide to intrinsically stable workers to apply for primary employment (Nickell, 1976; Lazear, 1981). Finally, to the extent that improved labour quality permits secondary workers to move into primary jobs, the lack of a return to education and training in the secondary segment is by no means inconsistent with orthodox analysis (Cain, 1976).

The thrust of the orthodox critique is thus to deny the economic distinctiveness of the institutional generalisations of the LMS (particularly dualist) literature. At best LMS is given credit for the institutional flesh of labour analysis; the bones are however reserved for a generally competitive version of orthodoxy.

A distinctive approach?

The orthodox critique has helped to clarify the requirements for a specifically segmentationist analysis of labour markets. Three features clearly differentiate the LMS approach.

The first distinguishing attribute of segmentationism is a view of the labour market as systematically differentiating the job rewards achieved by comparable individuals. Thus the high pay of primary workers cannot be explained simply in terms of higher quality of labour. Many secondary workers are capable of performing well in primary jobs but the rationing of access to good jobs denies them the opportunity to do so. The labour market is thus seen as a key ingredient in the generation of economic inequality and not a passive mirror of the inequalities which people bring to it from family and social class.

This is not to argue that all secondary workers are as good as all primary workers. Labour quality will in general be higher in primary jobs. The key points are rather that the difference in labour quality across jobs is less than that in pay; and that the direction of causality between pay and labour quality is reversed. Wage structure is taken as given, differentiated by employer characteristics rather than worker attributes. Under such conditions high-paying employers can take their pick from the applicant queue and rationally hire labour of high quality. The compensation, however, is only partial, with the difference in job-rewards exceeding that in worker-quality.

Labour-quality and labour-productivity must therefore be carefully distinguished. Productivity is seen as an attribute of the job rather than the worker, depending upon the equipment available and the product market served. Primary workers have higher productivity than do their secondary counterparts because of the jobs in which they work rather than because of who they are. Were they confined to secondary employment, with its labour-intensive techniques and unfavourable product markets, their productivity would be correspondingly lower.

A similar divergence of interpretation occurs for employment stability. While the roles of many secondary workers in the family (youths and married females) or society (inner-city non-whites) may mean lower intrinsic job-stability than for primary workers, in an LMS interpretation the instability of jobs is the more important influence. Many secondary workers, particularly married females, are interested in and available for steady work but are denied access to it. Thus while the supply side does indeed exert an influence, it is seen as less important than the demand side and social institutions in explaining the differentiation of outcomes in the labour market (Doeringer and Piore, 1971, p. 167).

The second distinguishing attribute of LMS follows from the first. The role of market forces in affecting labour outcomes is not denied; however, their locus is the *product* rather than the *labour* market. The part played by labour-market influences, particularly excess demand but also trade unions, is seen as subsidiary to such attributes of the product market as demand variability, employer power and production technology (section 7.3).[2] Similarly, internal labour markets are seen as the result not so much of technology and skills as of power relationships and control strategies within the enterprise.

The final *differentia* involves the widening of the scope of the analysis. In contrast to the orthodox assumptions of given tastes and indeterminate public policy, LMS treats both tastes and policy as endogenous. Thus the instability of inner-city employment is attributed to an adverse interaction between worker-attitudes and job-attributes: the experience of unstable jobs cumulatively disposes secondary workers to high quit rates. Similarly, the common confinement of youths and married females to secondary jobs reflects preferences that are not just exogenously determined but rather moulded by their subordinate positions within both family and society.

These attributes distinguish the LMS approach and contradict the charge that it is simply descriptive, taxonomic and compatible with a competitive interpretation.

IS THIS ?
THE CASE ?

7.3   THE SOURCES OF SEGMENTATION

Theories of labour market segmentation all focus upon the interaction between organisations and product markets, and in particular on the way their relationships have evolved over time.

Interpretations of LMS which centre around stability and mobility analyse the responses of firms to product market instability. Piore's approach centres upon the evolution of product markets from the competitive and the localised to the producer-dominated and the national. Technological change makes possible capital-intensive methods of production. However, employers are unwilling to undertake large-scale investment unless product demand is stable and predictable. When demand is variable labour-intensive techniques are preferred. A growing division is found between firms which cater for stable markets (or the stable portion of demand in unstable markets) and those which do the opposite. This adaptation of Smith's dictum that the division of labour is limited by the size of the (product) market carries implications for the labour market. Firms which cater to stable product demand create primary conditions of employment, including notably job-security; firms which face unstable demand operate in the secondary segment of the labour market (Berger and Piore, 1982).

Instability of product demand is not the only reason for secondary status. Employers are unwilling to invest in declining industries. Elsewhere, production may be technically unsuited to mass production, particularly where the size of the market is limited by customer service requirements. In such situations, Piore observes that some work tasks remain complex and require substantial skill, while others are reduced to low skill requirements and allocated to secondary status. The gap in skill levels prevents upward mobility between these categories. In such cases the frontier between primary and secondary segments cuts through the workplace itself.

The contours of segmentation, defined according to stability, fluctuate with the state of the economy. When labour markets are tight and product markets favourable, employers seek to tie workers to the firm by expanding their provision of primary jobs. However, when the opposite is the case, and particularly when a downturn proves longer and deeper than anticipated, employers seek to increase the share of secondary jobs, proclaiming the virtues of flexibility (Sengenberger, 1981).

The theory of segmentation advanced by radical economists in the USA takes a different tack, focusing upon changing systems of organisation within the capitalist firm. The key to segmentation is sought in the varied employer-strategies for the control and motivation of their workforces – i.e. for the setting of the undetermined component of the labour contract: the work to be provided in return for wages. Previous systems of labour control, notably the personalised discipline of 'simple control' and the impersonal machine-pacing of 'technical control' proved decreasingly effective as firms turned into giant corporations and worker organisation become more insistent. Large employers turned instead to 'bureaucratic control', erecting impersonal procedures and providing job-security and career prospects in order to win the loyalty of employees. Thus emerged the internal labour market and the difference between its job-rewards and those of employers who lacked the incentive to abandon the secondary segment (Edwards, 1979; Gordon *et al.*, 1982).

The forces which led some employers to create primary jobs begin with the emergence of the large corporation. Simple control, or the open, highly visible, direct command-rule by supervisors over subordinates, proved unviable in large plants: the interdependence between workers in mass production made it difficult to measure the output of individuals. The power wielded by large firms over product markets permitted them to take a longer view and to provide superior job-rewards. The high turnover associated with previous systems of control was found to involve high costs. Last, but by no means least, worker-solidarity was to be undermined by status differentiation along job-ladders, the rationale for whose existence lay in worker-motivation rather than skill-development. The internal labour markets of primary employers represent a sophisticated version of the traditional capitalist strategy of 'divide and rule'.

These theories of segmentation concentrate to a greater or lesser degree upon its stability and mobility attributes. Explanations which focus upon pay structure also look to the characteristics of employers and product markets. The key distinction, often neglected, is that between the internal and external (i.e. within and between organisations) dimensions of wage-structure.

Taking external wage-structure first, the source of much subsequent theoretical endeavour was the linking of labour-market outcomes to an underlying duality in industrial structure by Averitt (1968). Jobs in the primary segment are generated by employers in 'core' sectors, whose ability to pay is boosted by large size, high capital-intensity and profitability, as well as a degree of unexploited power in product markets. Secondary jobs are provided by firms located in the 'periphery', where firm-size and capital-intensity are lower and product-markets are highly competitive on price. Secondary work may also involve 'irregular' activities, i.e. those not included in the national accounts (odd jobs, crime).[3]

The advantages enjoyed by core firms however, are permissive rather than deterministic. Their implications for labour outcomes may even be indeterminate in some cases. Thus powerful employers may use their extra resources to deny special advantages to employees (e.g. through direct union-busting and relocation of production) as readily as to grant them to them (Hodson and Kaufman, 1982). Similarly, even highly competitive product markets may yield primary jobs if employees are well organised and able to fend off unorganised competition from home and abroad – as in the parts of the coal, trucking and construction sectors in the USA (Levinson, 1967). To take another example, public employment may involve superior job rewards under permissive political conditions, but inferior ones elsewhere.

In any event, core employers typically need not extend primary jobs to all their employees. As a range of functions, particularly in cleaning and catering, is generally limited to secondary status either within the firm or in subcontractors, the contours of segmentation run through firms, not simply between sectors (Rubery and Wilkinson, 1981). Similarly, jobs in small firms include not only the low pay and job-instability of the classic sweatshop, but also the high rewards offered by producers of speciality goods (Brusco and Sabel, 1981).

The latter point is developed in some accounts, particularly in Britain, into a central role for trade unions and professional associations, alongside employers, in the generation of primary employment conditions. The downgrading of skills by mechanisation led many craft unions to cushion their decline in two ways. They protected their bargaining power by expanding to include the semi-skilled workers who were displacing them in production. They used their bargaining power to encourage the growth of internal labour markets, restricting entry to the best jobs and facilitating the maintenance of their members' advantages in the labour market (Rubery, 1978). More generally, it has been argued that the attributes of core firms will provide superior job rewards for workers only when labour shows both energy and skill in turning such resources to their own ends (Hodson and Kaufman, 1982).

Turning to internal wage structure, the differentiation of pay within internal labour markets was initially explained primarily in terms of firm-specific skills which can only be developed through on-the-job training. The senior workers who possess such skills must be sufficiently well paid and secure in their jobs to ensure their willingness to train others (Doeringer and Piore, 1971).

A sharper differentiation from orthodox analysis, however, is achieved by elaborating a further factor suggested by Deoringer and Piore: custom. The stability of work groups within internal labour markets permits the generation of norms, foremost amongst which stand concepts of fair treatment. Employers must accommodate such values if production is to proceed without interruption (Piore, 1973). Custom is both the accumulated total of such norms and a norm in itself: the requirement that established practices be respected. Thus two groups of workers whom the worker-collectivity holds should be paid the same will often be paid the same, even if the presence of excess demand for one and excess supply for the other calls for different pay rates (Ryan, 1980). Similarly, the job-evaluation techniques which determine pay in many internal labour markets reward skill and responsibility in proportions which vary with the relative importance of craft and process employees (Theochorakis, 1988). The role of trade unions in formulating and enforcing such norms may be minimal.[4]

These theories of segmentation are diverse and even contradictory. They do however share a common emphasis upon the influence of organisation, power and norms, in contrast to an orthodox agenda which for the most part limits itself to the implications of technology and individual preferences.

7.4   THE EVIDENCE

The outstanding characteristics of the empirical evaluation of labour market segmentation are (i) the difficulty of attaining strong tests; (ii) the lack of support for a strict dualistic formulation; and (iii) the importance of indirect evidence from employment and turnover patterns.

Difficulties in testing

Strong tests have been difficult either because of a confusion concerning the nature of segmentation or as a result of the rarity of comprehensive data sets on the characteristics of both employers and workers. Both difficulties can be illustrated from the results of one of the earliest empirical studies of pay (Osterman, 1975). A national sample of male workers was classified into secondary and primary (lower and upper tier) segments according to occupational characteristics. Separate earnings functions were estimated for each category. As the returns to both schooling and work experience proved significant only in the primary segment, the presence of duality was inferred (Table 7.1).

TABLE 7.1 Illustrative earnings functions for primary and secondary segments of US labour markets

Variable[2]	Coefficient (standard error) for:[1]	
	Secondary segment	Primary[3] segment
Age	0.056[4] (3.357	6.644[4]* (0.527)
Age squared	0.005[4] (0.040)	− 0.069[4]* (0.006
Schooling	0.014 (0.022)	0.062* (0.003)
Race (white)	0.120 (0.133)	0.227* (0.032)
R^2	0.21	0.25
N	234	4130

Notes: * indicates significant difference from zero ($p = 0.05$)

Notes: 2. Controls for unemployment duration and hours worked, as well as the intercept, are not reported here.
3. Lower tier of primary segment only.
4. Coefficients on age and age-squared multiplied by 100.
Source: Osterman (1975) Table 4.

Osterman's study has been criticised for its subjective classification procedure – a difficulty avoided by more recent studies, some of which reach similar conclusions.[5] More fundamental problems arise however at two levels. In the first place, the absence of a return to human capital in a secondary segment (termed the 'incremental' formulation of segmentation) is neither necessary nor sufficient for the viability of a LMS interpretation (Ryan, 1981). It is not necessary because any two segments, each of which pays higher wages to more educated and experienced workers, may still differ greatly in the rewards which they offer to a given level of education or experience. It is not sufficient because in a competitive model differences in the returns which any two segments offer to experience are compensated for by lower starting-rates in the one which offers the higher returns to experience. The incremental formulation may capture neatly the concept of dead end secondary jobs, which provide no reward for additional education and training, but a wider assessment of segmentation need not depend upon this particular issue.

The importance of the incremental formulation is diminished still further to the extent that higher levels of labour quality provide a return through facilitating exit from the secondary segment. When a sample is truncated on the basis of variables highly correlated with the dependent variable (earnings), it is inevitable that the lower segment will contain predominantly low-wage occupations. By effectively standardising for occupation, such a procedure thus denies to schooling and training their effect on earnings through upward occupational mobility (Cain, 1976).

The more fundamental attribute of segmentation involves levels of, rather than increments in, labour quality. It asks whether comparable workers achieve different outcomes depending upon where and for whom they happen to work.[6] Osterman's results are also consistent with the 'levels' aspect of segmentation as well. His secondary segment contained many individuals the quality of whose labour was statistically comparable to that of, but whose earnings were roughly one-fifth lower than those of, their primary counterparts. The extent of 'levels' segmentation in pay structure has proved still greater in other US studies.[7] In the British context, the earnings gain from relocating a representative male member of a secondary segment defined on 'periphery' sectoral characteristics into its primary counterpart (in a 1975 General Household Survey sample) amounted to more than 30 per cent (McNabb, 1987).

Yet even then the sceptic is entitled to remain unconvinced. The limitations of the data permit divergent interpretations. An orthodox assessment would emphasise the limitations of years of schooling and work experience as indicators of labour quality, hypothesising that if the unmeasured dimensions (quality of schooling and experience, health, attitudes and ability) were to be included the difference between segments would disappear. For the segmentationist, however, the ability of high-wage employers to hire applicants with the highest prospective productivity means that some of the return to education and experience actually represents the underlying structural differentiation in the pay rates attached to jobs. The impossibility of a decisive test in the dispute between LMS and orthodoxy is clear.[8]

Nevertheless, evidence of a link between the attributes of employers, production technologies and product markets, on the one side, and labour-market outcomes on the other, is by now sufficiently extensive to underline the credibility of many segmentationist propositions. Studies of both pay and mobility find moderately strong and consistent associations with product-market concentration-ratios, capital–labour ratios, firm size and access to government contracts in a variety of advanced economies.[9]

The empirical analysis of segmentation has, moreover, begun to delineate and explain differences across time and place. Historically, the gap between the productivity and pay of workers in a core/periphery dichotomisation of US industry widened secularly between 1950 and 1980. The change has been attributed (speculatively, to be sure) to the consolidation of a long wave in capitalist development, following earlier waves in which labour was successively proletarianised and homogenised (Gordon *et al.*, 1982; Reich, 1984). The ensuing sequence of economic slump and currency overvaluation has seen considerable rearrangement in the industrial wage-structure, the difficulties of the giant steel and automobile firms being mirrored in an at-least-temporary reduction in the job rewards available to their employees (Mitchell, 1985).[10] Institutional rearrangement has proceeded on a wide front in the USA. A managerial offensive has sought the rescinding of the internal labour-market rules, bargained during the post-war 'labour accord', in order to regain greater control over the allocation of workers to jobs (Piore, 1982; Strauss, 1984; Edwards, Garonna and Todtling, 1986).

Important differences in the contours and sources of segmentation can be seen across countries. The centrality of the job and the occupation in US labour-market structuring contrasts with that of the employer and in Japan. Access to government purchases proves a particular source of advantage to employers and employees in the USA; centrality to the planning process, in Hungary (Cukor and Kertesi, 1986).

Indeed, the importance of the state has been brought to the fore by recent comparative work. The very existence of occupational markets in the face of pressures for internalisation depends crucially upon institutional support from public policy (Marsden, 1986). Where governments have responded to economic crisis in a corporatist manner, seeking consensual solutions (as in Sweden and Norway), labour-market inequality has remained low relative to that in countries (such as Britain and the USA) where government has espoused market ideology and undermined the statutory protection of secondary workers (Kalleberg and Hanisch, 1986). The weakening since 1977 of both incomes policy and the minimum-wage protection provided in Britain by Wages Councils has increased markedly the extent of segmentation in the British labour market (Brosnan and Wilkinson, 1987).

Strict duality?

Such differences across time and place in institutional structures and labour-market outcomes cannot realistically be attributed mostly, let alone entirely, to the effects of differing worker-attributes as worked out through competitive markets. However the LMS approach has not had things its own way in other respects. In particular, interpretations of the labour market in terms of strict duality (i.e. including bimodality) have failed to muster adequate empirical support.

The high-water mark of strict dualism has been the finding of bimodality in distributions of industry characteristics in the USA (Oster, 1978), along with correlations between the latter and labour-market outcomes (Wallace and Kalleberg, 1981; Buchele, 1983). A representative example is provided by a factor analysis of sector attributes in Britain (Table 7.2). (McNabb and Ryan, 1986) Three independent dimensions of sectoral structure emerged. The first factor accounting for more than half the variation in the sample, loaded strongly on concentration, plant-size and capital-intensity. It corresponds to the producer-power factor which typically dominates in US studies. The second factor, accounting for a further 25 per cent of the variance, was closely associated with

TABLE 7.2 Factor analysis of sector characteristics

Variable	Factor 1	Factor 2	Factor 3
Seller concentration (five firm)	0.9779		
Plant size	0.8363		−0.4222
Capital expenditure per Employee	0.7715		
Import penetration		0.9424	
Collective bargaining coverage	0.3949	−0.7596	−0.3295
Productivity growth			0.9712

Notes: data (for a year as close to 1978 as possible) refer to a 23 sector
breakdown of the British economy; factor scores less than 0.3
are not reported.
Source: McNabb and Ryan (1986) Table 1.

exposure to import-competition (generally absent from US studies)
and, inversely, with bargaining coverage. The third factor indicates
a subsidiary role for productivity growth, particularly in sectors
with small plants and low bargaining coverage.

The distribution of sector scores on the first factor suggests a
division between a 'core' composed primarily of heavy industry,
transport and communications, business services and public administration and a 'periphery' dominated by light manufacturing,
construction, distribution and personal services. Earnings functions estimated for males in the two sector groupings (holding
labour-quality constant, insofar as is possible) indicated an advantage in 1978 annual earnings of 30 per cent for core- over
periphery- workers – suggesting a moderately strong degree of
segmentation in the British labour market (Table 7.3).

Such evidence does not however establish the existence of strict
duality.[11] Bimodality is typically found, if at all, in only one of the
several dimensions of industrial structure (factors), while the
classification of sectors as core or periphery (and labour segments

TABLE 7.3   **Earnings functions for British employees in a dualist classification by sector characteristics**

Variable[2]	Coefficient (standard error) for:[1]	
	Core[3]	Periphery[3]
Intercept	3.81*	3.52*
	(0.06)	(0.06)
Schooling	0.026*	0.030*
	(0.003)	(0.003)
Experience[4]	0.027*	0.027*
	(0.002)	(0.001)
Experience squared	− 0.0004*	− 0.0004*
	(0.00003)	(0.00003)
Race (non-white)	− 0.033	− 0.017
	(0.042)	(0.055)
R^2	0.202	0.398
N	3780	2690

Notes: * indicates significant difference from zero ($p = 0.05$)
   1. Dependent variable is the log of weekly earnings of males in 1978 (derived from the General Household Survey).
   2. Controls for broad occupational category, marital status and health were also imposed but not reported here.
   3. Sectors classified as to scores on factors 1 and 2 in Table 1
   4. Age minus years of schooling minus five.
Source: McNabb and Ryan (1986), Table 3.

as primary and secondary) relies on only one of those dimensions. Even though the factor upon which the classification is based typically both shows bimodality and leads the explanation of variance, the link between product and labour market remains unacceptably oversimplified.

For example, the removal of mining, construction and transportation from an application of the core/periphery duality developed by Oster (1978) is justified by Reich (1984, p. 74) in terms of the implausibility of the periphery status to which a unidimensional classification based upon an 'employer-power' factor would assign them, given the large numbers of firms, small plant sizes and low capital-intensities found in these sectors. The minumum price to be paid for establishing strict dualism proves then to be the exclusion of more than half of national employment. It would be preferable to extend the classification and attempt to develop a factor representing the combination of high labour-organisation and restricted producer-entry which underlies high earnings in such sectors. Strict dualism, however, would prove a casualty in such a move, as there is no reason to expect parallel bimodalities in the distributions of sectors across these two factors, let alone others.[12]

In any event, the bimodality established in such studies refers to product-market attributes rather than to labour-market outcomes. The labour-market consequences of bimodal dualism (in studies attempting to establish strict duality) have been limited to differences between earnings or turnover in the two segments. No one has established the existence of a bimodal duality in pay or turnover parallel to that in industrial characteristics – for the simple reason that they do not exist.[13] Thus even the strict dualists have implicitly accepted that duality applies to the labour market only in the heuristic sense (Figure 7.1, above).

The plain fact is that the links between product and labour markets are too multidimensional and complex for a strict dualist formulation to prove viable (Wallace and Kalleberg, 1981; Hodson and Kaufman, 1982).[14] Analytic effort would be better devoted to the elaboration of the linkages between product and labour markets. For example, the position of trade unionism requires particular attention. To treat union-membership density simply as another component for a factor analysis of industrial structure is to ignore its own dependence upon industrial attributes, as an intermediate linkage between product- and labour-markets. This complex issue has received more attention in the orthodox than in the LMS literature.

As has been argued above, failure to establish strict duality does not however scupper the entire LMS enterprise. The distinction between primary and secondary jobs will still be used as a convenient shorthand for segmentation as we turn to employment and mobility patterns for indirect evidence of its presence.

Employment patterns

A central observation in the LMS literature is that secondary jobs are filled not randomly but rather by particular types of worker, notably non-whites, females and youths. The various secondary segments defined in empirical work show extensive over-representation of each of these three groups. In one particular (non-dualist) formulation, the share of youths in manual employment is found to vary inversely across sectors with the pay of adult males in all EEC economies (Table 7.4). The pay of adult males is taken as a broad indicator of the standing of a sector in the industrial dimension of segmentation; its inverse association with youth employment shares corresponds to LMS predictions.

LMS analysis holds further that confinement to bad jobs reflects not lack of human capital but rather discrimination. In support of this proposition LMS writings point to the considerable skill attained by secondary workers in sectors such as cutlery, and jobs

TABLE 7.4 **Regression analysis of the share of young workers in manual male employment in mining and manufacturing, various European economies, 1972**

Country	Intercept	Adult male pay	Relative pay	$\bar{R}^2$
Belgium	3.57* (0.62)	−2.37* (0.42)	−0.24 (0.88)	0.50
France	3.61* (1.96)	−2.38* (0.68)	−0.25 (1.74)	0.38
West Germany	5.69* (0.73)	−2.41* (0.63)	−2.81* 0.79	0.47
Italy	5.59* (1.96)	−2.96* (0.69)	−1.98 (1.81)	0.34
Netherlands	6.05* (0.84)	−3.37* (0.54)	−2.88* (1.06)	0.57
UK	5.39* (0.78)	−2.65* (0.52)	−3.00* (0.77)	0.47

Notes: Employment share an adult pay variables normalised to mean of unity in each country.
* denotes significant difference from zero ($p=0.05$)
Source: Marsden and Ryan (1986), Table 4.

such as catering (Craig *et al.*, 1982); to the low skill-requirements of many primary jobs (Blackburn and Mann, 1979); to the tendency for skills to be learned on the job rather than being a condition of access to the job (Doeringer and Piore, 1971; Thurow, 1975); and to the fact that primary jobs frequently require dependability and reliability, as well as compatibility with existing work groups, rather than technical skills (Edwards, 1976).

To some extent the difficulties of secondary workers involve lack of these personality traits – as in the incompatability between the street culture of urban non-whites and the requirements of good jobs. 'Primary employment requires the individual to abandon street life and conform to an ethical code which is not recognised in the street' (Doeringer and Piore, 1971, p. 176). Similarly, marginal status in the family and society, reinforced by limited access to social security, disposes many youths, immigrants and married females to offer their labour-power at low supply prices.

However, while the characteristics of secondary workers may indeed to some extent run parallel to those of secondary jobs, the LMS interpretation is valid only if the variation in worker traits is significantly less than that in jobs. Many young workers, non-whites and (particularly) married females must be available for stable employment and interested in high earnings but unable to gain access to primary jobs.

Explanations of such employment patterns have tended to rely upon discrimination, with primary employers favouring adult male white applicants for jobs because of either their prejudices or statistical discrimination. Thus the poor prospects of females are attributed partly to widespread hostility – associated with patriarchal male attitudes – to the improvement of female employment conditions (Humphries and Rubery, 1984). While the part played by prejudice in setting employment patterns is undoubtedly important, only intermittently has recognition been granted to that expressed by primary workers intent upon guarding their own privileges in the labour market and able to impose sanctions upon employers who seek to undermine them (Cockburn, 1983).

However, in many situations employers are both free to hire whom they please from available applicants and interested in cutting employment costs. In such cases an explanation of employment patterns may be based upon a combination of the concepts of the job queue and statistical discrimination, the outline of which has been sketched by Thurow (1975). An exogenous wage-structure is postulated, highly differentiated across employers and unresponsive to the attributes of job applicants. Firms rank applicants in terms of their prospective trainability (more generally, productivity). Information about individual applicants is costly, as must be the case for example when not even the individual knows the likelihood of his or her remaining in the job. Youths, non-whites and females find themselves placed low in the queue for the best jobs because the average attitudes, skills and/or quit propensities of group members are expected (on the basis of experience, general knowledge or prejudice) to be lower than those of white adult males. Only in the lower regions of the job distribution do they find themselves at the top of the queue.

The uniformity of youth employment patterns across European industry (Table 7.4) is most readily explained in such terms. A negative relationship between adult male pay and the employment shares of youths could arise in a competitively determined industry wage structure only if high adult male pay were to reflect high skill levels, with youths as poor substitutes. However, adult pay is only weakly correlated with the skill mix across sectors (Marsden, 1979, ch 3). A more convincing interpretation involves segmentation, with profit-seeking employers faced with a given position in the wage-structure selecting the prospectively-most-productive applicants for jobs (Marsden and Ryan, 1986). The average youth might be only slightly less productive than the adult male counterpart, but small differences in labour quality would still be capable of producing large differences in employment patterns in such a world.[15]

Mobility and turnover

The issue of mobility has been more central to LMS writing than might be inferred from this discussion. The proposition that the poor are confined to the secondary segment suggests an extension of the inequality-creating effects of segmentation from the point in time to the individual life cycle. If workers cannot change places in the structure of earnings inequality over their working lives then the oppressive effects of segmentation are correspondingly greater.

The original 'confinement' proposition has received at most qualified support from the evidence. Dualist studies which define a clear frontier between primary and secondary segments have typically found both moderately high rates of mobility across that frontier and a significant role for human capital in determining the probability of individual crossings. Even when the secondary segment is limited to the original category of inner-city residents in menial work, typically one half or more of male workers who held secondary jobs on entry to the labour-force in the USA moved subsequently into primary employment, assisted in a somewhat uneven fashion by higher levels of schooling and work experience (Rosenberg, 1977, 1980).[16] For Britain, although lifetime mobility out of low-level occupations is indeed limited, significant amounts are still observable, again generally associated with schooling and experience (Mayhew and Rosewell, 1979).

The rate of exit from the secondary segment remains significant even when the criterion is tightened from the simple crossing of an arbitrary frontier to travelling a substantial distance along the spectrum of job-rewards. Thus the average change in relative earnings position within age cohorts (in the USA between 1957 and 1971) amounted to 21 percentage points and depended only weakly on initial positions in the distribution (Schiller, 1977). Elements of segmentation were indeed suggested in a rate of movement across an arbitrary dualist frontier roughly one half of what would be expected on a random basis; and in an average distance of travel for blacks in the lowest 5 per cent which was only one half that of whites.

Although such results have been interpreted as inconsistent with segmentation, the damage inflicted upon LMS analysis is again less extensive than some have claimed.[17] Accepting that 'the secondary segment is not airtight' (Rosenberg, 1980) does not require the abandoning of the broader LMS endeavour. The reasons may be examined at two levels: taking mobility first as an attribute of segmentation in its own right and second as indirect evidence of segmentation in pay structure.

Treating immobility as the intertemporal extension of segmentation, non-eligible inter-segment mobility does not imply that most or all secondary workers can attain primary employment. The foregoing studies all exclude females, many of whom may be unable to obtain primary jobs. Moreover, an unduly favourable view of male mobility rates may result from failure to control either for retirements from or for expansion in the primary segment. The retirement of older males from primary jobs undoubtedly creates opportunities for young men to enter. The fact that many men working in primary jobs started their careers in secondary jobs carries no implication that those who failed to make the transition when young can still do so in middle age (Osterman, 1980).

Similarly, most studies make no controls for the size of the primary segment, despite the presence of economic expansion in the period to which most of the data refer. A rough corrective is provided by comparing downward- with upward-mobility. The incidence of downward-mobility from primary jobs in Rosenberg's study (12 to 26 per cent across race/city groups) proved much lower than that upward from secondary employment (47 to 67 per cent; 1977, Table 7.1).

Nevertheless, mobility studies suggest that enduring imprisonment in secondary jobs applies, amongst males at least, only to the inner-city minorities whose experiences produced the proposition in the first place. Even so, the essence of the LMS approach – the existence of a hierarchy of rewards for comparable workers – survives the news unscathed. When mobility is considered as indirect evidence of segmentation and measured from the side of the job rather than the worker, i.e. through turnover rates, the presence of segmentation remains clearly visible.

In the LMS hierarchy of job-rewards, workers at the high end of the distribution are expected to affirm their position by taking pains to hold onto their advantages. A low quit-rate is the anticipated result. Conversely, low job-rewards at the bottom of the ladder imply high quit-rates. The concrete result is an inverse wage–quit relationship amongst comparable workers. (An inverse relationship may also hold for lay-offs and redundancies, in which case the relative job rewards of primary employees are wider than simply higher pay.)

Statistical assessment of the prediction is complicated by the tendency of high-wage segments to employ high-qualify labour-power – in this context, individuals or groups with low quit-propensities, such as 'prime age' males with dependents. The principal source of evidence is the distribution of quit-rates across sectors, ranging in 1960 in the USA from 0.39 per cent per month in petroleum refining to 2.65 per cent in confectionary (Pencavel, 1970, p. 60).[18] A highly significant inverse wage–quit relationship emerges, with an elasticity estimated at -0.9 in the presence of statistical controls for workforce composition (*ibid*, Table 1). The spread in quit-rates between the highest- and lowest-wage industries, controlling inter alia for workforce composition and unionisation, is estimated at nearly 100 per cent, ranging from 0.92 to 1.81 per cent per month.

Not only have the segmentationist implications of the wage–quit relationship generally gone unrecognised; it has even been construed as supportive of a competitive analysis, by confirming the 'allocative role assigned to voluntary mobility by economic theory' (Stoikov and Raimon, 1968). It is true that low-wage employers lose labour at a faster rate than do high-wage firms. This is however a necessary but not sufficient condition for a competitive interpretation. Sufficiency is attained only when the wage-structure adapts in the face of mobility – and, as institutionalists have insisted, this just does not occur (Ulman, 1965). Instead, secondary workers move largely amongst secondary jobs and only gain access to primary employment when retirement and expansion creates vacancies. A non-price rationing of access to primary jobs is therefore indicated by the low quit-rates of their incumbents.[19]

7.5 CONCLUSIONS

Recognition of segmentation in the labour market leads to interest in its magnitude. Although much of the controversy in the area remains qualitative (does LMS exist?), segmentation is clearly a matter of degree: you can have more or less of it. Instead of requiring a choice between competitive and institutional forces in labour markets, the economist is better advised to gauge the relative importance of the two sets of influences. Thus a relativistic approach might seek to understand why segmentation appears more marked in the Third World than in industrial economies; and in South Africa than in the USA, for example.

The claims made on behalf of segmentation must be limited. Dualism is not strictly applicable to the labour markets of advanced capitalist economies (with the possible exception of South Africa). Moreover, the constraints upon segmentation deserve elaboration, although they in turn involve institutional as well as competitive considerations.

The limits to segment-differentiation in the advanced economy may be illustrated by comparison with the international economy. The productivity and earnings of workers in many less-developed economies are held down relative to those in advanced economies by the higher rates of investment and productivity growth attained in advanced economies, as well as by the undervaluation of their output in a system of unequal exchange. Each of these phenomena has its counterpart within the advanced economy. The growth of physical productivity is greater in primary than in secondary employment, while output prices are inflated in the former as part of the higher returns achieved by both capital and labour. Yet the dispersion of labour outcomes is incommensurately greater in the international than within the advanced economy.

The narrower scope of segmentation within than between economies reflects to some extent the coincidence of obstacles to factor-mobility with national boundaries. Labour cannot move as readily from Hong Kong to the USA as it can from textiles to chemicals within the USA. However, there are two more powerful constraints upon the dispersion of value productivity growth and earnings within the advanced economy, each of which lacks a counterpart at the international level.

The first is the relocation of production. Sectors which achieve only slow growth in physical productivity either see production transferred to low-wage developing countries (in the case of tradeables) or revalued upwards by price rises (in the case of non-tradeables). As the international economy lacks an analogue to the former mechanism, its dispersion of value-productivity growth-rates is accordingly greater. Second, the world economy lacks any effective equivalents to the phenomena of relativity bargaining (for the unionised) and statutory wage protection and indexed social-security provision (for the unorganised) which limit segmentation within advanced economies. Although these constraints upon segmentation have been relaxed substantially in many advanced economies by the growth of both unemployment and deregulatory politics, the differentiation of labour outcomes within advanced economies which they permit has remained moderate relative to that at the global level.

Less than global, however, does not mean insignificant. Even when the limits to segmentation are recognised, the central LMS tenet remains intact: the labour market itself constitutes an important source of economic inequality.

8 The Economics of Discrimination: Theory and British Evidence

ZAFIRIS TZANNATOS

8.1 INTRODUCTION

This chapter is concerned with the economics of discrimination. Its purpose is threefold. First, to outline the case of sex discrimination in Britain; while it is true that other forms of discrimination are equally objectionable, sex discrimination in Britain, as elsewhere, may potentially affect a little more than 50 per cent of the population whereas race discrimination may apply to rather less than 5 per cent of the population – and to a lower percentage of the labour force (Mayhew and Addison, 1983, p. 311). Second, to introduce some aspects of industrial relations into this volume; positivism has greatly improved our understanding of how the labour market and its agents *may* operate but, at times, economists tend to forget that a whole range of theoretical abstractions and eventualities become redundant once information on real-life arrangements becomes available. Third, and finally, to evaluate the role that legislation can or should play with respect to issues such as equality.

In section 8.2 we present the explanations which have been put forward by economists for the inferior wage and employment characteristics of certain groups of workers, referred to below as 'discriminated groups'. Then we ask the question 'What are the costs of discrimination to society, and who benefits from it?'

Finally we examine the institutional framework within which sex discrimination used to take place and how and to what extent legislation has changed it. Our reference point will be women in Britain.

8.2   THE ECONOMIC THEORY OF DISCRIMINATION

Early thoughts on discrimination

Early statements on discrimination came mostly from the European side of the Atlantic and related to sex. Europeans somehow distanced themselves from other forms of discrimination at home, as unequal treatment of certain groups usually took place a few thousand miles away from the homeland, namely in the land of the other groups (in the colonies). Thus sex discrimination was the obvious candidate for a start, as other forms of discrimination were associated with geographical segregation.

As early as the mid-nineteenth century it was argued that:

> there is no natural inequality between sexes except perhaps in bodily strength ... if nature has not made men and women unequal, still less ought the law to make them so ... men and women ought to be perfectly coequal and a woman ought not to be dependent on a man, more than a man on a woman, except so far as their affections make them so (John Stuart Mill and Harriet Taylor Mill in Rossi, 1970, pp 73–4).

These avant-garde statements were made at a time when legislation and society made women and children the property of husbands and fathers; when a woman's possessions became her husband's automatically on marriage; when women could not sue for divorce on an equal basis and had limited access to children in the event of separation and when women could not vote. In addition, opportunities for the education of women were practically non-existent. Compare Mill's arguments to those from another author some fifty years later:

> it is more important to have done with the senseless cry for 'full equality', for even the malest [*sic*] woman is scarcely more than 50

per cent male, and it is only to that male part of her that she owes her special capacity or whatever importance she may eventually gain (Weiniger, 1906).

The pre-neoclassical debate on the issue of women's inferior position in the labour market concentrated mostly on wage differentials. The early analysts identified potential reasons for women's low earnings to be customs and public opinion, the woman's secondary nature of employment (*vis-à-vis* that of the husband, the conventional breadwinner), lower productivity, women's lack of trade-union support and lower standards of living, insufficient education and few opportunities for alternative employment (Webb, S., 1891; Collet, 1891; Fawcett 1892; Cannan 1914; Rathbone, 1917; Webb, B., 1919; the Atkin War Cabinet Committee on the Employment of Women in Industry, 1919).

These observations set the stage for the debate which followed. Edgeworth (1922) and Fawcett (1917, 1918) put forward the concept of crowding. According to this hypothesis, women are over-represented in certain sectors and this depresses female wages in these sectors *ceteris paribus*. Nevertheless this explanation, which was explicitly formalised by Bergmann some fifty years later (see below), was criticised by Florence (1931) as incomplete. Women's relative immobility in the labour market because of family and social conventions, and the refusal of men to work with or under the supervision of women were perceived by Florence to be more important factors for the explanation of sex wage differentials other than those caused by productivity differences between men and women.

Pigou added that 'unscrupulous or unthinking employers are able to pay women less than they are worth' because of the latters 'strategic weakness' (Pigou, 1952) and this explanation was also among those considered by Florence (1931). Joan Robinson (1933) eventually formalised this weakness of women using the well-known theory of monopsony (for an exposition see, for example, Addison and Siebert, 1979, pp. 225–8).

In the 'pre-Becker' era one should also mention here Myrdal's 'principle of cumulative causation' which saw the negro problem in the USA arising from the interaction and reinforcement of three causes moving in a vicious circle (Myrdal, 1944): first, the behaviour of whites against blacks; second, the conditions of poverty of blacks; third, the human capital and cultural characteristics of blacks. Few, if any, will challenge this view, but vicious-circle explanations tend sometimes to be circular arguments. What we learn from them (especially from authors in the area of development economics) is that there is a market failure and government intervention may be required to break the chain.

The pre-Becker (that is, pre-1957) literature is completed with two articles by Bronfenbrenner (1939, 1956) who examined monopsony and union – employer discrimination as sources for differential wages. An observation that should be made here is that Bronfenbrenner considered employers to be prepared to offer lower wages to the minority group (that is $w - x$ where w is the wage of the majority group and x is expected cost of employing workers from the minority group) in anticipation of higher costs which might arise from labour conflict, if the majority and minority groups were working together. This is interesting for three reasons:

(i) this analysis can be seen as an extension of the monopsony case (Lundahl and Wadensjö, 1984, pp. 13–14);
(ii) employing heterogeneous labour was seen as something which increases costs for the employer, although it could also be seen as either a form of diversification and risk-spreading or as a 'divide and conquer' tactic (Roemer, 1979);
(iii) the *mechanics* of Bronfenbrenner's analysis (that is, $w - x$) is, in effect, similar to the approach adopted by Becker who also assumed (though for different reasons) that employers will employ members from the minority group only if the latter's wages were lower than those of the majority group.

Becker

Becker's theory of discrimination is based on physical disutility, in the sense that individuals may prefer to incur costs rather than come into contact with members of certain groups. The disutility comes within the reign of tastes and in Becker's own words 'if an individual has a "taste" for discrimination, he must act *as if* he were willing to pay something, either directly or in the form of a reduced income, to be associated with some groups instead of others'. Becker argues further that 'when actual discrimination occurs, [the individual] must, in fact, either pay or forfeit income for this privilege. This *simple* way of looking at the matter gets at the essence of prejudice and discrimination' (Becker, 1957, p. 14) (italics added).

Whether Becker's theory, which lays emphasis on individual (rather than group) behaviour, 'gets at the essence' of discrimination may be questionable (see below). But this 'simple way of looking at the matter' has certainly resulted in an improvement of our understanding of the 'mechanics' of the issue. Its simplicity and power can now be dissected. We adopt here a different presentation from that presented in Becker's book; nevertheless, this exposition captures the essence of the model (Arrow, 1972a, 1972b, 1973). Define the employer's objective not as simple maximisation of profits, as it is usually assumed, but as:

$$\max U = f \text{ (profits, percentage of men in the firm's workforce)}$$

where U stands for the employer's objective (utility) function. The discriminating employer attempts to maximise his profits *and* the number of men in the firm's labour force. This reverts us to the standard two-commodity space with convex indifference curves defined over profits and the sex-mix of the firm's labour force. Assume also that all the other usual conditions hold with respect to the production function and competitiveness in the product and labour markets. Consider Figure 8.1 where monetary profits are depicted on the vertical axis and the sex-mix of the labour force on the horizontal axis.

The representative indifference curve of the employer is shown as *IC* in Figure 8.1. The more an employer dislikes women, the steeper the slope of the indifference curve becomes. On the assumption that women and men are perfect substitutes in production and are paid the same wage rate, total profits would be given by a horizontal line like P_1P_1. Had the employer been sex-blind, *IC* would have been horizontal and the equilibrium position would be indeterminate under the assumptions of the model (that is, it would depend on factors such as chance and not on the parameters of the model). As *IC* is drawn, the discriminating employer would prefer to employ only men. The reason given by the model is that the employer, due to his taste for discrimination, incurs a psychic cost from employing women. Although the monetary cost from

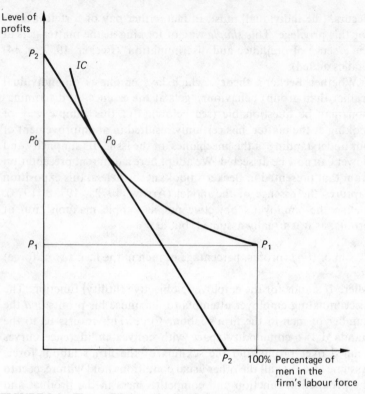

FIGURE 8.1   The equilibrium of a discriminating employer: men and women perfect substitutes in production

employing women is as much as that from employing men (that is the wage rate, w), the *net* cost to him is $w(1 + d)$, where d $(d > 0)$ is the disutility caused by the presence of women in the labour force. Becker called d the *discrimination coefficient*.

The value of d can be anything from minus infinity to plus infinity. Negative values of d imply favouritism or *nepotism* if the employer is a member of the group in question, while positive values imply *discrimination*. When d is zero there is no distinction between different groups of workers and we are back to the conventional analysis. The term wd indicates the deviation of *net* costs from *monetary* costs to the employer when women are employed. It can be thought of as the exact money equivalent of the employer's psychic cost from women's employment. Thus

Becker's discrimination coefficient has made it possible to incorporate explicitly the *act* (but not cause) of discrimination into an economic model and allows the study of its *effects*. The fact that discrimination has now become potentially measurable on a continuous scale comprises the power of Becker's analysis. Let us go back to Figure 8.1 and examine the implications of the presence of discrimination.

If the same wage rate applies to both men and women, the discriminating employer will achieve the highest level of utility by employing only men, as the monetary and net costs coincide only in the case of men. The discriminating employer's equilibrium is shown at point P_1. If, however, the women's wage rate were lower than that of men, (again under the assumption of perfect substitutability between the sexes in production) then the higher the percentage of men in the labour force, the lower profits would be. As a matter of fact, profits will become negative before the firm's labour force becomes all-male (under the competitive conditions assumed earlier). This relationship is shown by the new profit curve P_2P_2 in Figure 8.1. The equilibrium position of the discriminating employer now becomes P_o and the employer forfeits profits equal to the difference P_2P_0'.

The foregoing analysis leads to a number of predictions. First, the higher the discrimination coefficient (d), the more convex the indifference curves will be and the firm will employ higher percentages of men. Second, the bigger the wage differential against women, the more expensive it becomes to discriminate against women and the percentage of women in the firm's labour force will rise (though it would still be less than the non-discriminatory outcome). Third, the less substitutable women and men become in production, the higher the percentage of women in the labour force would be (as small deviations from the optimal sex-mix would result in a sharp decline in profits: the profit curve in Figure 8.1 falls faster than P_2P_2).

One can show the implications of the model in a different way with reference to Figure 8.2. Assuming perfect substitutability in production between women and men, *MM* indicates the values of marginal product (and is also the demand-for-labour curve) for both factors in the absence of discrimination. If tastes work against women, this would result in an inward shift of the demand curve for women's labour (to *FF*) and by an amount equal to $-wd$ (to

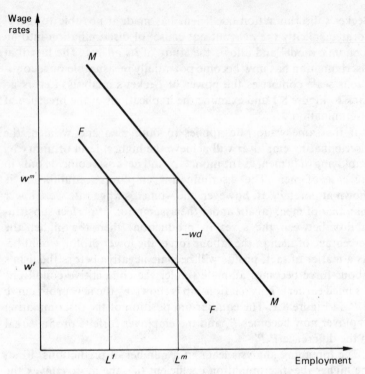

FIGURE 8.2   Employment and wages of the discriminated group

compensate for the psychic cost, namely *wd*, which derives from
the discrimination coefficient). If one thinks of the inward movement as a vertical shift, this would imply that the employer would
be prepared to hire as many women as men (point L_m) only if the
female wage rate were equal to w^f. Alternatively, if one thinks of
the inward movement as an horizontal shift, the employer would
hire only L_f women, had the wage rate been the same for both
sexes, namely w^m.

   One can further derive the following predictions from the model.
First, in the long-run the discriminating employer will be driven
out of the market by the money-cost-minimising non-discriminating employer. Second, before the 'fittest survives' (that is, in the
short run), there would be both wage and employment differentials. The discriminated group will be employed in smaller proportions by the discriminating firms and will tend to join non-

discriminating firms. One should place a warning here: the model is cast in terms of neoclassical full employment and does not explain differences between the unemployment or labour-force-participation rates of women and men. As a result, the model predicts that fewer women will be employed by discriminating firms, *not* that fewer women overall will be employed in the economy. The story takes place within a general equilibrium framework with perfectly inelastic factor supplies (see also section 8.3 below).

Extensions and evaluation. The foregoing presentation, albeit simple, captures the essential features of Becker's theory. The theory can be extended in various ways. Monopoly conditions in the commodity market (but competition in the capital market) result in the same predictions as before with respect to wage and employment differentials (Becker, 1959). If the discriminator is not the employer but fellow-workers, wage differences should be observed in both the short run and the long run if the two groups are not perfect substitutes in production (or if they are complements). If they are perfect substitutes, then there will be wage differences neither in the short run nor in the long run. Under all the above assumptions about the substitutability of women and men in production there will exist segregation. Finally, if consumers have a taste for discrimination, then again wage and employment differentials will prevail in the short run; the long-run outcome will depend on whether there is a possibility of segregation between different groups of consumers (for an exposition of all eventualities, see Lundahl and Wadensjö, 1984).

We have examined the consequences of the existence of tastes for discrimination upon workers' wages and employment. As a general conclusion workers from the majority group benefit in terms of better wages, while members of the minority group lose. What happens to employers' profits? Of course, as far as an individual employer is concerned, his profits will depend on whether he discriminates or not and the implications of this have been already shown. However, the overall share of profits (*vis-à-vis* wages) in the economy is not easy to predict. Becker (1957, pp. 21–2) claimed that:

There is a remarkable agreement in the literature on the proposition that [employers] . . . are the major beneficiaries of prejudice and discrimination ... [T]he *non sequitur* in the mistaken analyses is the conclusion that ... the difference between wage rates must accrue as profits to [employers] ... This profit would only exist if this wage differential resulted from price discrimination (due to monopoly power), rather than from a taste for discrimination.

Thus, one is led to believe that under the assumptions of Becker's model employers overall lose as a group (or, class?). This is hard to believe and, as a matter of fact, Becker's conclusion was found to rest on a mathematical error (Madden, 1973). That employers may lose is possible, but analyses which consider them as benefactors from discrimination have not been proved wrong by Becker's theory. In Thurow's (1969, p. 112) words: 'if [Becker's] deduction is correct, empirical impressions are amazingly false. Do the whites of South Africa or United States have lower standards of living as a result of their discrimination?'. We pursue this point later in this chapter.

The difference between the pre- and post-Beckerian theories of discrimination may be more in appearance than in substance. In particular all possible causes of discrimination that were *formalised* by Becker (and by others who were inspired by his work) had been previously discussed and, in some cases, presented albeit in simple diagrammatic expositions. Many have argued that Becker broke with the earlier tradition by making a 'sharp distinction between the *causes* and the *act* of discrimination' in that 'the existence of a taste for discrimination serves to explain the *act* of discrimination [and its effects]' while 'little notice is taken of the causes for discrimination' (Lundahl and Wadensjö, 1984, pp. 4 and 20). Nevertheless, it is true that the advantages of the Beckerian formulation are great, as discrimination became potentially measurable on a continuous scale rather than simply being present or absent. It is also true, however, that tastes or preferences or prejudices or whatever one wants to call d can be found implicitly as early as 1891 in S. Webb, as well as in the writings of the other authors mentioned earlier. In addition Becker's d is directly equivalent to the x of Bronfenbrenner.

The important contribution of Becker is in the incorporation of d into an economic model, where the mechanics of the standard optimisation procedures can apply. However, a problem appears in Becker's '*as if*' assumptions in the definition of a taste for discrimination. Thus discrimination *is assumed to exist* and operate in a certain way but *its origin* still remains a 'black box' (Dex, 1986, p. 21). This may create little concern within positivist analysis. Theories are usually evaluated, on the one hand, on the frugality of their assumptions and, on the other hand, on the performance of their predictions. Many of Becker's results conform with common sense.

Perhaps the greatest shortcoming of Becker's analysis is its failure to examine discrimination in the wider economic (and social) context. The physical-distance assumption is not necessarily an important or *probable* one especially in the case of sex discrimination, though *possible* it may be. The assumption becomes of relevance only if the firm and the owner–employer coincide; the separation of management from ownership gives little concern to the owner about the characteristics of the labour force. Also, customer discrimination can only cover a limited number of cases such as direct personal services.

Another concern relates to the fact that the model examines the effects of tastes only at the place of employment. Consider, for example, a discriminating employer who forfeits profits in order to satisfy his tastes at the work-place. Is it reasonable to assume that this may be his only objective? If by forfeiting profits he cannot live in a 'white' area (because house prices are higher than those in the black ghettos), or if he cannot educate his children in establishments with fewer or no blacks because of his limited income (thanks to his enjoyment of discrimination at the work-place), then there are potential clashes between behaviour at work and at home which are not explored by the theory. Discrimination has to be considered in a broader context and should be examined simultaneously with consumption (demand for goods) patterns. The appropriate analysis should be developed in terms of expenditure functions rather than only in terms of *levels* of profits.

Other Analysts

Becker provided an analysis based on an assumption about the act of discrimination. Nevertheless the analysis was coherent and served as a point of departure for many other studies. The level of theoretical debate was raised both by those who expanded the theory and by those who were critical of it.

According to Becker's theory, if there exists a taste for discrimination by some (but not all) employers there will be segregation in the short run. However, as firms which have the lowest or zero discrimination coefficients hire successively more of the members of the minority group, in the long run the non-discriminatory employers will drive the discriminating ones out of the market. As a result, Becker's theory cannot explain why discriminatory wage differentials can persist in the long run. Arrow (1972a, 1972b, 1973) accommodated this inconsistency by taking into account adjustment costs. If there are costs of hiring and firing, it may not be cost-efficient to change the mix of the workforce as quickly as the paradigm of perfect competition suggests. The discriminatory wage differentials will be eliminated through natural wastage and/or the emergence of new firms only after a significant period of time. Arrow's extension tells us that the process of equalisation of wages and integration of the labour force will be slow but it still does not explain why differentials have persisted and are with us even today after so many decades of market functioning.

Even if the market were working as postulated by neoclassical economists, economic outcomes do not depend entirely on market forces. A lot is decided by administrators who are part of central government and municipal bodies. For these agents there is no pressure to become monetary-cost-minimisers. Their existence and survival does not depend on economic performance but is guaranteed by decree. Sowell (1981) highlighted this point with reference to the exclusion of blacks from certain occupations in the USA and Tzannatos (1986) made reference to the 'marriage bar' (prohibition of employment of married women) and other impediments which were utilised to exclude women from the Civil Service in Britain. Thus state monopolies may aggravate the problem. The same also applies to types of monopolies which are associated with 'no market for entrance', such as professional associations of craft unions (Demsetz, 1965). Regulating entrance to these monopolies has zero costs to those who belong to them, although there are efficiency losses associated with such actions.

Becker argued that private monopolies will be more inclined not to pursue discriminatory policies: a monopoly is worth potentially more to somebody who does not discriminate! But, do monopolies (or firms in other market structures) try to maximize profits? Alchian and Kessel (1962) deny this for the case of monopolies, as such a behaviour may attract either entry of other firms or government action under the provisions of competition policies. Thus it may not make the possession of a monopoly more profitable for a non-discriminating employer than for a discriminating one. As a result, the symptoms of employment segregation between the majority and minority groups of workers and wage differentials may persist, though again not in the long run. In the models outlined so far, labour supply is assumed to be fixed at full employment. Gilman (1965) extended the analysis to include employment effects. If there is wage rigidity, there may be excess supply or demand in various sectors. If wage discrimination is not allowed (say, because of anti-discriminatory legislation or minimum-wage provisions) the monetary cost of discrimination will be zero and there will be unemployment. Queuing for jobs in the discriminating sectors will make it possible for discriminating employers to offer lower wages in these sectors. The discriminated group will have to search for employment in the least-covered sectors and wage-differentials *not within* but *across* sectors will arise. Obviously, segregation will again persist.

An early statement of how social origins and class may affect individual behaviour is found in Adam Smith:

> We rarely hear ... of the combinations of masters, though frequently of those of workmen. But whoever imagines, upon this account, that masters rarely combine, is ignorant of the world as of the subject. Masters are always and everywhere in a sort of tacit, but constant and uniform, combination, not to raise the wages of labour above their actual rate (Smith, 1776, Book 1, ch. 8).

We also mentioned earlier that the early British debate on discrimination paid due respect to the role of traditions and customs. However, Cassel's (1918) paradox had to wait a few decades before an answer was found. The paradox refers to the obvious neoclassical question 'How can one factor of production generally and permanently receive a lower wage than it is worth?' It took time before answers were formulated into a concrete model: why should firms adhere to a given tradition and not maximise profits by employing more of the cheap factor? Akerlof (1976, 1980, 1983) showed that discrimination as a social custom is compatible with stable economic solutions as long as individuals perceive that non-adherence to social rules implies expulsion from the group to which they belong, the membership of which carries certain benefits. The important point here is the interdependence of the two transactions involved, namely the transaction between the employer and the worker *and* the transaction between the employer and other fellow-employers. This interdependence is overlooked by Becker. Non-discrimination in an otherwise discriminating world incurs costs as there may be 'penalties' for such rule-breaking. Opposing the rule may be *economically* profitable but it may not at the same time be *overall* advantageous.

Another line of reasoning is that of 'imperfect information'. If an employer wants to provide training to an employee of his, will he be indifferent between a woman and an otherwise identical man? Women *as a group* share disproportionately the reproduction cycle of a family and, as a result, they are less attached than men to the labour market. Recovery of the costs of training is less certain in the case of women. The inferior labour-market characteristics of women as a group give rise to so-called 'statistical discrimination'. Firms do not know in advance the precise productivity and commitment of a particular worker. Consequently sex, marital status, race, ethnicity or other characteristics become inexpensive screening devices for the firm's employment decisions (Phelps, 1972; Aigner and Cain, 1977). These considerations can explain why some groups receive on *average* lower wages than others, or why they tend to be employed in certain sectors. However, no insight is offered as to why an *individual* member of a minority group does not advance towards the characteristics of members in the majority group after some period of time, when the employer has had the opportunity to assess his/her individual productivity. Perhaps one can explain the *under*-representation of women or blacks in managerial tasks today, but it is hard to offer a statistical explanation for the *total* absence of women and blacks from such ranks only a few years ago. One has to go back to Adam Smith's and Akerlof's theories to explain this rigidity.

Finally another group of theories come under the headings of 'dual', 'segmented', 'radical' and 'Marxist'. Their common characteristic is the emphasis on the way the firm, or the labour market as a whole functions. These 'alternative' theories (Cain, 1976) which are closely identified with Piore (1975), Reich (1981) and Roemer

(1979), are along the lines of the well-known 'divide and conquer' rule: the bargaining power of employees is greater the more homogeneous the labour-force of the firm becomes. Firms decide on the optimal composition of their workforce in order to minimise labour disputes (compare this explanation with that of Bronfenbrenner). The dual and segmented labour-market approach is explained elsewhere in the volume (see Chapter 7 by McNabb and Ryan) and the reader has only to interchange the words 'sex' and 'race' for upper or lower segments to make that analysis relevant to the present context.

8.3 THE COSTS OF DISCRIMINATION

Assume that there are two identical factors of production, say men and women, which are employed separately in two identical industries. Assume for simplicity that factor supplies are equal and perfectly inelastic. This is shown in Figure 8.3. Under competitive conditions and assuming that there are neither costs of adjustment nor non-pecuniary differentials between the two occupations, a common wage will prevail, namely w^*. If an arbitrary wage differential ($w^m - w^*$) is imposed or if employment in the industry employing all men is artificially restricted (from M to M'), displaced male workers from industry 1 will seek employment in the industry previously employing only women, namely, industry 2. This will lower wages in the latter industry to w^f. Thus the remaining workers in the male industry will benefit by $w^m - w^*$ while displaced male workers and all female workers will suffer a reduction in wage equal to $w^* - w^f$. The market is now characterised by wage differentials, the non-discriminated group gains, the discriminated group loses and there exists partial segregation.

These predictions are very much in line with most of the theories outlined in the previous section. Discrimination benefits some members of the society and harms others. From the point of view of an economist this is not a moral issue (only?). If those who gain from discrimination do not gain enough to compensate the losers, then the discriminating economy has moved away from a potentially Pareto-situation to an inferior one. As a matter of fact, all economic theories of discrimination lead to the prediction that there are welfare losses associated with any kind of discrimination,

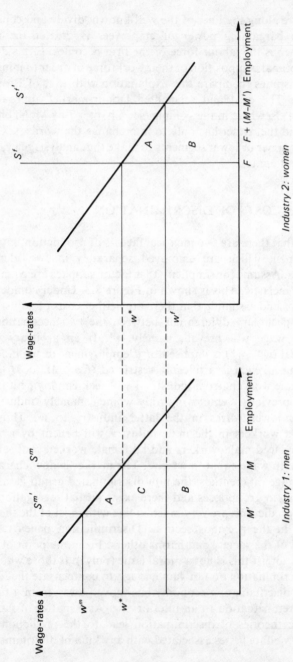

FIGURE 8.3 The welfare cost of discrimination: partial equilibrium

irrespective of the particular assumptions of the model. In Figure 8.3, the reduction in employment in industry 1 resulted in loss of output equal to the trapezoid $A + B + C$. The gain in output from the additional employment (crowding) in industry 2 is only $A + B$. Thus there has been a welfare (deadweight) loss equal to that indicated by the area of the rectangle C in industry 1. As we saw, male workers gained in wages while women workers lost. What has happened to employers' profits? This can be shown most clearly in a general equilibrium framework.

Figure 8.4 represents the conventional Edgeworth–Bowley box in our case for two industries (one producing a capital-intensive good, G, and the other producing a labour-intensive good, H) and three factors of production (capital, K, and identical male and female labour, L^m and L^f respectively). The vertical axis measures total capital stock and the horizontal axis the labour stock. Assume, however, that labour is not randomly distributed between the two industries but, instead, that all men are initially employed in industry G and all women in industry H. The initial general equilibrium point is depicted by point A and is on the Pareto-

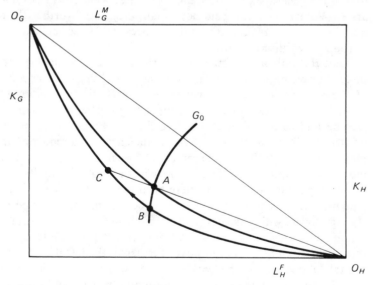

FIGURE 8.4 Effects of discrimination on wages and profits: general equilibrium

efficient contract curve. Men and women receive as wages the value of their marginal products, which is the same for both industries, and the owners capital (employers) earn normal profits.

Wages cannot be lowered in both sectors below their respective marginal products (this is ruled out by Walras's law). Neither can employment be reduced in both sectors. One can then introduce discrimination into this model as an attempt either to reduce wages below their initial marginal product in one sector (say, industry H) or to restrict employment in the other sector (the G industry). If the former were introduced and if the level of output in the male industry, G, were to stay initially the same as before, a new equilibrium would be reached at, say, point B. Point B lies on the original isoquant G_0 for industry G but on a new contract curve away from the diagonal except at its extreme points (see Tzannatos, 1987a, pp. 24–5). Production is now inefficient. At point B women are definitely worse-off (the capital–labour ratio has decreased), men are better-off (the capital–labour ratio has increased) and employers may be better-off or worse-off depending on the quantities of goods G and H which they consumed originally (as, now, the price of good H relative to good G has changed). Notice that in the general-equilibrium analysis Cassel's paradox does not arise. Women are not paid less than they are 'worth' (their marginal product): they are paid less because of the inefficiency introduced by discrimination.

Point B is only a temporary equilibrium. Given the income and price changes induced by changes in wages and prices in industry H, the production of good G will decrease, while the production of good H may increase or decrease depending on the magnitude of income and substitution effects (recall from Figure 8.4 that an arbitrary differential results in loss of efficiency and a reduction in *total* output; hence, less production in G does not necessarily imply more production in H). Thus there will be another equilibrium point to the north-west of B where both men and women will be paid more relative to B (men will always be paid more than at point A). Employers will in general be better-off, unless the final equilibrium point is *sufficiently* far away from point B. Point C illustrates this: if the equilibrium point moves further to the left than C, the capital–labour ratio in the female industry will also be higher than at A. In this case, female post-discrimination wages will be higher than at A (and male wages will be even higher). Of course, as said before, the allocation of factors as well as the allocation of production and consumption among the two industries will be inefficient. The economy is suffering a deadweight loss.

Thus, a discriminatory differential will definitely favour the non-discriminated group and may harm employers *or* the discriminated group depending on factor-intensities, prices and initial consumption patterns. One study which addresses the question found that it is more likely that the employers' (rather than the discriminated) group gain from discrimination than *vice versa* (Tzannatos 1987a). This is more in line with Akerlof's theory than Becker's. One thing, however, is certain: arbitrary wage or employment differentials result in net welfare losses and the winners cannot compensate the losers. The magnitude of gains and losses to individual agents and the social cost of discrimination cannot be answered by theory alone, even if the applicability of the theory were beyond doubt.

One has to resort to empirical studies to estimate the effects of discrimination on wages, employment and output. We next ask three interrelated questions:

(i) how much of the sex wage differential is due to discrimination;
(ii) how much of the employment misallocation is affected by sex wage differentials;
(iii) what would the gain in output be, if both the wage and employment distributions of men and women were alike.

How much of the sex wage gap is due to discrimination?

If discrimination against women were eliminated, one should not expect that women would be paid *equally* or would be employed on the same basis as men. This would be so, only if women and men were the *same*. Notice the difference between *equal* and *same*.

Consider, for example, the case of a disabled person. To admit that he is *equal* to a fully able person has very little implications. The fact remains that unless he is in a position himself to restrict the effects of his disability (by means say, of crutches or a wheelchair) and unless there are environmental provisions which allow him to exercise his potential (by special entrances and other facilities in public places) he will not be able to circumvent the effects of his disability. Think of one's own provisions to combat one's disability as the supply-side of the labour market, and the environmental provisions as the demand-side. To claim that a disabled person has *in general* an equal right with able-bodied people to visit public places would not eliminate differences between him or her and the rest of the population. What the disabled person needs is a *special* right which will enable him to have access to improved (and costly) facilities for the disabled. Is such a right an automatic one? The answer to many is no. If this sounds strange consider another example: do slow learners have a right to receive grants for a six-year period for a university undergraduate course?

To the extent that women and men can be taken as *equal* but not the *same*, one would expect differences in labour-market outcomes (among others) between the sexes. Some differences will be due to women's own decisions as well as those deriving from their family environment. This is the supply-side and in Western societies individuals are considered to be the ultimate judges of their own best interests. Other differences will be due to the environment. Some may be overt, such as discrimination. Others will be indirect; for example lack of provisions for maternity matters are generally more of an impediment for women than they are for men. In line with our previous discussion, maternity rights are special (to women) rights; the right for equal pay is a general right irrespective of sex. In order to formulate public policy on the issue, one has to find out which part of the sex wage-gap is due to inequality of treatment and which part is due to dissimilarity of characteristics. The usual line of argument is to relate inequalities to discrimination and dissimilarities to competitive outcomes (valuations) of the market.

A study which specifically addressed the issue for Britain is that of Zabalza and Arrufat (1985). Wages of men (W^m) and women (W^f) are taken to depend respectively on a number of observed characteristics X^m and X^f in the following way:

$$W^m = aX^m$$
$$W^f = bX^f$$

where a and b are coefficients which indicate how these characteristics are transformed into wages. Following Oaxaca (1973), for a given set of characteristics the differences in wages can be decomposed (after simple manipulation of the two wage equations above) into those which are due to different characteristics $(X^m - X^f)$ and those attributable to different rewards to a certain characteristic $(a - b)$ according to the following formula:

$$W^m - W^f = a(X^m - X^f) + X^f(a - b)$$

The first part on the right-hand side of the last equation measures that part of the pay differentials which is due to dissimilarity and will persist even if productive attributes of men and women were paid the same. The second part is the pay differential due to different valuation of productive attributes (inequality) and can be attributed to discrimination.

The characteristics of interest in the study of Zabalza and Arrufat were years of schooling, labour-market experience, race, health, occupation and industry. Using regression analysis and data for married women from the *General Household Survey* for 1975, they estimated the increase in female earnings which would be necessary to make a equal to b in the above formulation. One interesting feature of this study was its estimate of the proportion of the earnings differential which was due to women's breaks in their labour force participation because of family and fertility commitments. One can summarise their results as follows.

In their sample the ratio of female to male pay was 62 per cent and men had, on average, 24.5 years of labour-market experience while women had only 15.9. Correcting for labour-market experience would increase the ratio of female to male pay to almost 80 per cent. Put alternatively, almost 50 per cent of the earnings differential was due to the fact that women had less experience than men in the labour market. Differences between the sexes with respect to other attributes (such as schooling) explained another 8 percentage points (or 20 per cent of the gross sex wage-differential). Finally the remaining 12 percentage points (30 per cent of the differential) were unaccounted for by the model and, as a result, were seen as the upper bound of wage discrimination against women in Britain at the time.

These results have been confirmed by a recent study which examined the pay characteristics of a much more homogeneous group of workers than those of the *General Household Survey* utilised by Zabalza and Arrufat. Joshi and Newell (1987) used data from the Medical Research Council's *National Survey of Health*

and Development and estimated again, that 30 per cent of the sex
wage-gap for the 1946 cohort of women was unexplained by
human capital variables or job characteristics in 1977. This finding
is in line with the results of Zabalza and Arrufat. In another study,
Stewart and Greenhalgh (1984) examined the work-pattern, history and occupational attainment of women, using data for 1975–6
from the *National Training Survey*. They concluded that if
women's work-patterns did not suffer from less attachment to the
labour force, female earnings could increase by at least 40 per cent.
This is quite close to Zabalza's and Arrufat's estimate with respect
to the dissimilarity between male and female employment histories.
All three of the above studies refer to data relating to years after
Equal pay legislation was enacted. However, as will be seen later,
one can perhaps feel fairly confident that these estimates are likely
to be reasonably accurate for the 1980s as well.

There are two possible interpretations of these results. According to the first (narrow) interpretation, the elimination of wage-
discrimination in Britain should result in an increase of the ratio of
average female to average male pay to 74 per cent (62 + 12).
According to a broader interpretation, part if not all of the
depreciation effect on women's human capital due to breaks in
labour-force-participation may be discriminatory. For this argument to be valid, either or both of the following conditions must
hold:

1. in the sphere of *production*, employers must use women's labour-
market interruptions as a reason for paying women less than
otherwise equivalent men;
2. the prevailing attitudes and norms must work disproportionately against women during the process of society's *reproduction*.

Neither of these two conditions sounds improbable. Thus, according to the broad interpretation, non-discrimination should result in
an increase in the ratio of average female to average male earnings
to around 90 per cent. As a matter of fact, this is the ratio of female
to male earnings in Sweden which is, perhaps, the most advanced
country with respect to egalitarian public policies between the
sexes both in the family and the work-place.

In conclusion, women in Britain would be paid less than men

even if demand for labour were sex-blind. However, the empirical evidence suggests that a large part of the difference between female and male wages is still unaccounted for by differences in the productive characteristics of the two sexes. The evidence suggested that the ratio of female to male wages in 1975 could potentially improve to anything between 72 and 92 per cent from their level of 62 per cent at that time. The former increase would occur if men and women were the same in the market; the latter if men and women were the same in the family. Zabalza and Arrufat, however, did not offer an opinion as to which figure is more appropriate and the reader can make up his/her own mind on the issue about where to put the knife in the 72 to 92 range.

How much is the misallocation of employment due to discrimination?

This is even more difficult to answer then the previous question. Here one has to identify not only the extent of unjustified under-payment of female labour, but also the extent of effective exclusion of women from employment in certain sectors. One way to proceed is to assume that the sex wage-differentials are due to overrepresentation of women in a few sectors either because of direct wage-discrimination or because women are effectively excluded from some sectors.

Researchers in Britain have typically adopted Bergmann's 1971 model to tackle this question. To illustrate this approach, consider an industry – for example the car industry – which employs both men and women but not within the same occupations (for example, men do a wide range of 'masculine' jobs such as tasks relating to mechanical and electrical engineering). Assume, perhaps not unreasonably, that men are paid more than women, who tend to be crowded into a few 'feminine' tasks (such as upholstery). Recall from our discussion on the general equilibrium theory of discrimi-nation that workers in both sectors were paid their respective marginal products. Women are, of course, paid less under con-ditions of crowding than the competitive outcome. However, at the non-discrimination equilibrium workers were paid the same. Referring back to our example of the car industry and asking the question 'How many women should leave their occupations and join male occupations so that wages across occupations are equalised?' We see that the answer will be valid only if the wage differentials are due to crowding and apply to otherwise identical workers.

Two studies Pike, 1982 and Tzannatos, 1989) have addressed the problem using different data sets. The difference between these two studies is that the former allowed for labour-supply responses due to changing wages, while the latter introduced adjustment in the capital stock due to changes in factor prices. Nevertheless, the results are fairly comparable and indicate that female employment in male-dominated occupations would need to increase by up to around one-third to achieve equality of wages. What is an interesting finding in both studies is that wages in the previously female-dominated occupations will increase significantly (on average by around 50 per cent), while this need not be accompanied by a reduction of more than a few percentage points in the previously male-dominated industries. This happens because there are efficiency gains from the elimination of crowding.

As in the three studies mentioned in the previous section, these estimates are only upper-bound estimates of the possible effects of discrimination. To the extent that human-capital investment and employment decisions are dependent only on women's preferences and their own prospects prior to their entry into the labour market and providing there is no discrimination after they join the labour market, then over-employment in some sectors does not indicate misallocation but simply that some workers prefer to work in some sectors more than in others (Mincer and Polachek, 1974).

The welfare cost of discrimination

The analyses of Pike (1982) and Tzannatos, (1989) provide, as a by-product, estimated changes in total output (efficiency gains) which result from the hypothetical reallocation of female labour towards male-dominated occupations. A key parameter for this simulation is the elasticity of substitution between male and female labour. There are no direct estimates for this elasticity. Therefore, both authors estimated the effect upon output (the welfare gain) using a range of values for the elasticity of substitution. Pike experimented with elasticities up to the value of 3 and found welfare gains up to 3 percentage points.

Tzannatos (1989) extended the analysis to cases where the

elasticity of substitution took a value of up to 10, as empirical evidence suggests that the elasticity is substantially greater than unity, ranging usually between 3 and 9 (see, for example, Bowles, 1970; Dougherty and Selowsky, 1973). As a matter of fact, such a hypothetical exercise can safely assume an elasticity of substitution equal to infinity as it rests on the assumption of identical factors. However, it may be wise to allow for a smaller value of the elasticity of substitution as there is bound to be some degree of complementarity or discontinuity between the employment of men and women in production. Tzannatos found that potential gains may be up to 10 percentage points if the use of capital is ignored or, if changes to capital utilisation are taken into account, gains may be around 5 to 6 percentage points.

Inevitably, all three questions posed in this section have been answered in a tentative way. There is no clear winner among the competing theories of discrimination and the quality of empirical estimates are constrained by the availability of data. Nevertheless, the picture points to the facts that, from an economist's point of view, a good part of the wage and employment differentials between men and women in Britain are unjustified. The emerging picture is that the discriminated group loses while the majority group gains a little and employers benefit. The welfare cost of discrimination is thus disproportionately borne by workers rather than employers. This perhaps conforms to reality more than does the Beckerian analysis.

8.4 THE EFFECTS OF BRITISH ANTI-SEX-DISCRIMINATION LEGISLATION

Despite the fact that the women's question was first and most profoundly analysed in Britain, the introduction of legislation has been extremely slow and piecemeal. Nevertheless, the effect of anti-sex-discrimination legislation in Britain has been striking at least on the wage front. Employment effects are, however, more difficult to establish. Let us examine these issues in turn.

History

In 1888 the Trades Union Congress unanimously passed a motion that 'where women do the same work as men, they shall receive the same payment'. This was reiterated by Congress on more than forty occasions in the following seventy-five years, but it was not until 1963 that Congress called for legislation to enact equal pay. In the meantime, the issue was examined by three Royal Commissions (1912–16; 1929–31, and 1944–6), three Governmental Committees (1918, 1919 and 1923) and was also raised on numerous occasions in parliament and extra-parliamentary circles (Hepple, 1984). The introduction of equal opportunities legislation was delayed – usually on the grounds that the nation (employers) could not afford it.

Equality of pay in the Civil Service was achieved in 1961 and the Labour Government elected in 1964 set up the appropriate motions for equality of pay in the private sector. As a result, the Equal Pay Act was enacted in 1970 with the aim of eliminating differences in pay *for the same or broadly similar work or for work related as equivalent under a job-evaluation study*. The Act provided for gradual five-year implementation (to 29 December 1975) in order to avoid the disruptive consequences of a sharp reduction in the long-established sex differentials. In addition, the Sex Discrimination Act 1975, outlawed unequal treatment on the grounds of sex and marital status in aspects of employment other than pay. The latter Act became operative on the same day as the Equal Pay Act 1970.

In the meantime the United Kingdom had become a member of the EEC and Article 119 of the Treaty of Rome sets forth the principle that 'men and women should receive equal pay for *equal work*'. In the mid-1970s it was clarified that 'equal work' in the Treaty means 'equal value' (EEC Directive 75/117). The wording of the British legislation was then successfully challenged before the European Court as too restrictive. Recall that the *letter* of the original British law provided for cases where women and men do the same or like work and *in practice* very few women and men are actually doing the same thing in the same establishment. As a result a new legislative piece came into force in January 1983 under the title 'Equal Pay (Amendment) Regulations', which consolidated and broadened the previous two Acts of 1970 and 1975. However, there was considerable scope for improvement in female pay prior to 1970 under the provisions of the 1970 Act, despite the narrow wording of the earlier legislation, as the way female pay was then determined was anachronistic, arbitrary and overtly discriminatory.

The effect of legislation on relative pay

It is too early to assess the effects of the broadening of legislation in 1983. Nevertheless the effects of the original legislation are both clear-cut and impressive. The ratio of female to male hourly earnings increased from around 60 per cent to 70 per cent in the five-year transitory period which started in the early 1970s. Up to 1970 female relative pay had been remarkably stable for the whole recorded history of wages in Britain (since 1886) and since 1976 has also been equally stable, albeit at a higher level (Table 8.1). The gradual implementation of equal pay started in 1970 and was completed by 1976. Was this a coincidence?

TABLE 8.1   Ratio of female to male pay 1886–1987 (%)

	1886	1960	1970	1976	1987	Source
Adult manual workers						
Weekly earnings	51·5*	51·4	49·9	60·6	61·1†	Department of
Hourly earnings	—	60.5	60.1	71.4	69.5†	Employment
Adult full-time workers, hourly earnings excluding overtime						
Manual	—	—	61.7	71.1	70.7	*New*
Non-manual	—	—	52.5	62.6	62.1	*Earnings*
All	—	—	63.7	73.5	74.1	Survey

* From *British Labour Statistics, Historical Abstract 1886–1968*, Table 35.
† Refers to 1984, the latest available.

Early researchers (Chiplin, Curran and Parsley, 1980; Pike, 1982) studying the effects of legislation upon female pay in Britain laid more emphasis on the egalitarian flat-rate provisions of the incomes policies of the early- and mid-1970s. These studies unavoidably suffered from lack of post-Equal-Pay-Act observations as they were carried out more or less at the same time as the incomes policies were in operation. However, later studies observed that the increase in female wages in the early 1970s was permanent (Table

8.1) and the effect of incomes policies was, on the one hand, negligible and, on the other hand, short-lived (Ashenfelter and Layard, 1983). The once-for-all improvement in female relative pay was found to be attributable neither to incomes policies, nor to a deterioration in male pay, nor indeed to changes in female employment from low-pay to high-pay sectors, nor to sudden changes in the demand for female relative to male labour (Tzannatos and Zabalza, 1984; Zabalza and Tzannatos, 1985a). The only explanation for the increase in female relative pay during the period 1970–6 remained in a residual way, the Equal Pay Act 1970.

A characteristic of the British legislation on the issue of discrimination is the lack of penalties for those who are found in breach of the law. In contrast, penalties in the USA often reach six-figure sums; yet there is no discernible change in female pay in the USA since their equal pay legislation (Dex and Shaw, 1986). The claim that legislation is responsible for the increase in female wages in Britain would be difficult to sustain unless one could show *how* the provisions of the law became operative, especially in the absence of infringement procedures. Tzannatos and Zabalza (1984) examined the system of wage determination in Britain and found that prior to 1970, collective agreements as a general rule prescribed female pay either *pro rata* to male pay, or as a differential to male pay or, if a single rate were prescribed, it was meant to apply to an activity almost solely undertaken by one sex only! Under the circumstances, enforcement took the form of a stroke of a pen and affected the pay of at least 70 per cent of women workers covered by collective agreements. A corroborative argument to this explanation is that the pay of female teachers and other women employed in the narrowly or broadly defined public sector was the only one which did not experience any change in the period 1970–5 (or immediately before or after). A near-identical story can be found in the case of Australia (Gregory and Duncan, 1981) and, to a lesser extent, in the case of Greece (Tzannatos, 1987b, 1988, 1989). Both countries used to have the same kind of wage-determination system as that of Britain prior to 1970.

This story also explains the constancy of female relative pay for a century before Equal Pay. The reasons why female relative wages have shown little variation since 1976 is, however, a question that no study has yet addressed. An explanation could be along the lines suggested in Section 8.2 (Arrow, 1972). Imperfect information and market imperfections make quick adjustments costly and established patterns may prevail in the short run and the 'longer' run (Phelps, 1972). Perhaps the answer is that changes in wage differentials from 'within the market' causes are slow and gradual, as in the American case. This intensifies the thesis that sudden disruptions of wage differentials should be sought outside the labour market.

The effect of legislation on relative employment

The employment response to legislation is difficult to predict theoretically and estimate empirically. In theory there are two offsetting effects. On the one hand, if legislation (the Equal Pay Act) is successful in raising female wages and making female labour dearer, then there will be substitution of other than female labour for the now-expensive women workers. On the other hand, if legislation (the Sex Discrimination Act) is successful, employers should not be able to respond negatively to higher pay for women as they should treat men and women equally. Thus the net effect of legislation is indeterminate.

There are a number of alternative theories which may apply and make the employment response to legislation tilt towards the positive side. One is the possibility of monopsonised labour markets for female labour, a factor often discussed but rarely found to be empirically relevant. Another relates to the issue of efficient wages which may become important when women's pay becomes unconstrained from norms and female labour is utilised as it deserves. Having to offer higher wages, employers may find better use of female labour, on the demand side, and women may become more productive in response to better wage and employment prospects, on the supply side. Both aspects ameliorate the negative prediction of the standard neoclassical theory of the demand for labour. Finally, in the longer run, better wage and employment prospects for women may have a considerable impact upon their expectations for their prospective roles in the labour market and the family.

There are only a limited number of studies which have undertaken to examine the employment response to legislation. It is only a few years since legislation was fully implemented and it is always difficult to proxy a qualitative variable (such as legislation) in regression analysis of the demand for inputs. Given these limitations, Pike (1985) concluded that equal opportunities legislation has been unable to play a substantial role in halting the decline of relative employment in manufacturing during the period 1973–82. However, Zabalza and Tzannatos (1985a) estimated that for both the whole economy and the private sector separately there was little evidence to suggest that the response to equal pay was detrimental to female employment. In another study (Tzannatos and Zabalza, 1985) the authors estimated that the variability of female employment after the introduction of legislation was somewhat lower than before. This applied to estimates for the whole economy as well as for the manufacturing and non-manufacturing sectors separately. Clearly, this is an issue which has to receive more attention in the future before any firm conclusions may be drawn.

8.5   CONCLUDING COMMENTS

The issue of discrimination has long haunted economists. To analyse discrimination has proved a daunting task. Discrimination is not only an economic issue, since social preferences and political interventions play an important role in shaping outcomes. In addition, discrimination is a qualitative issue and its incorporation in the neoclassical theory did not formally occur until Becker's model appeared in 1957. As we have seen, Becker's theory proved especially useful for the fresh look at the issue which it provided. However, the *act* of discrimination needs to be more than an assumption to enable theory to explain the long-run persistence of differentials.

On the issue of policy, it is not easy to provide answers. To the extent that discrimination could not be accommodated in theory (Cassel's paradox), the orthodoxy denied its existence and hence avoided the need to prescribe policies, if not solutions. With Becker, discrimination became part of tastes, that is part of the individual's preferences whose formation and consequences are considered to fall within the reign of individual freedom in market economies. Opinion is divided on two grounds. Should one intervene? Should interventions be within the market system or is it the market system which needs changing?

One thing which is certain is that legislation (that is, government intervention) in Britain did not prevent the competitive functioning of the labour market. On the contrary, wage-setting is now more competitive than before. The market prior to Equal Pay was subjected to an unjustified wage-differential whose origins go back a few thousand years. Here one has a concrete case where interventions may not always be undesirable. Perhaps there are many more cases of this kind. If there are not such cases, perhaps this is the time to try to create them. Section 8.4 showed that it is probable that policies and actions which improve the position of women in the labour market will be self-financed in that there will be efficiency gains as a result of these policies. After all, half of the nation's intelligence is in the heads of women and women still contribute less than a third to the country's recorded output.

9 The Labour Market in the Open Economy

GEORGE ALOGOSKOUFIS

9.1 INTRODUCTION

The 1970s have seen many developments in macroeconomics, that have in many ways transformed the way in which open economies are analysed. Among these is an increasing emphasis on the role of relative prices like real wages (relative price of labour), competitiveness (relative price of imports), the relative price of oil, real interest rates and others.

A leading open-economy macroeconomics textbook written at the end of the 1970s, like Dornbusch's *Open Economy Macroeconomics* (1980), differs in many ways from one written at the end of the 1960s, like Mundell's *International Economics* (1968). This partly reflects the move to flexible exchange rates, but also the increased emphasis on relative prices referred to above.

How can macroeconomic policy affect such relative prices, and through them, and possibly other channels, output, unemployment, inflation and the current account? These considerations are at the forefront of the concerns of macroeconomists and policymakers alike, and the role of labour market adjustment is pivotal in the conclusions one can draw.

The observation that the labour market fails to adjust adequately in the short run has been with us for a long time. The analytical implications of this are perhaps the most important message contained in Keynes's *General Theory of Employment, Interest and Money* (1936), the book that in many ways created macroeconomics as a separate subdiscipline. The central assumption is that wages will not fall sufficiently in the presence of unemployment to eliminate it. Thus, economies may find themselves stuck in equilibria with a high level of unemployment, in which case there may be an argument for policy intervention to reduce it.

This chapter is concerned with the simple analytics of wage rigidity, competitiveness and macroeconomic policy in an open economy. Wage rigidity is sometimes taken to mean that *nominal* wages will not adjust and sometimes that *real* wages will not adjust. The very concept of the real wage is ambiguous in an open economy. Thus, I shall be using a distinction between the *product real wage*, which is the nominal wage deflated by the price of domestically produced goods, and the *consumption real wage*, which is the nominal wage deflated by the consumer price index. The former is the relative price of labour that concerns firms in their employment decisions, while the latter is the relative price of labour that concerns workers in their labour-supply decisions. In the absence of taxation, that would introduce a further wedge between them, product and consumption wages differ to the extent that the relative price of imports is different from unity. These relations are examined in section 9.2. In section 9.3, I examine the supply side of open economies, in the presence of three alternative assumptions about wage-adjustment: namely equilibrium-adjustment, consumption-wage rigidity, and nominal-wage rigidity. In section 9.4 I bring in the demand side, and examine monetary and fiscal policy, concentrating on the case of consumption-wage rigidity, which many macroeconomists (e.g. Bruno and Sachs, 1985) think is an important aspect of some European economies, including that of the United Kingdom. In section 9.5 I examine supply-side policies, chiefly changes in tax-rates, which directly change the wedge between product and consumption wages, and in section 9.6 I briefly examine various extensions as well as the empirical evidence. Conclusions are summarised in the final section.

9.2 THE RELATIONSHIP BETWEEN REAL WAGES AND COMPETITIVENESS

Consider the simple case of an economy that has completely

specialised in the production of a single tradeable commodity. Denote the price of this commodity by P. The price of imports in domestic currency is equal to EP^*, where E is the exchange rate (units of domestic currency per unit of foreign currency) and P^* is the price of imports in foreign currency. The consumer price index in this economy can be represented as a geometric average of the prices of domestic and imported goods respectively:

$$P^c \equiv P^\delta(EP^*)^{1-\delta} \tag{9.1}$$

where P^c is the consumer price index and δ the share of domestic goods in the consumption of domestic residents.

It is convenient to apply a logarithmic transformation to (9.1). Lowercase letters demote natural logarithms.

$$p^c \equiv \delta p + (1 - \delta)(e + p^*) \tag{9.1^1}$$

Competitiveness in this simple model is defined as the relative price of imported goods, i.e. EP^*/P. In logarithms, with c denoting the log of competitiveness,

$$c \equiv e + p^* - p \tag{9.2}$$

From (9.1) and (9.2),

$$p^c \equiv p + (1 - \delta)c \tag{9.3}$$

The consumer price index is proportional to domestic prices, and depends on competitiveness with an elasticity equal to the share of imports in domestic consumption.

To look at the relationship between real wages and competitiveness we shall, as noted above, define two measures of the real wage. The first is the *product real wage*, which is none other than the nominal wage deflated by the price of domestic goods. This is the relative price of labour relevant for the employment decisions of firms. In logarithmic terms it is given by:

$$\omega \equiv w - p \tag{9.4}$$

where ω denotes (the log of) the product wage, and w the nominal wage.

The second measure of the real wage is the *consumption real wage*, which is the relative price of labour relevant for the decisions of workers. This is the nominal wage deflated by the consumer price index. In logarithms:

$$\omega^c \equiv w - p^c \tag{9.5}$$

where ω^c denotes (the log of) the consumption wage.

Having defined the relevant concepts in this simple model, let us briefly look at the relationship between them.

Note that by substituting (9.3) into (9.5) the consumption wage is equal to the product wage, minus competitiveness, the latter multiplied by the share of imports in total consumption:

$$\omega^c \equiv \omega - (1 - \delta)c \tag{9.6}$$

Expression (9.6) is an identity among the relevant variables. It has no empirical content, unless one makes some further assumptions. As our interest is in labour economics, let us consider two simple assumptions about the determination of wages.

First, consider the case of consumption-wage rigidity. This would obtain if workers (or unions) were only concerned with the purchasing power of wages, and aimed at ensuring a target consumption wage. Without loss of generality let us normalize this target to unity, in which case ω^c (the log) is equal to zero. Then:

$$\omega = (1 - \delta)c \tag{9.7}$$

In the case of consumption-wage rigidity, the product wage is positively related to competitiveness, with an elasticity equal to the share of imports in total consumption. This is because, when the price of imports rises relative to domestic prices, nominal wages also rise, in order to maintain a constant consumption wage.

Second, consider the case of product-wage rigidity. This could obtain in a number of circumstances. For example, in competitive models with Leontief technology, in oligopolistic models where the optimal price is a constant mark-up on variable costs, and in efficiency-wage models, among others. In that case, after normalising the constant ω to zero, one obtains:

$$\omega^c = -(1 - \delta)c \tag{9.8}$$

For a constant product wage, there is a negative relationship between competitiveness and consumption wages. This is because any change in nominal wages is fully reflected in domestic prices.

Having clarified the relationship between competitiveness and alternative measures of real wages, let us move on to examining one of the most widely used models of the labour market in open-economy macro-models.

9.3 THE LABOUR MARKET AND AGGREGATE SUPPLY

One of the most widely used specifications of the determination of employment in macroeconomic models is the labour-demand model. According to this employment always lies along a down-ward-sloping labour-demand function of firms.

To consider this model, assume that domestic output is produced according to the following Cobb–Douglas production function:

$$Y = K^{a}L^{1-a} \tag{9.9}$$

where L is employment, K the capital stock, a the share of capital in output, and $1 - a$ the share of labour, assumed to be constant.

Assume that the capital stock is fixed in the short run, and that firms are competitive profit-maximisers and choose employment so as to maximise profits subject to given wages and prices.

Profit-mazimisation implies that the marginal revenue product of labour will be equal to the product real wage. In this case:

$$(1 - a)K^{a}L^{-a} = \frac{W}{P} \tag{9.10}$$

where W is the nominal wage, and P the price of domestically produced goods.

From (9.9), taking logarithms:

$$\log(Y) = a\log K + (1 - a)\log L$$

and assuming $K = \bar{K}$ in the short run, we get:

$$y = a\bar{k} + (1 - a)l \tag{9.11}$$

where lower-case letters denote natural logarithms. $\bar{k}$ is the logarithm of the assumed constant capital stock.

From (9.10), taking logarithms and solving for employment, we get:

$$l = l_0 + \bar{k} - \lambda\omega \quad ; \quad \lambda = 1/\alpha, \ l_0 = \log(1-\alpha) \tag{9.12}$$

(9.12) is a conventional downward-sloping neoclassical demand function for labour. The elasticity of labour demand with respect to the product wage depends positively on the share of labour in total output $(1-\alpha)$.

Substituting (9.12) in (9.11), one gets the following short-run aggregate-supply function:

$$y = (1-\alpha)l_0 + \bar{k} - (1-\alpha)\lambda\omega \tag{9.13}$$

According to (9.13), when real wages go up, output falls, because labour becomes more expensive and firms employ fewer workers.

The next step is to look at the determination of unemployment. For this we must consider the supply side of the labour market. Assume that (the log of) labour supply is positively related to the consumption wage:

$$n = n_0 + \varepsilon\omega^c \tag{9.14}$$

where n refers to the log of labour supply, n_0 depends on demographic characteristics, labour market institutions, social custom etc, all assumed constant, and ε is the elasticity of labour supply.

The unemployment rate is approximately equal to the difference between the logarithm of labour supply and the logarithm of employment. From (9.12), (9.14) and (9.6):

$$u = (n_0 - l_0) - \bar{k} + \varepsilon\omega^c + \lambda\omega = (n_0 - l_0 - \bar{k}) + (\varepsilon + \lambda)\omega - \varepsilon(1-\delta)c \tag{9.15}$$

The unemployment rate therefore is positively related to the product wage, because, *ceteris paribus*, the product wage increases labour supply and reduces labour demand. It is negatively related to competitiveness because, *ceteris paribus*, competitiveness reduces the consumption wage, and hence reduces labour supply.

We now have almost all the elements required to put together the supply side of an open-economy macro-model. The behaviour of the economy and the effects of macroeconomic policy will depend on the nature of wage adjustment.

Wage adjustment mechanisms

Three alternatives will be considered. First, consider the benchmark of continuous equilibrium in the labour market. In equilibrium, there is a positive relationship between product wages and competitiveness, given by (set $u = 0$ in (9.15)):

$$\omega = -\frac{(n_0 - l_0) - \bar{k}}{\varepsilon + \lambda} + \frac{\varepsilon(1 - \delta)}{\varepsilon + \lambda} c \qquad (9.16)$$

Equation (9.16) reflects the requirement for equal movements in demand and supply of labour to keep the labour market in equilibrium. If competitiveness rises, causing a reduction in labour supply, the product wage must also rise to bring about an equal reduction in labour demand. In the case of continuous equilibrium in the labour market classical neutrality will obtain, unless aggregate-demand policies can affect competitiveness, and hence the equilibrium product wage. Although the unemployment rate will not be affected, the level of employment and output will be affected by such policies.

A second benchmark case is that of *consumption-wage rigidity*, already referred to in the previous section. If wage-setters aim at, and succeed in maintaining, a constant consumption wage (equal to unity, say) the relationship between product and competitiveness is now constant, and unemployment is given by:

$$u = (n_0 - l_0 - \bar{k}) + \lambda \omega \qquad (9.17)$$

The similarity between this case and the case of equilibrium in the labour market is that the only channel through which aggregate demand policies can affect real variables is competitiveness. The difference is that now the unemployment rate will also be affected.

Finally, a third benchmark case is that of *nominal-wage rigidity*. If the nominal wage is constant, then the product wage is negatively related to the domestic price level, while the consumption wage is negatively related to both the domestic price level and competitiveness:

$$\omega = \bar{w} - p \tag{9.18}$$

$$\omega^c = \bar{w} - p - (1 - \delta)c \tag{9.19}$$

where $\bar{w}$ is the assumed constant nominal wage. Now there is a different channel of real effects of aggregate demand policies, which is none other than the traditional Keynesian channel. An increase in the price level reduces product wages and thus increases employment and output, and reduces unemployment.

We can now consider the supply of output under the three alternative assumptions about wage adjustment.

First, consider the case of labour-market equilibrium. Substituting (9.16) into (9.13), we obtain the following supply-side relationship between output and competitiveness:

$$y = y_1 - \frac{(1 - \alpha)\lambda(1 - \delta)\varepsilon}{\varepsilon + \lambda} c \tag{9.20}$$

where $y_1 = (1 - \alpha)l_0 + \bar{k} + [(1 - \alpha)\lambda/(\varepsilon + \lambda)] [n_0 - l_0 - \bar{k}]$.

Second, consider the case of consumption-wage rigidity. Substituting (9.7) into (9.13), we obtain the following supply-side relationship between output and competitiveness:

$$y = y_2 - (1 - \alpha)(1 - \delta)\lambda \ c \tag{9.21}$$

where $y_2 = (1 - \alpha)l_0 + \bar{k}$.

Notice by comparing (9.21) with (9.20) that the elasticity of aggregate supply with respect to competitiveness is higher under real-wage rigidity than under labour market equilibrium. This is because real-wage rigidity corresponds to an infinitely elastic short-run labour-supply function at the given consumption wage.

Finally, under nominal-wage rigidity, output supply is positively related to the price level. Substituting (9.18) in (9.13) gives:

$$y = y_3 + (1 - \alpha)\lambda p \tag{9.22'}$$

where $y_3 = (1 - \alpha)l_0 + k - (1 - \alpha)\lambda\bar{w}$.

Under fixed exchange rates, an increase in the domestic price level reduces competitiveness equiproportionately. Thus, under fixed exchange rates ($e = \bar{e}$, say), (9.22′) could be written as:

$$y = y_3 + (1 - \alpha)\lambda(\bar{e} + p^*) - (1 - \alpha)\lambda c \qquad (9.22)$$

Note from (9.22) that the elasticity of output supply with respect to competitiveness is higher under nominal-wage rigidity, than under either of the other two labour-market regimes. This is because nominal-wage rigidity corresponds to an infinitely elastic short-run labour-supply function, at the given nominal wage. In contrast to the other two cases, an increase in competitiveness does not affect the wage demands of workers in the short run, and does not therefore cause a change in product wages through that channel.

The three alternative output-supply functions under fixed-exchange rates are depicted in Figure 9.1. Labour-market equili-

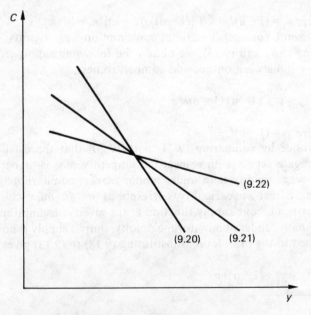

FIGURE 9.1 Aggregate supply curve

brium provides the steepest one, with nominal-wage rigidity providing the flattest. In what follows we shall concentrate on the case of consumption-wage rigidity.

9.4 MONETARY AND FISCAL POLICY

Consider now the demand-side in an open economy. Assume an IS curve, mapping the combinations of income and the domestic interest rate that make planned savings plus imports equal to planned investment plus exports, and an LM curve, mapping the combinations of income and the domestic interest rate that make the stock of money willingly held. In log-linear form we can write them as:

IS
$$y = \varphi_0 - \varphi_1 i + \varphi_2 c + f \tag{9.23}$$

LM
$$m - p = y - \psi i \tag{9.24}$$

where φ_1 depends on the interest-rate-elasticity of investment, φ_2 on the relative price elasticities of imports and exports, f is an index of fiscal policy, with an increase indicating a fiscal expansion, m is the logarithm of the money stock, i the domestic interest rate and ψ is the interest elasticity of the real demand for money.

Assuming zero international capital mobility, we can solve the IS–LM system for an aggregate-demand function, that would give the combinations of income and competitiveness that ensure the consistency of planned savings plus imports with planned investment plus exports, *and* money-market equilibrium. Solving (9.24) for i and substituting in (9.23), we get the following aggregate-demand function:

$$y = \frac{1}{\psi + \varphi_1} [\varphi_0 \psi + \varphi_1(m - p) + \varphi_2 \psi c + \psi f] \tag{9.25}$$

An increase in competitiveness increases the demand for exports and decreases the demand for imports. To maintain aggregate consistency savings must rise and investment must fall. An increase in income achieves both, as savings rise through the consumption function, and investment falls through the interest-rate increase, which comes about to maintain money-market equilibrium. This mechanism is summarised in (9.25).

Also consider the condition for equilibrium in the current account. If export demand depends positively on competitiveness, and import demand negatively on competitiveness and positively on domestic income, then there is a negatively sloped relationship between output and competitiveness, which will keep the current account in equilibrium. This relationship which we shall term the NX curve (for Net Exports) is given below:

NX
$$y = \chi_0 + \chi_1 c \qquad (9.26)$$

Equation (9.26) is the locus of combinations between income and competitiveness that keep the current account in balance. Its parameters depend on the parameters of the export- and import-demand functions.

We can now consider short-run equilibrium. We consider three aggregate consistency requirements. First, the supply function (9.21), which depicts the combinations of output and competitiveness that make the employment decisions of firms consistent with the wage demands of workers. Second, the demand function (9.25), which depicts the combinations of output and competitiveness that make planned savings plus imports, equal to planned investment plus exports, and money demand equal to the money supply. Finally, we consider the external balance condition (9.26).

The three conditions are depicted in Figure 9.2. An increase in aggregate demand (through a monetary or fiscal expansion) will cause a fall in competitiveness, and an increase in output and employment. Assume that the economy was initially at point E, which is associated with a balanced current account. An aggregate demand expansion (from AD to AD') will take the economy from E to E'. The transmission mechanism will be an increase in the domestic price-level, brought about by excess demand, which, because of openess, triggers a less-than-proportional increase in nominal wages, even when the consumption wage is rigid. Thus, product wages fall, and employment and output rise. This expansion is associated with a current-account deficit and a higher price-level. As one can see from the left part of Figure 9.2, unemployment will fall.

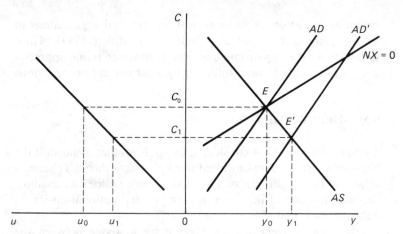

FIGURE 9.2 An aggregate demand expansion

It is interesting to note that an aggregate demand expansion brings about a fall in unemployment through an increase in inflation and a current-account deficit. In addition, for a fiscal expansion, domestic interest-rates will rise, possibly reducing investment. These are the familiar tradeoffs between internal and external balance, between inflation and unemployment, and the crowding-out effect of fiscal policy.

Under perfect capital mobility and fixed exchange rates things do not change much. The LM curve is now replaced by the condition of parity between domestic and world interest rates, which is achieved through devoting monetary policy to the defence of the exchange rate. The IS curve itself becomes the aggregate demand curve, with the world interest rate i^* replacing i in (9.23). The properties of the model will be quite similar to what they were before. A fiscal expansion will again cause inflation, this will reduce competiveness, increase output and employment, and reduce unemployment. The current account will deteriorate.

Where the theory becomes more complicated is under perfect capital mobility and flexible exchange rates. Under such circumstances the role of expectations about the future path of the exchange rate becomes pivotal (see Dornbusch, 1976). Under rational expectations, a rise in domestic interest-rates above world levels will only arise if there are expectations of future depreciations of the exchange rate. Following such a rise, say because of an expansionary fiscal policy, the exchange rate overshoots its equilibrium appreciation, in order to warrant rational expectations of future depreciations (see also Buiter and Miller, 1981). Thus, following a fiscal expansion, one expects to see an initial appreciation of the exchange rate, followed by a subsequent depreciation.

9.5 SUPPLY-SIDE POLICY

Up to now we have not considered any policies that could shift the aggregate supply curve or indeed unemployment through channels other than competitiveness. To consider such policies let us allow for the existence of income taxes, employers' national-insurance contributions, and indirect taxes.

Like competitiveness, such taxes drive a wedge between the product wage and the consumption wage.

Let us start with the product wage: if employers have to pay national-insurance contributions at a proportional rate, t_1 say, then the product wage relevant for their employment decisions is given by:

$$W(1 + t_1)/P$$

or in logarithms:

$$\omega = w - p + t_1 \tag{9.27}$$

where I have used the approximation $\log(1 + t_1) \simeq t_1$. for a small t_1.

On the other hand, if workers have to pay income taxes and national-insurance contributions at a rate t_2, and an indirect tax at a rate t_3 is levied on all goods, the consumption wage becomes:

$$W(1 - t_2)/[P^\delta (EP^*)^{1-\delta}(1 + t_3)]$$

or in logarithms:

$$\omega^c = w - p - (1 - \delta)\, c - t_2 - t_3 \tag{9.28}$$

Thus, taking the difference between the net-product wage (9.27) and the net-consumption wage (9.28), we find the wedge between the two to be:

$$\omega - \omega^c = (1 - \delta)c + t_1 + t_2 + t_3 \qquad (9.29)$$

Under net consumption wage rigidity, assuming $\bar{\omega}^c = 0$ we obtain,

$$\omega = (1 - \delta)c + t_1 + t_2 + t_3 \qquad (9.30)$$

Substituting (9.30) for ω in (9.17), gives,

$$u = (n_0 - l_0 - \bar{k}) + \lambda(1 - \delta)c + \lambda(t_1 + t_2 + t_3) \qquad (9.31)$$

Thus, under consumption-wage rigidity unemployment depends positively on competitiveness and the national insurance, income tax and indirect tax rates. All those factors increase the product wage and reduce labour demand.

The output supply function can be derived by substituting (9.30) for ω in (9.13). We then get:

$$y = y_2 - (1 - \alpha)\lambda(1 - \delta)c - (1 - \alpha)\lambda(t_1 + t_2 + t_3) \qquad (9.32)$$

Thus changes in the tax rates shift the aggregate supply function. Consider Figure 9.3. A decrease in the average tax rate, compensated to keep the aggregate demand-schedule constant will shift

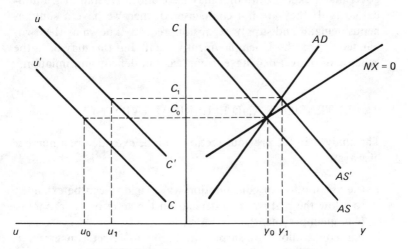

FIGURE 9.3 An aggregate supply expansion

both the aggregate supply curve (9.32) and the unemployment curve (9.31) to the right. In the new equilibrium, competitiveness and output rise, unemployment falls, and so does the price level. The current account will improve if the NX curve is flatter than the AD curve.

To recapitulate, both demand and supply policies can reduce unemployment and increase output in the short run, even when there is consumption-wage rigidity. The effect of supply-side policies would even go through in a closed economy, but the effect of demand policies depends crucially on the openess of the economy. Demand expansions are, however, associated with a fall in competitiveness, and rises in inflation and the deficit of the current account. Supply-side expansions are associated with a rise in competitiveness, and possible falls in inflation and the current-account deficit.

One should not forget in all this that the underlying problem is in any case the rigidity of consumption wages, which does not allow nominal wages to move and clear the labour market. Demand and supply policies are alternative ways of substituting other problems for the unemployment problems thus created. For example, demand policies substitute a current account and inflation problem for unemployment, while supply-side policies, compensated to keep the aggregate demand curve in place, may require cuts in government expenditure that may have allocative and distributional costs. If they are not compensated, then we have a simultaneous demand and supply expansion, recently known as the 'two-handed approach'. Unemployment will fall, but this may be at the expense of budget deficits, current-account deficits and inflation.

9.6   EXTENSIONS AND EMPIRICAL EVIDENCE

The analysis in the previous sections can be extended in a number of ways:

1. the assumption of consumption-wage rigidity can be extended to allow the real wage to depend on the state of the economy (e.g. unemployment);
2. one could allow for surprise inflation to affect consumption wages in the short run;

3. one could relax the assumption of perfect competition;
4. one could allow for supply-side effects of government expenditure;
5. one could analyse two sector models; an important example of such models is the open-economy model with traded and nontraded goods;
6. the effects of external price shocks (e.g. oil shocks) can also be straightforwardly considered;
7. dynamic considerations can be introduced.

These could arise as a result of the government budget constraint, partial adjustment in labour demand, investment, exchange-rate dynamics, current-account dynamics and so forth.

The extension to allow consumption wages to depend on the state of the labour market, is a characteristic of many types of models, ranging from equilibrium models of the labour market to disequilibrium and bargaining models (see Nickell, 1984). Algebraically, we could have an equation for consumption wages of the following form:

$$\omega^c = \bar{\omega}^c - \eta u \tag{9.33}$$

Equation (9.33) suggests that consumption wages depend negatively on unemployment. In the context of the so-called monopolyunion model (see Chapter 5), this could be because a rise in unemployment reduces the expected utility of members of the union who are laid off, and so mitigates the wage demands of unions (see also Oswald, 1982). An extension such as (9.33) would not modify the nature of the results arrived at in the previous sections, although it would change some of the details.

The extension to consider the effects of unanticipated inflation is also fairly standard, ever since the modification of the original Phillips curve by Phelps (1968) and Friedman (1968). The idea is that wages are negotiated periodically, and that workers can only bargain about a nominal wage, given their expectations of future inflation. When inflation turns out higher than expected, consumption wages unavoidably fall, and then firms are willing to employ more labour and produce more. This set-up can be modified to allow for some indexation of wages on inflation (see Gray, 1976, 1978), although full indexation brings us back to the consumption-wage-rigidity models. Open-economy models with indexation have recently been examined by many. A good example is Aizenman and Frenkel (1985).

The assumption of perfect competition in the product market could also be relaxed, in a way that would allow for different pricing rules. Normal cost pricing is such a rule (see Godley and Nordhaus, 1972). According to this, oligopolistic firms set prices as a mark-up on their normal costs. Explicit oligopolistic models and their effects have recently been examined by Dornbusch (1987). The implication seems to be that aggregate demand affects the mark-up of firms, and could thus directly increase employment, without necessarily reducing product wages; see also Layard and Nickell (1986).

Another supply-side effect that could be considered, is the direct-employment effect of government expenditure. The government is a major employer itself, and a large part of its expenditure is on wages and salaries. Thus, an increase in real government expenditure is to a large extent an increase in government employment and output. Recognition of this fact, would modify the labour-demand function, allowing it to depend directly on government expenditure as well. Thus, increases in government expenditure would shift the aggregate supply curve as well. This is taken into account in models by Andrews and Nickell (1982), Alogoskoufis (1985) and others. It would certainly modify the analysis in the previous section.

Another extension would be to assume that two types of commodities are produced: one internationally tradeable and the other non-tradeable. Two-sector models of this type have been produced in the international trade literature, and have also found their way into international macroeconomics (see for example, Dornbusch (1980), ch. 6). Alogoskoufis (1989) has analysed alternative monetary-policy rules in such a model.

The effects of external-input price-shocks have also been analysed extensively, starting with Findlay and Rodriguez (1977), Buiter (1978), Katseli (1980) and others. The admirable recent monograph by Bruno and Sachs (1985), analyses the macroeconomic implications of such shocks, and the role of the labour market, in a very detailed way.

In principle dynamic extensions are possible, although models with a rich structure become rather unwieldy once allowance is made for dynamics. Models of exchange-rate dynamics have been analysed quite extensively, following Dornbusch's (1976) important contribution, for example by Buiter and Miller (1981). Extensions to take account of the government budget-constraint, capital accumulation or adjustment costs in labour demand, have not yet been fully incorporated in the open-economy macroeconomics literature.

What about empirical evidence on the type of model suggested in the previous sections? From an empirical viewpoint, the model has two important testable implications. The assumption that employment lies along a downward-sloping labour-demand curve and the assumption of consumption-wage rigidity.

The labour-demand curve has been recently investigated for the UK by Nickell and Andrews (1983), Symons (1985), and Layard and Nickell (1986) among others. International evidence can be found in Symons and Layard (1984), Newell and Symons (1985), Bruno and Sachs (1985), Bean, Layard and Nickell (1986) and others. Almost all these studies find a negative relationship between product wages and employment, which suggests the presence of a downward-sloping labour-demand curve. The details differ, however, and many researchers report difficulties in finding such a relationship for the USA.

Most of the above studies, as well as the study of Alogoskoufis and Manning (1988), have also examined wage rigidity. The emphasis is on the coefficient η of an equation like (9.33). The value $\eta = 0$ implies complete wage rigidity, while as η goes to infinity we approach the case of competitive labour market equilibrium. The estimated coefficients are quite low, suggesting the presence of considerable consumption-wage rigidity, although there are considerable cross-country differences.

9.7 CONCLUSIONS

To sum up, if one acepts that employment lies along a downward-sloping labour-demand curve, and there is considerable consumption-wage rigidity, the main way in which macroeconomic policy can affect output and unemployment is through changing the wedge between product and consumption wages. Alternatively, if nominal wages are not fully indexed, a surprise inflation can reduce real wages and unemployment. However, such a policy cannot be systematically followed, as wage-setters will start out-guessing the policy authorities.

In an open economy, demand policies can change this wedge through their effects on competitiveness, while supply-side policies can change it directly. An aggregate demand expansion increases output, reduces unemployment and competitiveness, and during the adjustment path creates additional inflation. In the new short-run equilibrium the current account has worsened. On the other hand, an aggregate supply expansion through a cut in tax rates affecting the labour market, increases competitiveness at the same time as an output rises and unemployment falls. The current account may still worsen. The adjustment path will be character-ised by a fall in inflation.

These conclusions are somewhat special to the particular model, but for the most part carry over to many of the models referred to in the previous section. They are the type of conclusions that underlie the recent calls of many European economists for a coordinated, two-handed (demand, supply) approach to expand-ing the European economies and reducing unemployment.

10 Profit-Sharing

SAUL ESTRIN and SUSHIL WADHWANI

10.1 INTRODUCTION

Perhaps the most conspicuous evidence of malfunctioning in the labour market has been the 'stagflation' of recent years, in Western Europe and the USA. The problem has been so prolonged and so persisent that some analysts, in particular Martin Weitzman have become convinced that it can only be cured by altering the method by which pay is determined. In a number of forceful papers and a book (see Weitzman, 1984, 1985, 1986, 1987) Weitzman has proposed that governments should encourage the introduction of economy-wide profit-sharing to replace the traditional fixed-wage system. This proposal has attracted considerable interest, and was an important factor in the British government's decision to subsidise profit-related pay (PRP) in the 1987 Finance Act. Our aim in this chapter is to review Weitzman's proposals and the empirical evidence to date on the topic, as well as to consider the other effects of alternative remuneration systems.

Weitzman himself offers three reasons why the widespread introduction of profit-sharing may improve the functioning of the labour market. In the first place, the method of remuneration may affect the supply of labour. A link between pay and performance may act to stimulate increased effort from the labour force. These productivity effects can also have implications for the demand for labour, if they increase the marginal product of labour. Weitzman labels this argument 'soft-boiled'.

Profit-sharing is also about increased wage-flexibility, arguments referred to by Weitzman as 'medium-boiled'. In contrast to what

227

happens under the traditional wage system, remuneration under profit-sharing varies with product-market conditions. It might be expected that if pay varies rather more over the trade cycle, employment would vary rather less, thereby reducing unemployment during recessions.

These arguments in favour of profit-sharing have been around for many years and cannot, in themselves, explain the current vogue for the proposal. The protagonists' case has recently been given a shot in the arm by what Weitzman calls the 'hard-boiled' justification for profit-sharing, namely the hypothesis that a profit-sharing economy will always display excess demand for labour. According to Weitzman, stagflation is caused by the relative inflexibility of money wages in the face of product-demand shocks, with a monopolistically competitive market-structure underlying a wage-push inflationary spiral. In principle monetary policy can deal with unemployment or inflation but not both. By driving a wedge between the marginal and average cost of labour, Weitzman argues, economy-wide profit-sharing creates a persistent excess demand for labour which ensure that the economy stays at full employment. Since the unemployment problem has been 'solved' by the remuneration system, monetary policy can be effectively targeted at inflation alone. Hence profit-sharing 'cures' stagflation.

Before proceeding to a formal analysis, several points need to be borne in mind. Profit-sharing represents a change in the way that people are paid, but not in the way that firms are managed. It is assumed that these continue to be run on behalf of owners, who seek to maximise profits only. Weitzman is explicit in ruling out any increase in employee participation in decision-making, let alone employee ownership, associated with profit-sharing. Profit-sharing firms are therefore not participatory firms, along the lines analysed for example by Aoki (1980) or Svejnar (1982), nor do they have the income-maximising objectives and employment restrictive behaviour of labour-managed firms (see Meade (1986). They are simply conventional profit-maximising firms in which some predetermined element of profit is used to pay a part of employees' remuneration. The failure to link profit-sharing with employee participation in decision-making has been severely criticised by Nuti (1986), who points out that since workers are being made to bear some proportion of business risks, they deserve some say in the choices that are being taken.

The policy implications also merit attention. Weitzman has called for tax subsidies to encourage workers and firms to adopt and maintain the system, but it is hard to justify this without 'hard-boiled' arguments. If the main impact of profit-sharing is via motivational effects on company performance, it will be privately profitable for firms to introduce it. No significant externalities meriting public subsidy by the government are at stake. Increased labour-market flexibility may have some broader policy merit, but profit-sharing is neither the only nor necessarily the most effective way to improve the link between labour-market conditions and pay. Weitzman, however, claims that economy-wide profit-sharing will shift the economy into a permanent state of excess demand for labour, resolving the problem of stagflation. This is in the interests of the government and society as a whole, but not individual firms, each of which, as we shall see, have an incentive to revert back to fixed-wage contracts provided everyone else continues to profit-share. It is upon this externality, and the requirement for a substantial degree of profit-sharing to sustain the excess demand equilibrium in times of recession, that Weitzman hinges his case for the public subsidiy. From a policy perspective, the issue is therefore not merely about whether profit-sharing affects the functioning of the labour market, but also about the channels through which the mechanism operates. This motivates much of the empirical work discussed below.

Economists with complete faith in free markets might argue that, since profit-sharing is not widespread, it is unlikely in practice to enhance productivity. If firms knew of a remuneration system which improved labour effort, they would introduce it of their own accord. This view perhaps places excessive faith in the free trans-mission of information. More importantly, recent empirical work suggests that profit-sharing is more widespread than hitherto expected. A recent survey found that 21 per cent of companies have at least one all-employee scheme (Smith, 1986). The schemes are concentrated among the large, quoted companies, where 41 per cent have an all-employee scheme. Using the Workplace Industrial Relations Survey, Blanchflower and Oswald (1988) report that 40 per cent of workers in the private manufacturing and non-manu-facturing sectors were eligible to participate in a profit-sharing scheme in 1984.

The large number of firms in the UK already using some form of profit-sharing in part reflects tax policy. In the 1978 Finance Act, a Profit-Sharing Share Scheme was introduced, whereby employers can put shares in their company worth up to 10 per cent of pay into a trust, exempt of corporation tax. If the employee holds the shares for five years, s/he pays no income tax at all on them. The 1980 Finance Act in addition provided tax exemption on five-year 'save as you earn' contracts for the purchase of share options. There were 562 schemes under the 1978 Act and 541 under the 1980 Act in June 1986, but despite the significant tax-breaks involved, the number of workers participating in options schemes remained small. According to Blanchflower and Oswald (1988), some 25 per cent of private-sector workers were involved in a share-ownership scheme in 1984, 20 per cent in a profit-sharing scheme and 15 per cent in value-added bonus schemes, not approved for tax purposes by the Inland Revenue.

Weitzman's claims for profit-sharing are therefore bold and important. The existence of a significant degree of profit-sharing, much of it introduced without the benefit of public subsidy, suggests that there may also be something to the 'soft-boiled' case for profit-sharing. The policy implications of the analysis remain crucial, particularly with PRP growing in the UK. We divide our detailed analysis into the theoretical and the empirical. In section 10.2 we concentrate on theoretical issues while empirical evidence is reviewed in section 10.3. The findings are summarised in section 10.4.

10.2 THEORETICAL ANALYSIS OF PROFIT-SHARING
PROFIT-SHARING – THE WEITZMAN MODEL

The starting-point for Weitzman's claims about the advantages of the share economy is the argument that profit-sharing will boost employment. To illustrate his idea suppose that Anyfirm plc pays wages equal to £200 per week and therefore will employ workers to the point where the additional value added per worker exactly equals £200. Assume that the *average* value added per worker is £300 (to provide a cover for overheads, profits, etc.) and that it actually employs ten people. Suppose that the firm adopts a profit-sharing scheme instead, and pays a base wage of £160 per week (80 per cent of existing remuneration) and a share of gross operating profits equal to £40 [2/7 × (300 − 160)] per worker. As things stand, the worker is indifferent to the new arrangement. However, the firm now has an incentive to hire an extra worker because if it did so, its value added goes up by £200 as before, but its cost of hiring the extra worker only increases by the base wage of £160, plus 2/7 the extra gross operating profits of £40 (= £200 − £160), or a total of £171.43.

Therefore, if the company hires an extra worker, it stands to clear a profit of nearly £30 (£200–£171.43). Under this new contract, Anyfirm plc has an incentive to resist lay-offs and to expand production. When production is expanded, Anyfirm's prices must come down, because more of the product can only be sold if the price is lowered. The expansion of Anyfirm creates an external benefit to other firms. Therefore, if many firms in the economy go over to profit-sharing, there will be a built-in bias towards eliminating unemployment, expanding output, and lowering prices. It is this macro effect which Weitzman has emphasised.

More formally, the key properties of a profit-sharing economy, can be summarised in the simple model of Weitzman (1985). We represent aggregate demand as:

$$Y = \alpha G + \beta \; \frac{M}{P} \tag{10.1}$$

where Y is aggregate real output, G represents total government real spending on goods, M denotes money balances, and P is the aggregate price level. The total supply of labour is exogenously fixed at L^* and production occurs with constant marginal product, a, providing a labour-supply-constrained maximum for GDP, denoted Y^*.

Considering the wage economy first, suppose that the money wage is exogenously fixed, for each of the n monopolistically competitor firms, subscripted i:

$$W(L_i) = W \tag{10.2}$$

Now, if the availability of labour is not a binding constraint, a profit-maximising firm equates marginal revenue to marginal cost, which, in the aggregate, yields the implication:

$$P = \frac{\mu W}{a} \tag{10.3}$$

where prices are a mark-up of the money wage which depends on the elasticity of demand and the marginal product of labour. Using the aggregate demand schedule, (10.1), target output, $\hat{Y}$, is given by

$$\hat{Y} \equiv \alpha G + \frac{\beta M a}{\mu W} \tag{10.4}$$

Define the tautness of the system as

$$T \equiv \hat{Y} - Y^* \tag{10.5}$$

where $(T > 0)$ is a region of positive demand for labour and $(T < 0)$ is a region of negative excess demand for labour. Table 10.1 summarises the behaviour of Y and P in the two regimes. The economy in regions $(T < 0)$ exhibits textbook Keynesian behaviour – prices are just a simple mark-up on wages, and are unaffected by government policy except through wages. However, output responds directly to changes in G and M.

TABLE 10.1   Short-run behaviour of a major macroeconomic variables in a wage system

Variable	$T < 0$	$T < 0$
Y	$\alpha G + \dfrac{\beta M a}{\mu W}$	Y^*
P	$\dfrac{\mu W}{a}$	$\dfrac{\beta M}{Y^* - \alpha G}$

In the excess demand for labour $(T > 0)$ region, aggregate output is constrained by the maximum feasible amount, Y^*, and P is then determined from the aggregate demand condition, (10.1). In this region, the economy displays classical characteristics – government aggregate-demand management has no influence on real output, but does influence the price level *directly*. Weitzman (1985) asserts that 'the *realpolitik* of wage capitalism, with its less-than-perfect labour markets and downard-inflexible wages, has the system residing in region ($T < 0$) most of the time ... The relevant region for most short-term policy analysis is the Keynesian region ($T < 0$) (Weitzman, 1985, p. 16).

Turning to the profit-sharing economy, assume that each firm pays its workers according to

$$W(L_i) = \theta + \lambda \left[\frac{R_i(L_i) - \theta L_i}{L_i} \right]$$ (10.6)

where $R_i(L_i)$ denotes total revenue as a function of labour, θ denotes the base wage, and $\tau > 0$, represents the profit-sharing coefficient. In the spirit of the comparison that is being undertaken, θ and τ are treated as exogenously fixed in the short run. Net profits may be rewritten as:

$$\Pi_i(L_i) \equiv (1 - \lambda) [R_i(L_i) - \theta L_i]$$ (10.7)

and if unlimited amounts of labour are available to be hired on contract (10.6), the firm will choose to hire workers up to the point where:

$$R'_i(L_i) = \theta$$ (10.8)

where $R'_i(.)$ denotes the marginal revenue product of labour. This is to be compared with the wage economy, where it is wages which are equated to the marginal product.

The analysis for the determination of Y and P parallels that of the wage economy, except that in the expressions in Table 10.1, we need to replace W with θ. If W^* is the market-clearing wage (in the sense that tautness $T = 0$) and

$$\theta < W^* \leqslant W$$ (10.9)

we shall have the wage economy residing in the ($T < 0$) region, while the profit-sharing system will operate in a region of *positive excess demand for labour*.

This is at the heart of Weitzman's propositions, and it yields the implications (see Table 10.1) that a wage economy operates like a textbook Keynesian model – output responds to aggregate demand policies, while prices are a simple mark-up on costs and do not respond *directly* to government policy. In contrast, a profit-sharing economy displays classical characteristics, despite the pay parameters being fixed, with output at the full employment level, while prices respond directly to monetary and fiscal policies. Hence, the profit-sharing economy is more likely to resist stagflation. For example, a rise in oil prices has no short-term macroeconomic effects in a share economy (we may represent the effects of an adverse supply shock by a deterioration in the marginal productivity parameter), but it increases prices and reduces output in the wage economy.

Some problems

The wage system and the profit-sharing one have the same long-run equilibrium (see Weitzman, 1983) but Weitzman does not provide a discussion of the transition from short run to long run. The different short run properties in part derive from the implicit assumption that firms could lower the existing total compensation of workers in a share economy, but not in a wage economy. Notice (as is clear from the case of Anyfirm plc), that when an extra worker is hired, the total pay of each existing worker falls (in our example by 1.3 per cent). Therefore, existing workers in Anyfirm plc will be made worse-off in the short run. It is therefore crucial that employers feel able to reduce average total remuneration (in the first instance) for, if they were to feel that they must continue to pay the same amount to each worker as in the existing wage system, introducing profit-sharing will not alter hiring behaviour. For example, in the ace of Anytime plc, if the firm felt that it must continue to pay its workers £200 per week (say this is the going rate for the job), then the extra cost of hiring an additional worker remains £200, and it no longer has an incentive to expand production. If firms felt committed to paying a certain total amount, the manner in which this amount was divided into the two components: base wage and profit-linked pay, would become irrelevant. This would be merely labels.

   To see this a little more formally, merely note that constrained profit-maximisation of the form:

$$\max_{L} \Pi = (1-\lambda)\,[R(L) - \theta L] \qquad\qquad (10.10a)$$

subject to

$$\theta + \lambda \left[\frac{R(L) - \theta L}{L} \right] = W \qquad (10.10b)$$

is equivalent to

$$\max_{L} \Pi = R(L) - W(L) \qquad (10.11)$$

This is trivially demonstrated by rewriting (10.10b) as

$$\theta = \left[\frac{1}{1-\lambda} \right] \left[W - \lambda \frac{R(L)}{L} \right] \qquad (10.12)$$

and, substituting (10.12) into (10.10a), to obtain

$$(1-\lambda)[R(L) - \left(\frac{1}{1-\lambda} \right) WL + \left(\frac{\lambda}{1-\lambda} \right) R(L)] = R(L) - WL, \text{ as}$$

required.

As an example of a theoretical model of wage determination where employers would feel committed to pay a fixed amount, consider the following. Suppose that wages are 'too high' today, and the reason that they do not fall in spite of mass unemployment is that firms believe that lower wages would be counter-productive. This could occur if workers' productivity depends on the wage that they are paid, and firms may not, then wish to lower the wage if doing so were to significantly reduce productivity. This intuition has been formalised in the so-called 'efficiency wage' theories (see Stiglitz, 1984, and Yellen, 1984). For example, a cut in wages might be more than offset by an increase in costs associated with a greater turnover in employment or lead to a significant deterioration in the average quality of a firm's labour force as better workers leave. In light of such factors, a firm will choose an optimal level of remuneration which will not be affected by profit-sharing. If firms do feel committed to paying a particular amount, their hiring behaviour will not be altered by profit-sharing (see Appendix).

There is evidence that this is what firms are saying themselves. For example, Incomes Data Services recently quoted the following response from a firm:

As we understand the Chancellor's proposals, if the company goes into difficulties the payroll costs would be cut automatically by the need to no longer pay out a profit-share. Presumably this would result in the earnings of the employees falling below the going market rate – a position which cannot be sustained for other than a very short period. This would inevitably result in a demand from the employees for an increase in basic wages, which would no doubt be conceded by a management who are concerned about the demotivation of a rapidly shrinking labour force.

In this case, the wage and profit-sharing systems will have the *same properties in the short run*.

To be completely convincing, Weitzman's model must therefore be supplemented with a description of how wages are set. As things stand, one must agree with Nordhaus 1986 that 'in an equilibrium setting, the excess demand-for-labour proposition is still unproven' (Nordhaus, 1986, p. 25).

Does profit-sharing reduce wage pressure?

Weitzman (1987) and Jackman (1987) have argued that profit-sharing reduces the non-accelerating inflation rate of unemployment (NAIRU). In order to understand what follows, it is convenient to summarise Weitzman's (1987) argument on why profit-sharing will reduce unemployment in a unionised economy.

A key feature of the model is the distinction between 'insiders' (i.e. those who already have a job) and 'outsiders' (those who are unemployed or laid off, see also Lindbeck and Snower, 1986). Now, if lay-offs occur by seniority (which is empirically plausible in the UK, see e.g. Oswald and Turnbull, 1985), and the union's preferences are those of the steady-state median voter, we can think about bargaining taking place between a firm that is interested only in profits, and a representative tenured worker who is interested only in pay. In this case, wages are assumed to be set by maximising the function:

$$\varphi = W^b \, \Pi \tag{10.13}$$

where W = manual wages, Π = profits, and b might be interpreted as resulting from asymmetries in the bargaining procedure or parties' beliefs on this, see Binmore, Rubinstein and Wolinsky, 1985.

This wage-setting process is grafted onto the simple macroeconomic model which has been employed in Weitzman (1985), and which is discussed above.

In this section, Weitzman (1987) shows that for *b* sufficiently large, the economy will have an equilibrium rate of unemployment:

$$\bar{u} = 1 - \frac{b\mu F/L^*}{b(\mu - 1) - 1}$$

In contrast, remuneration could be determined by a profit-sharing system where, recall, workers are paid by the formula (10.6) where $\lambda > 0$ is now used to denote the profit-sharing coefficient:

$$W(L_i) = \theta + \lambda \left[\frac{R_i(L_i) - \theta L_i}{L_i} \right]$$

Under this contract, a profit-maximising firm will employ workers (if they are available) up to the point at which $R'(L) = \theta$, instead of $R'(L) = W$, as in a wage economy.

Figure 10.1 illustrates the effects of varying total remuneration on the objective function, φ. Initially, in a wage economy, ($\lambda = 0$), φ is represented by the curve *BAG*, which is maximised at wage W_o, which is greater than the competitive wage, W^*. Therefore, we have unemployment. If we introduce profit-sharing, the new curve is *BHCJ*.

The reason why the curve drawn for positive λ (the profit-sharing firm) is below that drawn for $\lambda = 0$ (the wage firm) is that, at any given level of total remuneration, $W > W^*$, the profit-sharing firm employs more workers than the corresponding wage firm. Specifically, it employs workers beyond the point at which $R'(L) = W$ (since it equates $R'(L)$ to the lower base wage, (θ) and, thereafter, at any given level of W, it makes lower profits than the corresponding wage firm. Hence, since $\theta = W^*\Pi$, at any given level of W, the value of φ for a profit-sharing firm must be lower than that of a wage firm. To see why the curve under profit-sharing is *BHCJ*, start at point *B*. In a wage economy, this represents full

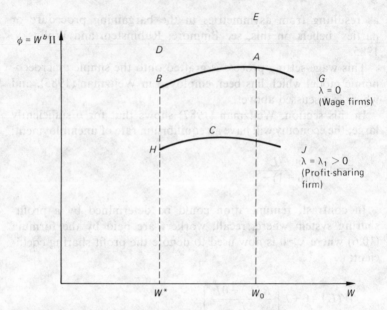

FIGURE 10.1   The effects of varying total remuneration

A   Initial equilibrium (with employment) in the wage economy
B   Full employment equilibrium
C   Analogue of A in a profit-sharing economy (albeit, dominated by B)
D B with tax incentives
E A with tax incentives

employment ($l^* = L^*/n$) with wage W^*. Now, if we convert to a profit-sharing economy such that:

$$\hat{\theta} + \lambda \left[\frac{R(l^*)}{l^*} - \hat{\theta} \right] = W^*$$

we shall remain at point B, for although $R'(l^*) > \hat{\theta}$, the firm cannot attract any extra workers. Hence, total remuneration and employment are as in the wage economy.

Suppose, now, that the firm raises its base wage to $\hat{\theta} + \varepsilon$. At employment l^*, total remuneration is $W^* + \varepsilon$. Since all other firms are assumed to continue to pay W^*, this firm can now attract workers from other firms (and it wants to, since $R'(l^*) > \hat{\theta} + \varepsilon$).

Therefore, employment rises in this firm, and workers continue to be hired as long as total remuneration falls back to W^*. In this new equilibrium, the firm's profits are lower than they were are point B since it is employing more than is warranted by $R'(L) = W^*$. Therefore, the new outcome lies vertically below point B (somewhere along the segment BH).

The point H is reached when total remuneration equals W^* and $R'(L) = \theta$, for, therefore, if θ is raised, total remuneration does increase, for it is not diluted by the entry of new workers. Hereafter, we move along the curve HCJ (which is the analogue of BAG).

As drawn on Figure 10.1, the corner competitive solution, B, dominates a point like C. (which is the analogue of A). This will be true for sufficiently large λ (see Weitzman, 1987, for a formal proof). Hence Weitzman asserts that the introduction of profit-sharing can lead us to a situation of full employment. If, starting at point B, the unions pressed for higher wages, they would, initially, be frustrated by the firm taking on more workers; and φ would fall along BH. Eventually, at point H, further union demands would not be resisted, but the lower level of profit caused by taking on more workers, means that the size of the 'cake' has shrunk. Therefore, the union will realise that it is in its interest to stick to the competitive wage.

However, the reader will have noticed that, evaluated in terms of φ, the wage economy is preferred (by the individual union and firm) to the share economy, and, specifically, the initial situation, A, is preferred to the competitive equilibrium, B. Therefore, it is not in the interests of an individual union and firm to switch to a profit-sharing system. Weitzman proposes the use of tax-incentives to deal with this problem, and we analyse this issue next.

Tax incentives and profit-sharing

The British government is proposing the introduction of tax incentives to encourage profit-sharing. If these tax incentives are conditional on having profit-sharing, it is possible to make the competitive equilibrium (with profit-sharing) more attractive than the unemployment equilibrium with no profit-sharing. Under the proposals a slice of profit-sharing income will not be taxed. This is, of course, equivalent to a subsidy at the rate s to profit-linked income, and we shall, for convenience, represent it in that way.

Insiders will vote for a conversion to a profit-sharing system if:

$$\left[W^* + s\lambda \, \frac{\Pi(W^*)}{L(W^*)} \right]^b \Pi(W^*) > W^b \, \Pi(W\!o) \tag{10.14}$$

i.e., if point D is higher than point A. For sufficiently high s, this is always possible.

Wadhwani (1986) argues that the above analysis is seriously incomplete, because it ignores the possibility of a cosmetic profit-sharing scheme. To fix ideas, compare the point D with the simple alternative where the firm and union could proceed just as they do now, in agreeing on the total level of remuneration, W, with the firm then determining employment on the assumption that W represents its marginal cost. Given the exogenously fixed profit-share parameter, λ, and the actual profit outcome, Π, the component $\lambda \, \Pi(W)/L(W)$ will then be called 'profit-sharing' income for the purposes of the Inland Revenue. This alternative could be preferable to point D even at the current level of total remuneration, W_o, if

$$\left[W_o + s\lambda \, \frac{\Pi(W_o)}{L(W_o)} \right]^b \Pi(W_o) > \left[W^* + s\lambda \, \frac{\Pi(W^*)}{L(W^*)} \right]^b \Pi(W^*) \tag{10.15}$$

which would correspond to point E being higher than point D in Figure 10.1. Now, condition (10.15) will hold in a wide variety of cases, and it clearly cannot be ruled out on an *a priori* basis. Note, of course, that we do not get full employment in this situation provided that a condition like (10.15) holds for some W (instead of $W_o) > W^*$.

Formally, all this just relies on the already-mentioned (trivial) fact that profit-maximisation subject to a remuneration constraint in a profit-sharing economy is equivalent to being in a wage economy.

We should emphasise that none of this depends on the union imposing any explicit hiring restrictions that impede the maximisation of profits on the part of the firm. Instead, it is merely the recognition by both parties that they are jointly better-off if the firm chooses employment to maximise profits under the assumption that it must pay a certain level of total remuneration, W. In this case, of course, its incentive to hire has not changed. Further, this alternative arrangement does not merely make both parties better-off, but it is something that they can both achieve quite easily. Specifically, this is quite different from the standard argument that both parties can be made better-off by bargaining over employment.

In the British context, there are already some signs that some of the profit-related pay schemes will be cosmetic – for example, the TUC's guidelines for negotiations includes an Appendix with a fully worked-out example of a cosmetic scheme!

Thus, it seems likely that tax incentives will lead to cosmetic profit-sharing schemes, for this will be in the self-interest of firms and workers. However, a legitimate question that one might ask is whether this result is robust to changes in the specification of the model. One possible extension is one where unions care about employment, and it is to this that we turn next.

Models in which unions care about employment

In an imaginative paper, Jackman (1987) has argued that introducing profit-sharing will induce a union that cares about both wages and employment to choose a lower wage. The reason for this is that profit-sharing changes the trade-off between wages and employment that the union faces. In a wage economy, a 1 per cent cut in total remuneration leads to an *h* per cent (where *h* is the elasticity of demand for labour) increase in employment, while, in a share economy, only a 1 per cent in the base wage is needed to achieve the same effect on employment. Therefore, the union will, in general, choose a wage that yields higher employment than in a wage economy. However, Wadhwani (1986) argues that Jackman does not give sufficient weight to the possibility that the union and firm might prefer the wage economy to a profit-sharing economy because, at any given level of total remuneration, the latter is associated with lower profits (largely because it is not true in the very special model which he considers).

Wadhwani's arguments regarding the possibility of a cosmetic profit-sharing scheme may continue to apply. To see this, simply replace φ in (10.13) by :

$$\varphi^1 = (WL^\varepsilon)^b \, \Pi \qquad (10.16)$$

for some small $\varepsilon > 0$, with (10.13) being a special case of (10.16) as $\varepsilon \to 0$. Now, provided, that ε is sufficiently small, it is still true that, at any given level of remuneration, the value of φ^1 is higher in a wage economy compared to a profit-sharing economy. The reason for this is that profits, Π, are higher in a wage economy, and the extra employment in a profit-sharing economy does not, for sufficiently small ε, increase the value of φ^1 enough to offset this effect. Provided that the wage economy is privately optimal, the union and the firm would still prefer a cosmetic profit-sharing scheme over a genuine one. On the other hand, for sufficiently large ε a profit-sharing system is preferred to a wage system, for the union utility derived from the extra employment in a profit-sharing economy may be enough to offset the fact that profits are lower. However, in this case, one still needs to explain why profit-sharing does not arise autonomously, for, if it is preferred by the two parties, there must be a presumption that they would introduce it. Thus, in this situation, one cannot justify the introduction of tax incentives to encourage profit-sharing.

Another result of interest in this area is that of Johnson (1986) (see also Pohjola, 1986). He asserts that even if firms and unions only bargain over wages and not employment, the introduction of profit-sharing enables them to achieve the 'efficient bargain' outcome. To the extent that the 'efficient bargain' level of employment is higher than the one which comes out of the 'right-to-manage' models, profit-sharing is seen to increase employment, and leads to a Pareto-improving change. However, one then has to explain why profit-sharing does not arise autonomously. Presumably, the reason why one cannot attain the efficient bargain outcome by bargaining about employment is that workers feel that the firm may 'cheat'. However, given 'creative accounting', the firm can 'cheat' in a profit-sharing system as well.

Finally, note that the firm and the union prefer the wage to the share system, and if they bargain over both wages and employment, then the introduction of profit-sharing in this situation is even more certain to lead to a cosmetic scheme for workers now can directly restrict the hiring of new workers to dilute their pay (as Weitzman, 1987, concedes).

The effects of sharing on employment variability

Sometimes, a distinction is made between the effects of profit-sharing on employment stability, and the level of employment (see e.g. the UK Green Paper, 1986). Within Weitzman's framework, this distinction is artificial and misleading. In Weitzman (1983 and 1985) the excess demand for labour leads to full employment, and once there, employment is stable – so, in fact, the two go hand in hand. Equally, at the other extreme, if wages are determined according to the efficiency wage theories, the wage and share systems are isomorphic in both the short run and the long run. In this case, sharing has no effect on either the level or stability of employment.

Of course, one can construct a different argument for the view that profit-sharing enhances macro-stability. It would be based on the fact that profit-sharing makes the remuneration of labour respond more *quickly* to macroeconomic shocks (see e.g. Mitchell, 1982, who argues that it would help to make a disinflation programme less costly by making wages more directly responsive to aggregate demand). Specifically, wage contracts in the USA often run for three years, and if major unexpected macroeconomic shocks occur during the contract period (e.g. the oil shocks of 1983 and 1979) firms have to wait for the end of the contract before they can make a plea for a change in wages. Hence, in the interim, the burden of adjustment falls on quantities (e.g. employment). Having a proportion of wages linked to profits (which some US firms report on a quarterly basis) would enable some of the burden of adjustment to be borne by prices. Therefore, profit-sharing might be viewed as a way of increasing the frequency of wage adjustments without the attendant additional negotiating costs which would be necessary in a fixed-wage system.

The above argument is quite sensible. However, in the UK, 95 per cent of private-sector settlements occur on annual basis, while firms report profit figures on a half-yearly basis. Therefore, the advantage gained through a quicker response to unexpected shocks is much smaller in the UK.

Could profit-sharing lead to higher inflation or unemployment?

When arguing for the introduction of profit-sharing, Weitzman amongst others, has made much of the fact that there are models in which it does some good but 'it is difficult to imagine scenarios where profit-sharing damages economy' (see Weitzman, 1986). This justification – i.e. that there is no downside risk – takes too sanguine a view of such a fundamental institutional change. It is worth noting the fact that profit-sharing will lead to a greater decentralisation of wage decisions, and it is possible that this may actually end up by *worsening*, rather than improving stagflation (this argument is developed further in Wadhwani, 1987b). For example, one reason why greater decentralisation may be harmful is the fact that the demand-for-labour curve facing the union is likely to be less elastic (because of the lower share of labour costs in total costs). This will induce the union to demand a higher wage.

It is also of interest that many employers are voicing fears that PRP may, in the end, be inflationary. This arises from their view of the British psychology of wage-determination. There is a deeply-ingrained notion among British workers that the fixed wage should be enough for them to maintain their standard of living, and that PRP or any gains accruing from an employee share scheme are no more than the 'cream' on top. This is, of course, hardly surprising. However, were workers to continue to expect to get wage increases at the same rate, with the PRP component not influencing wage negotiations (and there is survey evidence suggesting that payments from employee share schemes do not influence wage negotiations) total remuneration would rise. There is no point in arguing (as the Chancellor does) that employers would never allow this to happen. For example, in an efficiency wage context, if the workers' notion of the total remuneration that was 'fair' went up (as it would here), the employer would find it in his interests to pay more. We shall be examining the empirical evidence regarding this later.

Profit-sharing and productivity

In this section, we will briefly survey the effects that economic theorists have suggested profit-sharing could have on company performance. The bulk of authors have argued for a positive relationship but an important body of literature argues the reverse – that profit-sharing will reduce productivity. It should be noted that the theory in this area remains for the most part discursive, with attention devoted to isolating the performance variables which might be affected by a change in remuneration system and to specifying ways of measuring the changes.

Profit-sharing might be expected to influence corporate performance via (i) the supply of the labour force; (ii) the productive skills of the labour force, and (iii) greater identification between workers and management. Let us consider each in turn.

(i) The supply of labour

Profit-sharing is a particular sort of group incentive scheme, with rewards to performance assessed at the level of the enterprise and distributed to all employees. This is in contrast to a fixed wage-payment, which offers workers no direct economic interest in the quality or intensity of their work. To ensure an adequate supply of effort with fixed wages, firms must therefore set up a complex monitoring system of supervisors and foremen, possibly at considerable expense. If workers are materially motivated, they are likely to work harder under a scheme linking remuneration to effort, however indirectly. Moreover, since in a group incentive scheme, an individual's pay depends on the efforts of his/her peers as well as him/herself, people will be motivated to monitor the labour supply of their fellow-employees more keenly. Positive peer-group pressure to increase work intensity may replace the traditional tendency to overlook, or even encourage, colleagues' shirking.

This argument hinges on the existence of a clear and significant relationship between effort and remuneration. However, profits vary for many reasons other than labour effort – for example, because of fluctuations in raw materials prices or exchange rates. Moreover, an individual can have virtually no effect on the performance of a large enterprise. Hence individualised incentive schemes relating each worker's effort directly to his/her pay may be preferable. Jensen and Meckling (1979) have argued that, if profit-sharing is contrasted with individual incentive systems, it will be found to encourage shirking. While the latter scheme bases rewards on marginal products, profit-sharing gives each worker only a small fraction of the incremental profit derived from their additional effort. The trade-off between shirking and income is therefore distorted to favour shirking. The problem is magnified by the diffusion of property rights over the profit stream. It is argued that, with monitoring of labour-supply crucial to maintain effort-levels, the right to appropriate the surplus should be vested in a central monitor. Under profit-sharing, a part of the surplus is instead distributed to the labour force.

The property-rights problem associated with profit-sharing cannot be ignored. However, the fact remains that individualised incentive schemes are not always feasible or desirable. There are many forms of technology in which individual marginal products cannot be separately identified, or at least the cost of so doing is prohibitively expensive. Assembly-line-production processes are a case in point. In these circumstances, the appropriate comparison is between fixed wages and profit-sharing, and the latter *does* provide incentives in support of positive collusion to raise effort. Moreover, with certain technologies the benefits of individualised incentives may be more than offset by the losses induced by rivalry in the workplace and competitive disruption in search of private gain. To the extent that production is a team effort, with strong externalities from mutually supporting efforts, profit-sharing will be a valid and effective incentive system.

(ii) The productive skills of the labour force

Profit-sharing may increase the productive skills of the labour force via its effects on labour tenure. Improved group awareness and a heightened sense of responsibility flowing from the new remuneration system may generate superior conflict resolution, which is likely to reduce labour turnover (see Jones and Svejnar, 1985). The resulting increase in average labour tenure translates itself into higher productivity through its positive effects on firm-specific human capital; the skills and knowledge that workers acquire in association with the particular company in which they are employed. One might expect, for example, increases in the average rate of capacity-utilisation as familiarity with operating and repairing machinery improves, or better functioning of work groups as knowledge about the strengths and weaknesses of particular workers improves. Moreover, many productive skills are acquired with the help of fellow-workers, who will be more willing to help in the knowledge that some proportion of the resulting incremental profits will accrue to them. From the firm's point of view, finally, reduced labour turnover will cut recruitment and training costs. These effects are analogous to the 'voice' impact of trade unions on productivity (see Freeman, 1976).

The relationship between labour turnover and productivity is not necessarily monotonic however. As one comes down from initially high levels of labour turnover, the productivity effects are likely to be significant. They will then probably tail off, and may ultimately become negative if low turnover is associated with labour inflexibility. For example, the resulting insularity of attitudes could restrict the influx of new ideas, with the labour force becoming resistant to new work methods or to technological advance because of the impact on recruitment.

(iii) Greater identification between workers and management

The most-frequently-cited productivity-effects stem from the impact of profit-sharing on the character of the workplace. These effects were prevalent in the British government's thinking behind the introduction of PRP (see the *Consultative Document on Profit-Related Pay* (Green Paper, 1986)), and have been analysed best in the industrial-relations tradition (see Bradley and Gelb, 1983, 1986). To quote Cable and Fitzroy 'participatory firms ... will produce better outcomes than traditional firms if the *negative* collusion to maximise one party's share ... can be replaced by *positive* collusion to maximise joint wealth' (Cable and Fitzroy, 1980, p. 166). It is hoped that profit-sharing could change the character of the workplace by eliminating the traditional conflict between workers and manager – the 'them and us' attitude.

There are many ways in which an effect of this sort could be felt. Workers may be less likely to strike or undertake damaging industrial action, partly because of the impact on their own remuneration and partly because of improved employee–manager relations. Better labour morale will show up in lower rates of absenteeism, greater willingness to work together and improved labour flexibility with respect to work practices. The resulting improvements in communication channels from workers to management can also help to eliminate numerous microeconomic-level organisational inefficiencies that workers have no incentive to disclose in a non-cooperative setting, and may in fact promote. This better use of workers' organisational know-how could be coupled with a greater willingness to implement decisions from higher up, in particular with regard to new machinery and technical change. Indeed, rather than resisting technological advance, it is possible that workers will actually generate innovative proposals in their own areas of expertise.

In contrast, James Meade (1986) has argued that, far from reducing conflict between managers and workers, profit-sharing schemes will increase it because there are incentives for managers to cheat in the definition of profit. Management have ample scope for dissimulation in the construction of the profit figure upon which workers' pay will be based. Such problems could lead to conflicts over company accounts.

10.3 EMPIRICAL EVIDENCE

The propositions

The theoretical literature therefore makes a number of claims about the effects of profit-sharing, which can be examined empirically.

Proposition I

(i) Changes in money supply (or, more generally, aggregate demand) should not cause output to deviate from its 'full employment' level.
(ii) Oil price increases and 'wage push' should not lead to higher price inflation.

Proposition II

(i) the base wage (but not total remuneration) should be regarded as the marginal cost of labour.
(ii) Firms should wish to employ more workers at the current pay parameters.

Proposition III

Total remuneration per worker will be lower.

Proposition IV

Profit-sharing firms will have higher productivity.

Economy-wide profit-sharing – the Japanese case

Weitzman asserts that 'Japan offers a living laboratory for many of the ideas' and, further, that 'it displays all the broad tendencies predicted by the theory' (Weitzman, 1984, p. 76). Wadhwani (1987a) has attempted to shed some light on the validity of these implications by looking at the Japanese experience.

An aspect of Proposition II is that firms in a share-economy would wish to employ more workers at the current pay-parameters. Using data on the proportion of firms who report a shortage of labour, there is no evidence that Japan is special in this respect. Over the period 1964–84, the proportion in the UK is much higher than in Japan (22.5 per cent as opposed to 11.3 per cent). If we compare Japan with four other European countries (for whom comparable data is available), Japan had the smallest proportion of firms reporting a shortage of labour over the period 1976–83, i.e. 2.3 per cent in Japan, as against 3.8 per cent in France, 3.2 per cent in Italy, 7.1 per cent in the Netherlands and 4.7 per cent in West Germany. On the basis of these numbers, it is difficult to believe that Japan experienced a greater degree of excess demand for labour than other countries. Though official unemployment in Japan is low, the statistics seriously understate the extent of the underutilisation of labour; each percentage point of unemployment in Japan is associated with a shortfall in output that is five times as great as that experienced in the UK or USA.

Wadhwani (1987b) argues that it is important to recognise that there is a two-tier labour market in Japan. There are those who are covered by the 'lifetime employment' system. These workers are, typically, male, and are often unionised. Then, there are the so-called 'temporary' workers, who also receive a lower rate of pay (for example, they often do not qualify for the bonus payments). They consist, in the main, of females, or males with relatively little formal education. The mobility of these marginal workers is high, and very few belong to unions. Given this structure, it would appear that, as in Meade's Discriminating Labour Capital Partnerships, Japanese firms cannot be in an excess demand for labour regime, because the temporary workers are hired/fired just as in a wage economy.

Turning to Proposition I, which is directly related to the stag flation-resisting properties of an economy, it is worth reminding ourselves of the Japanese experience after the first oil shock. Among OECD countries, Japan experienced the sharpest slowing in the growth of output after the first oil shock, while inflation reached 19 per cent. According to Wadhwani (1987a) changes in the money supply did cause output to deviate from 'potential output' in Japan, and, this, therefore, constitutes evidence against Proposition I (i). As for Proposition I (ii), the effects of cost-shocks on inflation, his results are consistent with the view that rises in wages and input prices explain the current change in product prices, with changes in the money supply being relatively unimportant.

Freeman and Weitzman (1986) use Japanese data to focus on Proposition II. They reject the hypothesis that bonus payments in Japan, which constitute a quarter of workers' pay, are just another form of wage payment, on the grounds that the two behave differently over the cycle. Bonuses respond more to changes in profits and revenues than do wages. They estimate employment equations which include the base wage and the bonus on the right hand side. Their most general model yields

$$\ln L_t = 9.13 - 0.003t + 0.191 \ln Y_t + 0.421 \ln L_{t-1} + 0.121 \ln B_{t-1}$$
$$\quad (0.003) \ (0.04) \qquad (0.11) \qquad\qquad (0.06)$$
$$\qquad\qquad\qquad\qquad\qquad\qquad\qquad\qquad - 0.241 \ln W_{t-1}$$
$$\qquad\qquad\qquad\qquad\qquad\qquad\qquad\qquad\quad (0.08)$$

with bonus (B) and wage equations being estimated simultaneously where t denotes time and figures in parentheses are standard errors. They therefore find a positive significant coefficient on the bonus but a negative one on the wage, which supports the view that the bonus is not regarded as part of the marginal cost of labour.

These important findings are tested again by Estrin, Grout and Wadhwani (1987) who show that, though robust to many specification changes, the result is sensitive to one particular variation. If, instead of attempting to explain the employment decision conditional on output (Y) we include the capital stock, the result is not sustained. A specification which includes the capital stock (instead of output) is the traditional, neoclassical specification of the demand for labour, and has been estimated with some degree of success in recent years (see, for example, Symons and Layard, 1984). The results under this specification provide no evidence that the bonus depresses employment less than the base wage. Both the base wage and the bonus–wage ratio are statistically insignificant.

Our reading of the evidence for the Japanese economy on Propositions I and II, is therefore that the share economy scores, at most, one-half out of four. What inference should we draw: that the Japanese bonus systems are not really profit-sharing, or that Weitzman's algebra is flawed? The explanation favoured by Freeman and Weitzman appears closer to the former. They argue that only 2.25 per cent of a Japanese worker's total pay should be regarded as genuine profit-sharing income by estimating an impact elasticity of the bonus with respect to profits of 0.09, and then using the fact that about 25 per cent of total pay is in the form of a bonus payment (0.09 × 0.25 = 0.0225).

However, this significantly understates the true response of bonuses to profits. This is for two reasons:

(i) They only consider the *impact* elasticity of profits on bonuses – yet forward-looking employers might also be concerned with the dynamic effects.
(ii) When they relate the bonus to the base wage and profits, they ignore the fact that profits affect the base wage as well.

If we take these factors into account, Wadhwani (1987a) argues that a more reasonable estimate of the share of Japanese worker's total pay that can be regarded as genuine profit-sharing income is 15 per cent. Moreover, one cannot assert that the bonus component is not a part of the marginal cost of labour and also hold that most of the bonus is a 'disguised wage'.

The implication of this is that we should not use Japan as an argument for introducing profit-sharing elsewhere. Either Japan does not have a genuine profit-sharing economy, in which case its experience is not relevant, or it has, in which case we must explain why it does not appear to exhibit many of the desirable properties of such a system.

The effects of profit-sharing on employment in the UK

In this section, we attempt to learn from the experience of British firms that already experiment with various forms of sharing arrangements.

We begin with survey evidence. According to Proposition II, profit-sharing encourages wage moderation. Yet, as we have discussed earlier, some fear that it could be inflationary because workers could view it as a payment in addition to an adequate wage. In one survey regarding the efficacy of the UK government proposals for PRP, 81 per cent of trade unionists and 84 per cent of managers thought that it would have little effect on wages or employment.

The existing econometric evidence on employment effects is mixed. The basic methodology employed is to estimate labour demand and remuneration equations of the form:

$$\ln L = \alpha_0 \ln W + \alpha_1 \left(\frac{B}{W} \right) + \alpha_2\, PSDM + \gamma_1 X$$

$$\ln W = \beta_0 \left(\frac{B}{W} \right) + \beta_1\, PSDM + \gamma_2 N$$

where *PSDM* is a profit-sharing dummy, and X and N are other relevant determinants of employment and wages. We have deliberately concentrated solely on the coefficients of interest.

We may test Proposition II (i) by examining whether $\hat{\alpha}_1 = 0$. If we reject that hypothesis, we may test the view that the firm takes the total level of compensation as the marginal cost of labour by examining whether $\hat{\alpha}_0 = \hat{\alpha}_1$. A significant value for α_2 would suggest that profit-sharing affects productivity and, thence, employment.

In the remuneration equation, Proposition III would require that $\beta_0 < -1$, (when $\beta_1 = 0$) for it is this that would lead to a fall in total remuneration under profit-sharing. A value of $\beta_0 > -1$ would be consistent with the view that profit-sharing actually *raises* wages.

There are two studies using firm-level data in the UK on this subject. Estrin and Wilson (1986) use a sample of fifty-two medium-sized firms in the UK engineering and metal-working sectors over the period 1978–82. 10 per cent of these firms operate a profit-sharing scheme under the 1978 Act, and 30 per cent operate their own value-added scheme (which does not receive any tax privileges). No firm in the sample changes category from non-profit-sharing to profit-sharing over the period. The scale of profit-sharing is typically very small, with only 3 per cent of earnings on average in any year, though it reaches 10 per cent in some firms.

The other study, by Wadhwani and Wall (1988), uses data on larger firms (the average number of employees is 6000, as against an average of 1300 in the Estrin and Wilson sample). This sample contains ninety-nine firms, of whom eighteen have had a scheme of some kind over the sample period (1972–82). Some of these are schemes approved under the 1978 Act, while others precede it. Estrin and Wilson (1986) estimate a special case of this model, where $\alpha_0 = \alpha_1$, with interest being confined to α_2 in the employment equation. In addition, they set $\beta_0 = -1$, and estimate β_1 in the remuneration equation. They obtain $\hat{\beta}_1 = -0.038$ (1.97) (figures in parentheses are *t*-statistics) suggesting that remuneration in profit-sharing firms is, on average, 4 per cent lower than that in non-profit-sharing firms. This supports Proposition III. In the employment equation, $\hat{\alpha}_2 = 0.124$ (2.26) suggests that profit-sharing boosts employment by 12 per cent. Note, though, that because they set $\alpha_0 = \alpha_1$, the Weitzman effect (Proposition VI) and the productivity effect (Proposition II) are both subsumed within this estimate. In fact, because the labour-demand curve is estimated to be highly inelastic, of the total estimated increase in employment of 13 per cent, Estrin and Wilson suggest that less than 0.5 per cent can be attributed to a Weitzman-type wedge effect. The remaining 12.5 per cent is attributed to productivity effects.

The evidence in Wadhwani and Wall is somewhat different from that of Estrin and Wilson. In the first place, they can find no evidence for Proposition II (i), and cannot, in fact, reject the hypothesis that $\alpha_0 = \alpha_1$. In the remuneration equation, they find that they cannot reject the hypothesis is that $\beta_1 = 0$. Their point estimate of β_1, not only denies Proposition III, but also suggests that there is some merit in the view that profit-sharing *increases* total remuneration, and could therefore, be inflationary. However, they also obtain a positive value for $\hat{\alpha}_2$, (verging on significance). In terms of the overall impact on employment, this has to be set against a decline resulting from the rise in wages. In fact, this study concludes with the result that employment might be a little higher in profit-sharing firms, (although the estimates are very imprecise) but that this is, presumably, due to the productivity differences.

Blanchflower and Oswald (1986, 1987, 1988) have been responsible for a number of studies at the establishment level using the Workplace Industrial Relations Survey (WIRS). They find little evidence that profit-sharing affects any of the variables of interest – employment, investment or performance. Cross-tabulations describing the distribution of employment changes in private sector establishments with and without profit-sharing indicate no significant differences by form of remuneration (Blanchflower and Oswald, 1988). For example, 25 per cent of establishments without profit-sharing and 24 per cent of those with profit-sharing grew by more than 20 per cent between 1980 and 1984, while 22 per cent of establishments without profit sharing showed a decrease in employment of 5–20 per cent, as against 24 per cent of establishments with profit-sharing. More formal evidence comes from employment equations estimated on the 1980 WIRS data set. Unfortunately this identifies only the existence of a share-ownership scheme, and thereby conflates profit-sharing share-schemes under the 1978 Act with other types of employee share ownership. The equation contains employment in 1979 and 1975, controls for product demand and financial performance and regional and sectoral dummies. The share-ownership dummy is never statistically significant in numerous specifications of the equation.

It is hard at this stage to square the inconsistency of findings at the enterprise and establishment level. The Estrin–Wilson and Wadhwani data sets are relatively small, covering only one sector in the former case, but strong in economic information and longitudinal variation. WIRS is a far larger data set, but perhaps lacks the richness in economic information to tease out these relatively small profit-sharing effects. On the other hand, these studies may be suggesting that in relatively large firms and in particular sectors, profit-sharing may have a small effect on employment, probably via productivity. Much more research is needed here, and the new PRP scheme should, in principle, provide a good test-bed for future work in this area.

Evidence on profit-sharing and productivity

In the theoretical section, it was argued that profit-sharing might lead to greater productivity, through increased labour effort, reduced labour turnover or greater employee identification with their companies. Evidence on these issues is especially hard to interpret because of an identification problem. If only 'good' managers introduce profit-sharing and we cannot control for managerial ability, the postulated relationship with productivity may be picking up this rather than any performance effect. Thus there are problems with the direction of causality. Does profit-sharing promote greater cooperation and trust, or are the latter a necessary prerequisite for the introduction of profit-sharing? This identification problem bedevils interpretation of many of the studies.

There is some evidence for positive productivity effects (e.g. Cable and Fitzroy, 1980; Jones and Svejnar, 1985; Defourny, Estrin and Jones, 1985; Wadhwani and Wall, 1988, and Blanchflower and Oswald, 1987) but even here the case is not overwhelming. The strongest findings are derived from firms which have a significant degree of employee ownership as well as profit-sharing. The various effects have not yet been properly disentangled. Moreover, evidence on the effects of the post-1978 expansion in UK profit-sharing schemes is markedly less optimistic about the effects on productivity. More empirical work is needed in all these areas before any final conclusions can be reached.

10.4 CONCLUSIONS

We have argued that we have serious reservations about Weitzman's claims regarding PRP. On theoretical grounds, the models which take the wage parameters as fixed exogenously suffer from the serious flaw that they do not provide a story to link the short run to the long run. When a theory of wages is appended, it can cast serious doubts on Weitzman's conclusions.

If we believe that unemployment arises from the use of insiders of their economic power, profit-sharing attempts to moderate wage demands but does nothing to weaken their position. In these circumstances, which may describe large sections of the British economy, the only solution to the unemployment problem involves directly weakening the power of insiders. More generally, the persistence of the fixed-wage system despite repeated efforts to reform it point to deep-rooted preferences of both workers and managers. The reasons for these preferences are not yet well understood, though they are probably linked to attitudes to risk, equity and fairness. Suffice it to say that, as historical experience attests, attempts to change ingrained microeconomic behaviour by statute or financial incentive have typically failed. Therefore, it seems likely that attempts to graft this new system of remuneration in the British environment will lead to the emergence of cosmetic profit-sharing schemes.

Turning to the empirical evidence (which is, admittedly, scanty) we did not find much evidence in favour of Weitzman's propositions. The Japanese labour market does not appear to be characterised by excess demand for labour, and the data on UK firms suggest that they probably view total remuneration, not the base wage, as the marginal cost of labour. However, we note survey evidence which suggests that PRP will have little effect on wages or employment and some managers and union leaders have argued that PRP could be *inflationary*. It is, therefore, of some interest that one of the econometric studies on UK firms suggested that profit-sharing schemes in these firms had actually acted to increase total remuneration. There is more evidence for positive productivity effects but even here the case is not overwhelming. The strongest findings are derived from firms which have a significant degree of employee ownership as well as profit-sharing. The various effects have not yet been properly disentangled. Moreover, evidence on the effects of the post-1978 expansion in UK profit-sharing schemes is markedly less optimistic about the effects on productivity. More empirical work is needed in all these areas before any final conclusions can be reached.

APPENDIX

Profit-sharing in an 'efficiency wage' model
The analysis below is based on Wadhwani (1987b).

We assume that the firm chooses the wage, W, and employment, L, to maximise profits, π where

$$\pi = F[\delta(W)L] - WL \tag{10A.1}$$

and $\delta(W)$ is the efficiency of a worker receiving W. This implies that the firm chooses W to minimise $W/\delta(W)$, and the solution to this entails choosing W subject to:

$$\delta'(W) = \frac{\delta(W)}{W} \tag{10A.2}$$

Let W_o solve (10A.2) (W_o denotes the efficiency wage). Having chosen W_o, the firm will set employment by setting $\delta F'(\delta L) = W_o$. Suppose that, instead, we adopt a profit-sharing contract, i.e:

$$W = \theta + s \left[\frac{F[\delta(W)L] - \theta L}{L} \right] \tag{10A.3}$$

Now, the firm will

$$\max_{\theta, L} \{(1-s) \, (F[\delta(W)L] - \theta L)\} \tag{10A.4}$$

which is equivalent to

$$\max_{L^*, \theta} \{(1-s) \, [F(L^*) - \frac{\theta}{\delta(W)} L^*]\} \tag{10A.5}$$

where $L^* = \delta(W) \cdot L$

Now, (10A.5) implies that the firm will choose θ to minimise $\theta/\delta(W)$.

Therefore, we can think of the maximising (10A.5) in two stages – first, it chooses θ to minimise $\theta/\delta(W)$. Having chosen this, it then chooses employment to maximise profits, while *taking into account its choice of* θ.

Minimising $\theta/\delta(W)$ implies that:

$$\delta(W) = \theta \delta'(W) \frac{dW}{d\theta} \tag{10A.6}$$

However, from (10A.3)

$$\frac{\delta W}{\delta \theta} = \frac{(1-s)}{1-s \, \frac{F(L^*)}{L^*} \, \delta'(W)} \tag{10A.7}$$

Substituting (10A.7) into (10A.6) yields

$$\frac{\delta(W)}{W} = \delta'(W) \tag{10A.8}$$

which is the same as (10A.2) (i.e. the firm has to pay W_o).

Casual inspection of (10A.4) might suggest that the firm will set employment to equate $\delta F'(L^*)$ to θ, which would be consistent with Weitzman's view that profit-sharing increases employment. However, that would be misleading because the firm would know that such behaviour would cause it to violate the constraint that it has to pay W_o from (10A.8). Hence, to choose employment, it would maximise (10A.4) subject to this constraint, which, implies that its behaviour will be no different from that of a firm in a wage economy. Therefore, if wages are 'too high' today because of any of the reasons advanced by the 'efficiency wage' model literature, introducing profit-sharing will do nothing to alleviate it.

End-Notes

CHAPTER 2

1. See Becker (1965), Muth (1966). An influential parallel development is Kelvin Lancaster's 'characteristics approach', whereby the household is seen as mixing commodities with utility-yielding characteristics to achieve the desired balance; see Lancaster (1966).
2. Becker and disciples actually talk of market 'goods' and domestically produced 'commodities'. We prefer the more traditional usage of 'good' for something that yields direct utility (and which, as in the case of public goods, may not have a market), and of 'commodity' for something that can be bought or sold.
3. If there are several households in such a position, that will generate a market for domestic labour.
4. Besides, that would be an act of charity, not a mutually beneficial transaction, because all the transfers would be in m's favour.
5. This is also a way of formalising Becker's contention that the efficiency gain from marriage is due to 'complementarity of traits' between the spouses; see Becker (1973, 1974, 1981).
6. Division of labour applies not only to the allocation of each person's time between home- and market-work, as in our simplified model, but also to the allocation of home-time among the various domestic tasks. In their major survey of New York State households, Walker and Woods (1976) found a high degree of specialisation of the second type, even where the first was not much in evidence.
7. For empirical evidence, see for example, Mincer (1985) and several of the papers in Cain and Watts (1973). For an 'endogenous' explanation of the comparative advantage in terms of investments in specialised human capital, see Becker (1985).
8. In the UK, for example, the females/males wage ratio rose from around 60 per cent in 1960 to just about 70 per cent in 1980, while the ratio of the participation rates rose from under 50 per cent to over 66 per cent.
9. The number of births per woman of fecund age, which in 1950 was still between 2.5 and 3 for most of Western Europe, had fallen to well below 2 by 1984.
10. See Boskin and Sheshinski (1983).

11. See Cigno (1983, 1986).
12. For the transaction-cost approach to household formation and family behaviour, see Ben-Porath (1980) and Pollak (1985).
13. It rises with w if the elasticity of substitution of I for H (in the domestic production of X) is unity *and* V is zero, but it falls as w rises for various combinations of low elasticity and high property income.
14. Ermisch (1981) estimates the wage and the income elasticity of household size in the UK at -0.3 and -0.2, respectively. While there is no other direct evidence on wage elasticity, Hickman (1974) reports an income elasticity of household size in the US very similar to that estimated by Ermisch, suggesting that the wage elasticity too may be of the order estimated for the UK. Furthermore, Borsch-Supan (1986) and Ermisch (1987) estimate strongly negative effects of housing prices on the demand for individual accommodation. This is consistent with the theory and, since housing accounts for a large proportion (20–25 per cent in the USA and UK) of household expenditure, provides additional indirect evidence of negative wage elasticity of household size.

CHAPTER 4

1. We might also mention models with fixed prices, imperfect competition and search theory, (see Chapters 3, 5, and 7).
2. In the case of insurance, for example, one is not covered for theft if one is negligent, e.g. by leaving the safe unlocked. In the language of the economics of information these two problems are examples of what is known as *adverse selection* and *moral hazard* respectively.
3. Whether wages or employment fluctuates more depends on the slope of the labour-supply and labour demand curves.
4. We have assumed for convenience that if not employed by this firm the workers cannot go elsewhere. This might be because of some mobility costs.
5. In the UK virtually all wage contracts are annual (see Gregory, Lobban and Thomson, 1985). In the USA three-year contracts are the norm and this has been used to explain macroeconomic fluctuations (see Fischer, 1977; Taylor, 1980).
6. Note that this does not mean that there is no benefit from having implicit contracts; only that the optimal contract does not involve wage rigidity.
7. This may not be a problem if employers can identify those workers who are trying to get laid-off and pay no unemployment benefit to them.
8. There are other more common ways of making payments to laid-off workers, e.g. redundancy payments.
9. Indeed the model presented above had this feature as workers could not move to other employers if laid-off and employers could not hire other workers.
10. One way out of this may be to have profit-sharing as this can drive a

wedge between the marginal cost of a worker to the employer and the total income received by the worker. However, this requires profit-sharing parameters that vary with the firm's output price.

11. In the literature this is often justified by reference to anti-slavery provisions in labour law.

12. This may seem strange as the original idea behind implicit-contract theory was that risk-averse workers demanded insurance. But in many of the asymmetric-information models this is not necessary and for some it is more important that the *employer* is risk-averse (see Hart, 1984).

CHAPTER 5

* We are grateful to the editor and to John Beath, Simon Burgess, Jim Malcomson, Barry McCormick and Geoff Stewart for comments on an earlier draft. We are responsible for any remaining errors.

1. In this case r should be interpreted not as the level of benefit *per se*, but as the level of income which each individual would have to be given if working to make them as well-off as receiving the benefit and not working.

2. Thus if for a group of workers being unemployed and drawing benefit is less preferable than working in the competitive sector, then by studying the effects of a reduction in r on union behaviour we can understand how the growing threat of unemployment affects the wage/employment conditions for which the union is prepared to settle.

3. It is important to bear in mind in all this discussion that these 'production functions' are really 'real value-added functions' giving the maximum real value of revenue net of all other costs of production, conditional on a particular choice of labour by the firm. Thus there can be many other inputs, but the crucial assumption is that these can all be chosen by the firm, *and* this choice can be made after the amount of labour has been determined. This effectively rules out the possibility of fixed factors – at least in this very simple version of the model.

4. This assumption is not as restrictive as it might seem, since, in its absence, we could always redefine the production function as $\tilde{f}(n) \equiv f(n) - f(0)$, and everything would go through as in the text.

5. Strictly speaking, we should specify utility as a function of real income by deflating wages by some index of consumer prices. It is straightforward to introduce this, and other real-world features such as income taxation. Oswald (1982) contains a discussion of how these affect the bargain. The critical feature of the model though is that p does not directly affect utility, reflecting the reasonable view that whatever any one firm produces is likely to form such a small part of the consumer price index that it can be ignored.

6. Here, and throughout the paper, we will use the notation $g_x(x,y)$ to mean the partial derivative of the function g with respect to the variable x.

7. Of course acceptance of these restrictions in no way 'proves' the validity of the theory, since there may be alternative explanations for this relationship.

8. So, once again, an increased threat of unemployment leads unions to moderate wage demands and increase employment.

9. The fact that employment does not enter an explicit contract, does not prevent it forming some part of an implicit contract. If capital is taken as fixed, then control over manning levels is effectively equivalent to controlling employment.

10. In part this is because we have assumed membership, to be so large that any level of employment that is negotiated falls below it. But the problem is deeper than that, because when people think employment is related to union power, they surely have in mind more than just the fact that membership might be a binding constraint on employment.

11. Notice that it is only in terms of the (n,u) formulation of the models that we can claim the theory goes through. Given the complexity of underlying payment systems we allow for, the only unambiguous 'wage' which could be said to be determined in the model is the total payment $\psi(h,u)$. Typically this will not appear in a formal contract – since it depends on the choice of hours – and this may help to explain the poor performance of the 'contract wage' in some of the studies reported in the previous section, e.g. Ashenfelter and Brown (1986).

12. On the other hand if seniority is unrelated to any economic difference amongst workers, then it lacks any rationale, and the resulting theory is essentially *ad hoc*.

CHAPTER 6

* The first draft of this chapter was written whilst the author was Pitt-Cobbett Visiting Fellow at the University of Tasmania. Financial support from the Pitt-Cobbett Trust as well as the hospitality of the Department of Economics is gratefully acknowledged.

1. By which Rees (1952, p. 380) meant the coverage of disputes as between large units (companies and industries) and small units (departments and plants). As he points out, a cyclical pattern in the number of separate strikes may arise, without any variation in the propensity of given workers to strike, if the scope of strikes changes over the cycle in such a way that during downturns strikes tend to occur in large units, while in the upturn they tend to occur in small units. One issue not discussed in this chapter concerns the relationship between plant size and strike proneness: for a discussion see Prais (1978).

2. Regarding the observed tendency for the strike peak to precede the cycle peal, Rees conjectures that the strike peak probably represents a maximum in the divergence of expectations between unions and employers which, he suggests, arises because the union concentrates its attention on employment (which typically does not lead at the cycle peak) whereas the employer focuses his attention on a range of *leading*

indicators (Rees, 1952, pp. 381–2). Equally *ad hoc* is Rees's explanation for the lag at the trough which he sees quite simply as the result of a 'wait and see' attitude on the part of union leaders who wish to ascertain that the upturn is genuine before risking their members' jobs. For a formal analysis of the role of expectations in explaining cycles of strikes see Kaufman (1981).

3. For example, Shorey (1976) and Geroski, Hamlin and Knight (1982) analysed UK cross section data by industry, while Kaufman (1983) and Jones and Walsh (1984) analysed pooled time-series cross-section industry data from the US and Canada respectively. Swindinsky and Vanderkamp (1982) analysed a pooled cross-section time-series micro-data set relating to individual bargaining units in Canada, while for the USA Leigh (1984) used micro-data relating to individual workers to analyse inter-industry variations in strike frequency.

4. See Siebert and Addison (1981) for a related approach which views strikes as accidents, while likewise stressing the role of imperfect information.

5. Notice that Mauro (1982), like Farber (1978) before him, assumed that the union's resistance curve is convex, although Hicks's own union resistance curve (see Figure 6.1) contained a concave section.

6. Let X and Y denote vectors of variables of interest to the employer and union respectively and M denote the firm's product price and CPI the consumer price index. Mauro's argument can be written more formally as follows in the case where the union correctly perceives the vector X and the employer the vector Y:

$$ECC = f(X,M), \qquad UCC = f(Y,CPI)$$
$$ECC_u = f(X,CPI), \qquad UCC_E = f(Y,M)$$

More generally, Mauro (1982, pp. 525–7) goes on to consider circumstances under which misperceptions occur regarding not only the position of the opponent's concession curve but also its slope.

7. However, Booth and Cressy (1987) accuse Tracy of confusing the union's subjective probability of a strike (6.16) with the objective probability of the event occurring.

8. These predictions may be demonstrated by writing $\hat{P}_0 = P$ and substituting into (6.16) the following expression for the so called cut off point $\underline{\hat{P}}$ as a function of w_1^*:

$$\hat{P}(w_j^*) = R + k_1(\hat{P}_0 - R)$$

where

$$k_1 = \frac{1 + \delta_F + \delta_F C_2}{2(1 - \delta_F + \delta_F C_2) - \delta_u C_2} < 1$$

Letting the end points $\underline{P}$ and $\bar{P}$ be stretched by a mean preserving amount Δ_1 and differentiating yields:

$$\frac{\partial P(s)}{\partial \Delta_1} = (1-k_1)\,\frac{\bar{P}+P-2R}{(\bar{P}-P)_2} < 1$$

which shows that increasing the union's uncertainty raises strike probability. The effect of raising the value of workers' outside opportunities is as follows:

$$\frac{\delta P(s)}{\delta R} = (1-k_1)\frac{1}{\bar{P}-\underline{P}} > 0$$

Shifting the entire range $[P,\ \bar{P}]$ by an amount Δ_2, with R held constant, increases the total expected rents to be divided while leaving uncertainty unaltered and differentiation gives

$$\frac{\partial P(s)}{\partial \Delta_2} = -(1-k_1)\,\frac{1}{\bar{P}-\underline{P}} > 0$$

which demonstrates that strike probability declines as total expected rents increase.

9. By which is meant what amounts to a contingent contract, in the sense of being an agreement – either explicit or implicit – governing the procedures for negotiating agreements. Protocols cover a wide range of issues, including not only the wages and fringes to be paid relative to those set in other collective agreements and in response to cost-of-living variations, work rules, rates and methods of payment, but also such issues as the time and location of meetings, the conditions under which a previous contract continues to apply after its expiration pending negotiation of a new contract, conditions under which mediation and arbitration may be introduced into the area and so forth (Reder and Neumann, 1980, pp. 870–1).

CHAPTER 7

1. Segmentationism has also been espoused by empirical sociologists (e.g. Wallace and Kalleberg, 1981), while even orthodox economists have accepted that some degree of segmentation characterises labour markets (Taubman and Wachter, 1986).
2. The limited role attributed to trade unions preserves the distinction between labour market segmentation and the branch of orthodoxy (particularly well represented in modern Britain, if not in the USA) which accepts a major role for unions in differentiating outcomes in the labour market.
3. Although the core/periphery dichotomy has been adopted by radical analyses (Gordon *et al.*, 1982; Reich, 1984), their primary interest lies in explaining employment stability and promotion ladders (rather than high pay) in the internal labour markets of large corporations.
4. The importance of normative influences upon internal pay structure

was accepted by Hicks in a key revisionist postscript to his classic labour text (1963, pp. 316–19). See also Marsden (1986, ch. 4) and Brown and Nolan (1987). An orthodox analysis which provides a bridge to the LMS approach interprets the internal labour market as a means of avoiding continuous bargaining over the terms of the employment contract by employees who possess specific skills (Williamson, Wachter and Harris, 1975).

5. Negligible returns to education and experience in secondary employment have been found in several US studies which have classified workers into segments according to measured job characteristics (Bluestone, 1974; Buchele, 1976; Rumberger and Carnoy, 1980). Significant within-segment returns have however been found in other US studies (Alexander, 1974; Beck, Horan and Tolbert, 1978) and, despite initial impressions (Bosanquet and Doeringer, 1973) in all results for Britain (Mayhew and Rosewell, 1979; McNabb and Psacharopoulos, 1981; McNabb and Ryan, 1986; McNabb, 1987).

6. The outcomes achieved by workers of different levels of labour quality may of course involve segmentation as well. The high earnings of many professional, managerial and craft workers undoubtedly involve a return not just to greater ability, education and training but also to entry barriers based upon group power. However, when workers differ in labour quality, the part played by segmentation in the labour market is particularly difficult to disentangle empirically from that before the market. Moreover, as one of the advantages of many primary jobs is access to training, the comparison of workers of comparable quality may be possible only before access is gained to primary employment (Ryan, 1981).

7. Earlier studies by Wachtel and Betsey (1972) and Buchele (1976) – both of which adopt multisector classifications and estimate common earnings functions across workers – found that the earnings increase consequent upon statistically 'relocating' a manual male worker of average labour quality from the least to the most advantaged sector amounts respectively to 27–40 per cent (by skill level) and 21 per cent (mature men only). Higher estimates were provided by Bluestone (1974) who, classifying by occupation rather than industry, estimated that the gain in pay associated with a similar statistical transfer (essentially a move of two standard deviations, centring on the mean, up the distributions of segment characteristics) varied between 30 and 44 per cent of mean play. The higher size of Bluestone's estimates is presumed to reflect the inclusion of non-whites and women, resulting in a longer reach in the measurement of segmentation than in most other studies.

8. Empirical assessment has arguably been biased against labour market segmentation by the concentration of most micro-data sets upon individual rather than employer characteristics. The attributes of jobs and employers are invariably more poorly captured than are those of workers. Thus the influence of unemployment benefits upon unemployment – a theme much favoured in competitive orthodoxy – is largely eliminated when the characteristics of employers are introduced alongside those of workers (Osberg, Apostle and Clairmont, 1986).

9. In addition to studies cited elsewhere in this chapter, evidence of segmentation is provided for the USA by Beck, Horan and Tolbert (1978), Hodson (1978) and Baron and Bielby (1980); and for the UK by Woodward and McNabb (1978).

10. The effects upon pay structures of a similar combination of slump and overvaluation in Britain have however proved relatively minor (Ryan, Kumar and Osberg, 1986).

11. The limited number of sectors distinguished in the data used by McNabb and Ryan made it impossible to assess the case for bimodality in the British labour market.

12. Thus both personal services and clothing would score low on a factor which captures seller-concentration but only clothing would score high on one which picks up exposure to foreign competition.

13. Only one study (Dickens and Lang, 1985) can lay claim to demonstrating empirically the existence of strict duality in the labour market itself. Advanced statistical techniques are used to filter out two distinct earnings functions which not only show negligible returns to schooling and experience in the secondary segment but also lower earnings at all levels of schooling and experience. However, as the factors which sort workers between segments are limited to race and urban residence (*ibid*, Table 1), the contours of labour market structure prove painfully thin – and the suspicion that the dichotomy is a statistical artefact remains therefore anallayed.

14. Other objections to studies which have attempted to establish strict duality in the labour market include lack of consensus upon the content of sectoral classifications (Zucker and Rosenstein, 1981); and – particularly in the early studies – the circularity of worker classifications which partly depended upon the labour-market outcomes which they were expected to explain.

15. Although the significant relative pay effect for young males in Table 7.4 might be construed as evidence for competitive effects, such an interpretation fails to explain the institutional variation which permits young workers to be paid less than adult males in some sectors and countries but not in others (Garonna and Ryan, 1986).

16. Similar results, with a stronger role for schooling in escape from the secondary segment were reported by Andrisani (1976). In another study, fully 40 per cent of young men working in the lowest of five occupational categories in the US in 1966 had crossed the frontier by 1969; 33 per cent of this upward mobility was associated with education and training (Buchele, 1976). An important role for motivation – a personal trait which cannot be measured directly – is suggested by the finding that the earnings of immigrants overtake those of the black people born in the USA, after a few years in the labour force (De Freitas, 1985).

17. 'There is no support for ... immobility across variously defined boundaries for, say, low wage and black workers' (Cain, 1976, p. 1231). See also Addison and Siebert (1979, p. 192) and Taubman and Wachter (1986).

18. Although the industry provides an imperfect guide to the contours of segmentation, it is adequate for present purposes. Lack of data on quits prevents a comparable analysis for Britain, although evidence that turnover rates respond to wages in other sectors (Shorey, 1980) suggests a similar conclusion.

19. A more sophisticated competitive interpretation of quit-rates looks to postulated requirements for specific skills in high wage sectors (Parsons, 1972). The lack of measures of investments in specific skill prevents direct testing of this theory, but it suffers from evidence that such investments are limited in most manual jobs (Ryan, 1977, ch. 3); and from the fact that, even where employer investments in specific skills are significant, the result in competitive markets is primarily a strong seniority element in pay and only secondarily high average earnings (Becker, 1975).

References

Addison, J. and Siebert, W. S. (1979) *the Market for Labour: An Analytical Treatment* (Santa Monica, California: Goodyear).

Aigner, D. J. and Cain, G. G. (1977) 'Statistical Theories of Discrimination in the Labor Market', *Industrial and Labor Relations Review*, pp. 175–87.

Aizenman, J. and Frenkel, J. A. (1985) 'Optimal Wage Indexation, Foreign Exchange Intervention, and Monetary Policy', *American Economic Review*, 75, pp. 402–23.

Akerlof, G. A. (1976) 'The Economics of Caste and of the Rat Race and Other Woeful Tales', *Quarterly Journal of Economics*, vol. 90, pp. 599–617.

Akerlof, G. A. (1980) 'The Theory of Social Custom, of which Unemployment may be One Consequence', *Quarterly Journal of Economics*, vol. 94, pp. 749–75.

Akerlof, G. A. (1983) 'Loyalty Filters', *American Economic Review*, vol. 73, pp. 54–63.

Akerlof, G. and Miyazaki, H. (1980) 'The Implicit Contract Theory of Unemployment meets the Wage Bill Argument', *Review of Economic Studies*, 47, pp. 321–38.

Alchian, A. A. (1970) 'Information Costs, Pricing and Resource Unemployment in Phelps, E. S. *et al.* (ed.) *Microeconomic Foundations of Employment and Inflation Theory* (New York: Norton).

Alchian, A. A. and Kessel, R. A. (1962) 'Competition, Monopoly and the Pursuit of Money', in *Aspects of Labor Economics* (Princeton: National Bureau of Economic Research) pp. 157–83.

Alexander, A. J. (1974) 'Income, Experience and the Structure of Internal Labour Markets', *Quarterly Journal of Economics*, February 88, pp. 63–87.

Alogoskoufis, G. S. (1985) 'Macroeconomic Policy and Aggregate Fluctuations in a Semi-Industrialized Open Economy', *European Economic Review*, 29, pp. 35–61.

Alogoskoufis, G. S. (1989) 'Monetary, Nominal Income and Exchange Rate Targets in a Small Open Economy', *European Economic Review*, forthcoming.

Alogoskoufis, G. and Manning, A. (1987) 'Tests of Alternative Wage

268

Employment Bargaining Models with an Application to the UK Aggregate Labour Market', mimeo (London: Birbeck College).

Alogoskoufis, G. S. and Manning, A. (1988) 'On the Persistence of Unemployment', *Economic Policy*, 7, pp. 427–69.

Andrews, M. and Nickell, S. J. (1982) 'Unemployment in the United Kingdom since the War', *Review of Economic Studies*, 49, pp. 731–59.

Andrisani, P. J. (1976) Discrimination, Segmentation and Upward Mobility: A Longitudinal Approach to the Dual Labour Market Theory (Department of Economics, Temple University, Philadelphia).

Aoki, M. (1980) 'A Model of the Firm as a Stockholder–Employee Cooperative Game', *American Economic Review*, vol. 70, pp. 600–10.

Arrow, K. J. (1972a) 'Models of Job Discrimination' in A. H. Pascal (ed.) *Racial Discrimination in Economic Life* (Lexington, Mass.: D.C. Heath) pp. 83–102.

Arrow, K. J. (1972b) 'Some Mathematical Models of Race in the Labor Market' in A. H. Pascal (ed.) *Racial Discrimination in Economic Life* (Lexington, Mass.: D. C. Heath) pp. 187–203.

Arrow, K. J. (1973) 'The Theory of Discrimination' in O. Ashenfelter and A. Rees (eds) *Discrimination in Labor Markets* (Princeton: Princeton University Press) pp. 3–33.

Ashenfelter, O, and Brown, J. N. (1986) 'Testing the Efficiency of Employment Contracts', *Journal of Political Economy*, vol. 94 (Supplement) pp. S41–87

Ashenfelter, O. and Johnson, G. E. (1969) 'Bargaining Theory, Trade Unions and Industrial Strike Activity', *American Economic Review*, vol. 59, no. 1, pp. 35–49.

Ashenfelter, O. and Layard, R. (1983) 'The Effects of Incomes Policies Upon Wage Differentials', *Economica*, vol. 50 pp. 127–44.

Atkin, War Cabinet Committee on the Employment of Women in Industry (1919) *Report* (London: HMSO).

Atkinson, A. B.; Gomulka, J., Mickelwright, J. and Rau, N. (1984) 'Unemployment Benefit, Duration and Incentives in Britain: How Robust is the Evidence?' *Journal of Public Economics*, 23(1/2) February/ March, 3–26.

Averitt, R. T. (1968) *The Dual Economy* (New York: Norton).

Azariadis, C. (1975) 'Implicit Contracts and Underemployment Equilibria', *Journal of Political Economy*, vol. 83, pp. 1183–202.

Azariadis, C. and Stiglitz, J. E. (1983) 'Implicit Contracts and Fixed Price Equilibria', *Quarterly Journal of Economics Supplement*, 98, 1–23.

Baily, M. N. (1974) 'Wages and Employment with Uncertain Demand', *Review of Economic Studies*, 41, pp. 37–50.

Baily, M. N. (1977) 'On the Theory of Lay-offs and Unemployment', *Econometrica*, 45, pp. 1043–64.

Bamber, G. J. and Lansbury, R. D. (eds) (1987) *International and Comparative Industrial Relations* (London, Allen & Unwin).

Baron, J. N. and Bielby, W. T. (1980) 'Bringing the Firms Back In: Stratification, Segmentation and the Organisation of Work', *American Sociological Review*, October 45 pp. 737–65.

Bean, C. (1984) 'Optimal Wage Bargains', *Economica*, vol. 51, pp. 141–9.
Bean, C., Layard, R. and Nickell, S. (1987) 'The Rise in Unemployment: A Multi-country Study' in C. Bean, R. Layard and S., Nickell (eds) *The Rise in Unemployment* (Oxford: Basil Blackwell). Also published in *Economica* (1986) vol. 53 (Supplement) pp. S1–S22.
Bean, C. and Turnbull, P. J. (1987) 'Employment in the Coal Industry: A Test of the Labour Demand Model', *CLE Discussion Paper no. 274.*
Beck, E. M., Horan, P. M. and Tolbert, C. M. (1978) 'Stratification in a Dual Economy: A Sectoral Model of Earnings Determination', *American Sociological Review*, October, 43, pp. 704–20.
Becker, G. S. (1957) *The Economics of Discrimination* (quotations in chapter 8 are from the 2nd edition, 1971) (Chicago: University of Chicago Press).
Becker, G. S. (1959) 'Union Restrictions on Entry' in P. Bradley (ed.) *The Public State in Union Power* (Charlottesville, Va.: University of Chicago Press).
Becker, G. S. (1960) 'An Economic Analysis of Fertility', in National Bureau of Economic Research, *Demographic and Economic Change in Developed Countries* (Princeton: Princeton University Press).
Becker, G. S. (1964) *Human Capital: A Theoretical and Empirical Analysis* (New York: National Bureau of Economic Research).
Becker, G. S. (1965) 'A Theory of the Allocation of Time', *Economic Journal*, vol. 75, no. 299, pp. 493–517.
Becker, G. S. (1973) 'A Theory of Marriage: Part I', *Journal of Political Economy*, vol. 81, pp. 813–46.
Becker, G. S. (1974) 'A Theory of Marriage, Part II', *Journal of Political Economy*, vol. 82, (Supplement) p. S11–S26.
Becker, G. S. (1975) *Human Capital* (New York: National Bureau of Economic Research) 2nd edn. pp. 511–522.
Becker, G. S. (1981) *A Treatise on the Family* (Cambridge, Mass.: Harvard University Press).
Becker, G. S. (1985) 'Human Capital, Effort, and the Sexual Division of Labor', *Journal of Labor Economics*, vol. 3, pp. S33–58.
Benassy, J.-P., (1976) 'The Disequilibrium Approach to Monopolistic Price Settings and General Monopolistic Equilibrium', *Review of Economic Studies*, 43, pp. 69–81.
Bennett, J. and Ulph, A. (1988) 'Asymmetries in the Gains to Firms and Unions of Alternative Bargaining Structures' (mimeo, University of Southampton).
Ben-Porath, Y. (1980) 'The F-connection: Families, Friends and Firms, and the Organization of Exchange', *Population and Development Review*, vol. 6, no 1, pp. 1–30.
Berger, S. and Piore, M. (1982) *Dualism and Discontinuity in Industrial Societies* (Cambridge: Cambridge University Press).
Bergmann, B. (1971) 'The Effect on White Incomes of Discrimination in Employment', *Journal of Political Economy*, vol. 79, pp. 294–313.
Binmore, K. and Herrero, M. (1987a) 'Matching and Bargaining in Dynamic Markets', *Review of Economic Studies*, 55, pp. 17–32.

Binmore, K. and Herrero, M. (1987b) 'Security Equilibrium', *Review of Economic Studies*, 55, pp. 33-48.

Binmore, K., Rubinstein, A. and Wolinsky, A. (1985) 'The Nash Bargaining Solution in Economic Modelling', *Rand Journal of Economics*, vol. 17, pp. 176-88.

Blackburn, R. M. and Mann, M. (1979) *The Working Class in the Labour Market* (London: Macmillan).

Blanchard, O. J. and Summers, L. H. (1986) 'Hysteresis and the European Unemployment Problem, in S. Fischer (ed.) *NBER Macroeconomic Annual 1986* (Cambridge, Mass.: MIT Press.

Blanchard, O. J. and Summers, L. H. (1987) 'Hysteresis in Unemployment', *European Economic Review*, 31, pp. 288-95.

Blanchflower, D. and Oswald, A. (1986) 'Shares for Employees: A Test of Their Effects' (London: London School of Economics, Centre for Labour Economics) Discussion Paper no. 273.

Blanchflower, D. and Oswald, A. (1987) 'Profit-Sharing – Can It Work?', *Oxford Economic Papers*, vol. 39, pp. 1-19.

Blanchflower, D. and Oswald, A. (1988) 'Profit-related Pay: Prose Rediscovered', *Economic Journal*, vol. 98, no. 392 (1988) pp. 720-36.

Bluestone, B. (1970) 'The Tripartite Economy', *Poverty and Human Resources Abstracts* 5, 4, pp. 15-35.

Bluestone, B. (1974) 'The Personal Earnings Distribution: Individual and Institutional Determinants', unpublished Ph.D. dissertation, University of Michigan: Ann Arbor.

Booth, A. (1985) 'The Free Rider Problem and a Social Custom Theory of Trade Union Membership', *Quarterly Journal of Economics*. 100, pp. 253-61.

Booth, A. and Cressy, R. (1987) 'Strikes with Asymmetric Information: Theory and Evidence (Australian National University, Centre for Economic Policy Research) Discussion Paper no 178.

Booth, A. and Ulph, D. (1988a) 'Union Wages and Employment with Endogenous Membership' (mimeo, Bristol University).

Booth, A. and Ulph, D. (1988b) 'A Note on Union Amalgamation (mimeo, University of Bristol).

Borsch-Supan, A. (1986) 'Household Formation, Housing Prices and Public Policy Impacts', *Journal of Public Economics*, vol. 30, pp. 145-64.

Bosanquet, N. and P. Doeringer (1973) 'Is there a Dual Labour Market in Great Britain?', *Economic Journal*, 83, pp. 421-35.

Boskin, M. J. and Sheshinski, E. (1983) 'Optimal Tax Treatment of the Family: Married Couples', *Journal of Public Economics*, vol. 20, pp. 281-97.

Bowles, S. (1970) 'Aggregation of Labor Inputs in the Economics of Growth and Planning: Experiments with a Two-Level CES Function', *Journal of Political Economy*, vol. 78, pp. 68-81.

Bradley, K. and Gelb, A. (1983) *Worker Capitalism: The New Industrial Relations* (London: Heinemann).

Bradley, K. and Gelb, A. (1986) *Share Ownership for Employees* (London: Public Policy Centre).

Bronfenbrenner, M. (1939) 'The Economics of Collective Bargaining', *Quarterly Journal of Economics*, vol. 53, pp. 535–61.

Bronfenbrenner, M. (1956) 'Potential Monopsony in Labor Markets', *Industrial and Labor Relations Review*, vol. 9, pp. 577–88.

Brosnan, P. and Wilkinson F. (1987) 'A National Statutory Minimum Wage and Economic Efficiency', working paper, Department of Applied Economics, University of Cambridge.

Brown, C. V., Levin, E., Rosa, P., Ruffell, R., and Ulph, D. (1986) 'Payment Systems, Demand Constraints and their Implications for Research into Labour Supply', in Blundell, R. and Walker, I. (eds) *Unemployment, Search, and Labour Supply* (Cambridge: Cambridge University Press).

Brown, W. and Nolan, P. (1987) 'Wages and Labour Productivity: The Contribution of Industrial Relations Research to the Understanding of Pay Determination', unpublished paper, Faculty of Economics, University of Cambridge.

Bruno, M. and Sachs, J. (1985) *The Economics of Worldwide Stagflation* (Oxford: Basil Blackwell).

Brusco, S. and Sabel, C. (1981) 'Artisan Production and Economic Growth', in Wilkinson (1981).

Buchele, R. K. (1976) 'Jobs and Workers: A Labour Market Segmentation Perspective on the Work experience of young men', unpublished Ph.D. dissertation, Harvard University.

Buchele, R. K. (1983) 'Economic Dualism and Employment Stability', *Industrial Relations*, Fall, 22, 3, pp. 410–18.

Buiter, W. (1978) 'Short-run and Long-run Effects of External Disturbances under a Floating Exchange Rate', *Economica*, 45, pp. 251–72.

Buiter, W. and Miller, M. (1981) 'Monetary Policy and International Competitiveness: The Problem of Adjustment', *Oxford Economic Papers*, 33, pp. 143–75.

Burns, A. F. and Mitchell, W. C. (1946) *Measuring Business Cycles* (New York: National Bureau of Economic Research).

Cable, J. and Fitzroy, F. (1980) 'Cooperation and Productivity: Some Evidence from West Germany Experience', *Economic Analysis and Workers' Management?*, vol. 14, pp. 163–90.

Cain G. G. (1976) 'The Challenge of Segmented Labor Market Theories to Orthodox Theories 'A Survey', *Journal of Economic Literature*, vol. 14, no 4, pp. 1215–17.

Cain G. G. and Watts, H. (1973) *Labor Supply and Income Maintenance* (New York: Academic Press).

Cairnes, J. (1874) *Some Leading Principles of Political Economy* (London: Macmillan).

Cameron, S. (1984) 'The Stability of the Post-War Aggregate British Strike Function, *Scottish Journal of Political Economy*, vol. 31, no 1, pp. 28–43.

Cannan, E. (1914) *Wealth* (London: P. S. King).

Carruth, A. A. and Oswald, A. J. (1985) 'Miners' Wages in Post-War Britain: An Application of a Model of Trade Union Behaviour', *Economic Journal*, 95, pp. 1003–1020.

Carruth, A. A., Findlay, L., and Oswald, A. J. (1986) 'A Test of a Model of Union Behaviour: The Coal and Steel Industries in Britain', *Oxford Bulletin of Economics and Statistics*, 48, pp. 1–18.

Cartter, A. M. (1959) *Theory of Wages and Employment* (Homewood, Illinois: Irwin).

Cassel, G. (1918) *The Theory of Social Economy* (London: T. Fisher Unwin).

Chamberlain, N. W. (1951) *Collective Bargaining* (New York: McGraw-Hill).

Chiplin, B., Curran, M. M. and Parsley, C. J. (1980) 'Relative Female Earnings in Britain and the Impact of Legislation' in P. J. Sloane (ed.) *Women and Low Pay* (London: Macmillan).

Chiplin, B. and Sloane, P. J. (1988) 'The Effect of Britain's Anti-Discriminatory Legislation on Relative Pay and Employment: A Comment', *Economic Journal*, vol. 98, pp. 833–38.

Cigno, A. (1983) 'On Optimal Family Allowances', *Oxford Economic Papers*, vol. 35, pp. 13–22.

Cigno, A. (1986) 'Fertility and the Tax-benefit System: A reconsideration of the Theory of Family Taxation', *Economic Journal*, vol. 96, pp. 1035–51.

Clark, J. B. (1900) *The Distribution of Wealth* (New York: Macmillan).

Cockburn, C. (1983) 'New Technology in Print: Men's Work and Women's Chances', in G. Winch (ed.) *Information Technology in Manufacturing Processes* (London: Rossendale).

Collet, C. E. (1891) 'Women's Work in Leeds', *Economic Journal*, vol. 1, pp. 460–73.

Craig, C., Rubery, J., Tarling, R. and Wilkinson, F. (1982) *Labour Market Structure, Industrial Organisation and Low Pay* (Cambridge: Cambridge University Press.

Cross, J. G. (1969) *The Economics of Bargaining* (London: Basic Books).

Cukor, E. and Kertesi, G. (1986) 'Company Pay Level and State Regulation in Hungary', paper presented to annual meeting of International Working Group on Labour Market Segmentation, Cambridge, England.

Davidson, C. (1986) 'Multi-Unit Bargaining in Oligopolistic Industries', (mimeo, Michigan State University).

Davies, R. J. (1979) 'Economic Activity, Incomes Policy and Strikes – A Quantitative Analysis', *British Journal of Industrial Relations*, vol. 17, no 2, pp. 205–23.

Defourny, J., Estrin, S. and Jones, D. (1985) 'The Effects of Worker Participation upon Productivity in French Producer Cooperatives', *International Journal of Industrial Organisation*, vol. 3, pp. 197–218.

DeFreitas, G. (1985) 'Labour Market Outcomes of Immigrants in the US: Alternative Models and Recent Findings', in P. Cottingham (ed.) *The Labour market Impact of Immigration* (New York: Rockefeller Foundation).

Demsetz, H. (1965) 'Minorities in the Labor Market', *North Carolina Law Review*, vol. 43, pp. 271–97.

Dertouzos, J. N. and Pencavel, J. H. (1981) 'Wage and Employment

Determination under Trade Unionism: The International Typergraphi-cal Union', *Journal of Political Economy*, vol. 89, no 6, pp. 1162–8.

Dex, S. (1986) *The Costs of Discriminating: A Review of the Literature*, (London: Home Office) Research and Planning Unit paper no 39.

Dex, S. and Shaw, L. B. (1986) *British and American Women at Work: Do Equal Employment Opportunities Matter?* (London: Macmillan).

Dickens, W. T. and Lang, K. (1985) 'A Test of Dual Labour Market Theory', *American Economic Review*, September, 75, 4, pp. 792–805.

Doeringer, P. and Piore, M. (1971) *Internal Labour Markets and Man-power Analysis* (Lexington, Mass: D.C. Heath).

Dornbusch, R. (1976) 'Expectations and Exchange Rate Dynamics', *Journal of Political Economy*, 84, pp. 1161–76.

Dornbusch, R. (1980) *Open Economy Macroeconomics* (New York: Basic Books).

Dornbusch, R. (1987) 'Exchange Rates and Prices', *American Economic Review*, 77, pp. 93–106.

Dougherty, C. R. S. and Selowsky, M. (1973) 'Measuring the Effects of the Misallocation of Labor', *Review of Economics and Statistics*, vol. LV, pp. 386–90.

Douglas, P. H. (1923) 'An Analysis of Strike Statistics, 1881–1921' *Journal of the American Statistical Association*, vol. 18. no 143, pp. 866–77.

Douty, H. M. (1932) 'The Trend of Industrial Disputes, 1922–1930', *Journal of the American Statistical Association*, vol. 27, pp. 168–72.

Drèze, J. (1987) 'Work Sharing: Why? How? How Not . . .' in R. Layard and L. Calmfors (eds) *The Fight Against Unemployment* (Cambridge, Mass: MIT Press).

Dunlop, J. T. (1957) 'The Task of Contemporary Wage Theory', in G. W. Taylor and F. C. Pierson (eds) *New Concepts in Wage Determination* (New York: McGraw Hill).

Edgeworth, F. Y. (1922) 'Equal Pay to Men and Women for Equal Work', *Economic Journal*, vol. 32, pp. 431–57.

Edwards, R. C. (1976) 'Individual Traits and Organisational Incentives: What Makes a 'Good' Worker?', *Journal of Human Resources*, Winter, 11, 1, 51–68.

Edwards, R. C. (1979) *Contested Terrain* (New York: Basic Books).

Edwards, R. C., Garonna, P. and Todtling, F. (eds) (1986) *Unions in Crisis and Beyond* (Dover, Massachusetts: Auburn House).

Edwards, R. C., Reich, M. and Gordon, D. M. (1975) *Labour Market Segmentation* (Lexington: D. C. Heath).

Ermisch, J. (1981) 'An Economic Analysis of Household Formation: Theory and Evidence from the General Household Survey', *Scottish Journal of Political Economy*, vol. 28, no 1, pp. 1–19.

Ermisch, J. (1987) 'Impacts of Policy Actions on the Family', *Journal of Public Policy*, vol. 6, pp. 297–318.

Estrin, S. and Wilson, N., (1986) 'The Micro-Economic Effects of Profit-Sharing: The British Experience' (London: London School of Eco-nomics, Centre for Labour Economics) Discussion Paper no 247.

Estrin, S, Grout, P. and Wadhwani, S. (1987) 'Profit-Sharing and

Employee Share Ownership: An Assessment', *Economic Policy*, no 4, April, pp. 1–60.

Farber, H. S. (1978) 'Bargaining Theory, Wage Outcomes, and the Occurrence of Strikes: An Econometric Analysis', *American Economic Review*, vol. 68, no 2, pp. 262–71.

Fawcett, M. (1892) 'Mr Sidney Webb's Article on Women's Wages', *Economic Journal*, vol 2, pp. 173–6.

Fawcett, M. (1917) 'The Position of Women in Economic Life', in W. H. Dawson (ed.) *After War Problems* (London: Allen & Unwin) pp. 191–215.

Fawcett, M. (1918) 'Equal Pay for Equal Work', *Economic Journal*, vol. 28, pp. 1–6.

Feldstein, M. (1976) 'Temporary Lay-offs in the Theory of Unemployment', *Journal of Political Economy*, 84, pp. 937–57.

Fellner, W. J. (1951) *Competition Among the Few* (New York: Knopf).

Findlay R. and Rodriguez, C. (1977) 'Intermediate Imports and Macroeconomic Policy under Flexible Exchange Rates', *Canadian Journal of Economics*, 10, pp. 208–17.

Fischer, S. (1977) 'Long-Term Contracts, Rational Expectations, and the Optimum Money Supply Rule', *Journal of Political Economy*, 85, pp. 191–205.

Fitzroy, K. and Kraft, K. (1986) 'Profitability and Profit-Sharing', *Journal of Industrial Economics*, vol. 35, no 2, pp. 113–30.

Florence, P. S. (1931) 'A Statistical Contribution to the Theory of Women's Wages', *Economic Journal*, vol. 41, pp. 19–37.

Frank, J. (1985) 'Trade Union Efficiency and Overemployment with Seniority Wage Scales', *Economic Journal*, 95, pp. 1021–34.

Freedman, M. (1976) *Labour Markets: Segments and Shelters* (Montclair, New Jersey: Allanheld, Osmun).

Freeman, R. (1976) 'Industry Mobility and Union Voice in the Labour Market', *American Economic Review* (Papers and Proceedings) vol. 66, pp. 361–8.

Freeman, R. and Weitzman, M. (1986) 'Bonuses and Employment in Japan' (New York: National Bureau of Economic Research) Working Paper no 1878.

Friedman, M. (1968) 'The Role of Monetary Policy', *American Economic Review*, 58, pp. 1–17.

Fung, K. C. (1986) 'Labor Relations, Labor Market Policies and the National Advantage' (mimeo, Mount Holyoke College).

Gale, D. (1986a and b) 'Bargaining and Competition: Parts I and II', *Econometrica*, 54, pp. 785–806, and 807–18.

Garonna, P. and Ryan, P. (1986) 'Youth Labour, Industrial Relations and Deregulation in Advanced Economies, *Economia e Lavoro*, October, 20, 4, pp. 3–19.

Geroski, P., Hamlin, A., and Knight, K. G. (1982) 'Wages, Strikes and Market Structure', *Oxford Economic Papers*, vol. 34, no 2, pp. 276–91.

Gilman, H. J. (1965) 'Economic Discrimination and Unemployment', *American Economic Review*, vol. 55, pp. 1077–96.

Godley, W. and Nordhaus, W. (1972) 'Pricing in the Trade Cycle', *Economic Journal*, 82, pp. 853–82.

Gomberg, E. L. (1944) 'Strikes and Lock-outs in Great Britain', *Quarterly Journal of Economics*, vol. 59, no 1, pp. 92–106.

Gordon, D. F. (1974) 'A Neoclassical Theory of Keynesian Unemployment', *Economic Inquiry*, vol. 12, pp. 431–59.

Gordon, D. M., Edwards, R. C. and Reich, M. (1982) *Segmented Work, Divided Workers* (Cambridge: Cambridge University Press).

Gottfries, N. and Horn, H. (1987) 'Wage Formation and the Persistence of Unemployment', *Economic Journal*, 97, pp. 877–84.

Gray, J. A. (1976) 'Wage Indexation: A Macroeconomic Approach', *Journal of Monetary Economics*, 2, pp. 221–35.

Gray, J. A. (1978) 'On Indexation and Contract Length', *Journal of Political Economy*, 86, pp. 1–18.

Green Paper (1986) *Profit-Related Pay* (London: HMSO) Cmnd 9835.

Gregory, M, Lobban, P. and Thomson, A. (1985) 'Wage settlements in Manufacturing, 1979–84: Evidence from the CBI Pay Databank', *British Journal of Industrial Relations*, 23, pp. 339–57.

Gregory, R. G. and Duncan, R. C. (1981) 'Segmented Labour Market Theories and the Australian Experience of Equal Pay for Women', *Journal of Post-Keynesian Economics*, vol. 3, pp. 403–28.

Griffin, J. E. (1939) *Strikes: A Study of Quantitative Economics* (New York: Columbia University Press).

Grossman, G. (1983) 'Union Wages, Seniority and Unemployment', *American Economic Review*, 73, pp. 277–90.

Grout, P. (1984) 'Investment and Wages in the Absence of Legally Binding Contracts: A Nash Bargaining Approach', *Econometrica*, 52, pp. 449–460.

Hamermesh, D. S. (1973) 'Who "Wins" in Wage Bargaining?' *Industrial and Labour Relations Review*, vol. 26, no 4, pp. 1146–9.

Hansen, A. H. (1921) 'Cycles of Strikes', *American Economic Review*, vol. 11, no 4, pp. 616–21.

Harsanyi, J. C. (1956) 'Approaches to the Bargaining Problem Before and After the Theory of Games: A Critical Discussion of Zeuthen's, Hicks's and Nash's Theories', *Econometrica*, vol. 24, no 2, pp. 144–57.

Hart, O. D. (1982) 'A Model of Imperfect Competition with Keynesian Features', *Quarterly Journal of Economics*, 97, pp. 109–38.

Hart, O. D. (1984) 'Optimal Labour Contracts under Asymmetric Information: An Introduction', *Review of Economic Studies*, 50, pp. 3–35.

Hart, O. D. and Holmstrom, B. (1986) 'The Theory of Contracts', in T. Bewley (ed.) *Advances in Economic Theory* (Cambridge: Cambridge University Press).

Hart, R. A. (1984) *The Economics of Non-Wage Labour Costs* (London: Allen & Unwin).

Hayes, B. (1984) 'Unions and Strikes with Asymmetric Information', *Journal of Labour Economics*, vol. 2, no 1, pp. 57–83.

Hazledine, T., Holden, K. and Howells, J., (1977) 'Strike Incidence and

Economic Activity: Some Further Evidence', *New Zealand Economic Papers*, vol. 11, pp. 91–105.

Hepple, B. A. (1984) *Equal Pay and the Industrial Tribunals* (London: Sweet & Maxwell).

Hey, J. D. (1979) '*Uncertainty in Microeconomics* (Oxford : Martin Robertson).

Hickman, B. G. (1974) 'What Became of the Building Cycle?' in P. David and M. Reder (eds) *Nations and Households in Economic Growth: Essays in Honor of Moses Abramovitz* (New York: Academic Press).

Hicks, J. R. (1932) *The Theory of Wages* (London: Macmillan).

Hicks, J. R. (1963) *The Theory of Wages* (London: Macmillan) 2nd edn.

Hodson, R. (1978) 'Labour in the Monopoly, Competitive and State Sectors of production', *Politics and Society*, 8, pp. 429–80.

Hodson, R. and Kaufman, R. (1982) 'Economic Dualism: A Critical Review', *American Sociological Review*, December, 47, 6, pp. 727–9.

Holmstrom, B. (1981) 'Contractual Models of the Labor Market', *American Economic Review Papers and Proceedings*, 71, pp. 308–13.

Hopkins, S. V. (1953) 'Industrial Stoppages and their Economic Significance', *Oxford Economic Papers*, vol. 5 (New Series) no 2, pp. 209–20.

Horn, H. and Wolinsky, A. (1988) 'Worker Substitutability and Patterns of Unionisation', *Economic Journal*, vol. 98, no. 391, pp. 484–97.

Humphries, J. and Rubery, J. (1984) 'The Reconstruction of the Supply Side of the Labour Market', *Cambridge Journal of Economics*, December, 8, 4, pp. 331–6.

Hunter, L. C. (1973) 'The Economic Determination of Strike Activity: A Reconsideration', University of Glasgow Department of Social and Economic Research, Discussion Papers no 1.

Jackman, R. (1987) 'Profit-Sharing in a Unionised Economy with Imperfect Competition', *International Journal of Industrial Organisation*, vol. 6, pp. 49–59.

Jensen, M. and Meckling, W. (1979) 'Rights and Production Functions: An Application of Labour-Managed Firms and Codetermination', *Journal of Business*, pp. 469–506.

Johnson, G. E. (1975) 'Economic Analysis of Trade Unionism', *American Economic Review*, (Papers and Proceedings) vol. 65, pp. 23–8.

Johnson, G. E. (1986) 'Work Rules, Overmanning, and Efficient Bargains', University of Michigan, mimeo.

Joll, C., McKenna, C., McNabb, R. and Shorey, J. (1983) *Developments in Labour Market Analysis* (London: Allen & Unwin).

Jones, D. and Svejnar, J. (1985) 'Participation, Profit-Sharing, Worker Ownership and Efficiency in Italian Producer Cooperatives', *Economica*, vol. 52, pp. 449–66.

Jones, J. and Walsh, W. D. (1984) 'Inter-Industry Strike Frequencies: Some Pooled Cross-Sectional Evidence from Canadian Secondary Manufacturing', *Journal of Labor Research*, vol. 5, no 4, pp. 419–25.

Joshi, H. and Newell, M. L. (1987) 'Pay Differences Between Men and Women: Longitudinal Evidence From the 1946 Cohort' (London: Centre for Economic Policy Research) Discussion Paper No. 156.

Jurkat, E. H. and Jurkat, D. B. (1949) 'Economic Functions of Strikes' *Industrial and Labor Relations Review*, vol. 2, no 4, pp. 527–45.

Kalleberg, A. and Hanisch, T. (1986) 'Towards the Comparative Analysis of Labour Markets', paper presented to annual meeting of the International Working Group on Labour Market Segmentation, Cambridge, England.

Katseli, L. T. (1980) 'Transmission of External Price Disturbances and the Composition of Trade', *Journal of International Economics*, 10, pp. 357–75.

Kaufman, B. E. (1981) 'Bargaining Theory, Inflation and Cyclical Strike Activity in Manufacturing', *Industrial and Labor Relations Review*, vol. 34, no 3, pp. 333–55.

Kaufman, B. E. (1983) 'The Determinants of Strikes Over Time and Across Industries', *Journal of Labor Research*, vol. 4, 2, pp. 159–75.

Kerr, C. (1954) 'The Balkanization of Labour Markets', in E. W. Bakke (ed.) *Labour Mobility and Economic Opportunity* (Cambridge, Mass.: MIT Press).

Keynes, J. M. (1936) *The General Theory of Employment, Interest and Money* (London, Macmillan).

Kidd, D. and Oswald, A. (1987) 'A Dynamic Model of Trade Union Behaviour', *Economica*, vol. 54, pp. 355–65.

Killingsworth, M. R. (1983) *Labour Supply* (Cambridge: Cambridge University Press).

Komiya, R. and Suzuki, Y. (1977) 'Inflation in Japan', in L. Krause and W. Salant (eds), *Worldwide Stagflation* (Washington: Brookings Institution).

Lancaster, K. (1966) 'A New Approach to Consumer Theory', *Journal of Political Economy*, vol. 74, pp. 132–57.

Layard, P. R. G. and Nickell, S. J. (1986) 'Unemployment in Britain', *Economica*, Supplement, 53, pp. 121–69.

Lazear, E. (1981) 'Agency, Earnings Profiles, Productivity and Hours Restrictions, *American Economic Review*, September, 71, 4, pp. 606–20.

Lee, L.-F. (1978) 'Unionism and Wage Rates: A Simultaneous Equations Model with Qualitative and Limited Dependent Variables', *International Economic Review*, 19, pp. 415–33.

Leigh, J. D. (1984) 'A Bargaining Model and Empirical Analysis of Strike Activity Across Industries', *Journal of Labor Research*, vol. 5, no 2, pp. 127–37.

Leontief, W. (1946) 'The Pure Theory of the Guaranteed Annual Wage Contract', *Journal of Political Economy*, vol. 54, no 1, pp. 76–9.

Levinson, H. M. (1967) 'Unionism, Concentration and Wage Changes: Towards a Unified Theory', *Industrial and Labour Relations Review*, January; 198–205.

Levitt, T. (1953) 'Prosperity verses Strikes', *Industrial and Labor Relations Review*, vol. 6, no 2, pp. 220–6.

Lin, Ching-yuan (1984) *Japanese and US Inflation* (Lexington, Mass.: Lexington Books).

Lindbeck, A. and Snower, D. (1984) 'Involuntary Unemployment as an

Insider–Outsider Dilemma', seminar paper no 282. (Institute for International Economic Studies, University of Stockholm).

Lindbeck, A. and Snower, D. (1986) 'Wage Setting, Unemployment and Insider–Outsider Relations', *American Economic Review – Papers and Proceedings*, 76, pp. 235–9.

Lundahl, M. and Wadensjö, E. (1984) *Unequal Treatment: A Study in the Neoclassical Theory of Discrimination* (Beckenham: Croom Helm).

MaCurdy, T. and Pencavel, J. (1986) 'Testing between Competing Models of Wage and Employment Determination in Unionised Markets', *Journal of Political Economy*, vol. 94 (Supplement) pp. S3–40.

Madden, J. F. (1973) *The Economics of Sex Discrimination* (Lexington, Mass.: D.C. Heath).

Malcomson, J. M. (1983) 'Trade Unions and Economic Efficiency', *Economic Journal*, 93, 50–64.

Marsden, D. (1979) 'A study of Changes in the Wage Structure of Manual Workers in Industry in Six Community Countries Since 1966 ', mimeo, European Research Centre, University of Sussex.

Marsden, D. (1986) *The End of Economic Man? Custom and Competition in Labour Markets* (Brighton: Wheatsheaf).

Marsden, D. and Ryan, P. (1986) 'Where do Young Workers Work? The Distribution of Youth Employment by Industry in Various European Economies', *British Journal of Industrial Relations*, March, 24, 1, pp. 83–102.

Marshall, A. (1890) *Principles of Economics* (London: Macmillan) reprinted 1960.

Matthews, R. C. O. (1985) 'Review of "The Share Economy" ' *Journal of Economic Literature*, vol. XXIII, pp. 658–60.

Mauro, M. J. (1982) 'Strikes as a Result of Imperfect Information' *Industrial and Labor Relations Review*, vol. 35, no 4, pp. 522–38.

Mayhew, K. and Addison, J. (1983) 'Discrimination in the Labour Market' in G. S. Bain (ed.) *Industrial Relations in Britain* (Oxford: Basil Blackwell).

Mayhew, K. and Rosewell, B. (1979) 'Labour Market Segmentation in Britain', *Oxford Bulletin of Economics and Statistics*, 41, 2, pp. 81–116.

McDonald, I. M. and Solow, R. M. (1981) 'Wage Bargaining and Employment', *American Economic Review*, vol. 71, no 4, pp. 896–908.

McKenna, C. (1985) *Uncertainty and the Labour Market: Recent Developments in Job Search Theory* (Brighton: Wheatsheaf).

McKenna, C. (1987) 'Models of Search Market Equilibrium', in J. D. Hey and P. J. Lambert (eds) *Surveys in the Economics of Uncertainty* (Oxford; Basil Blackwell).

McNabb, R. (1987) 'Testing for Labour Market Segmentation in Britain', *Manchester School*, September; 55, 3; pp. 257–73.

McNabb, R. and Psacharopoulos, G. (1981) 'Further Evidence on the Relevance of the Dual Labour Market Hypothesis for the UK', *Journal of Human Resources*, summer, 16, 3, pp. 442–8.

McNabb, R. and Ryan, P. (1986) 'Earnings Determination and Labour Market Duality in Britain', paper presented to annual meeting of

International Working Group on Labour Market Segmentation, Cambridge.

Meade, J. E. (1986) *Alternative Systems of Business Organisation and Workers' Remuneration* (London: Allen & Unwin).

Mill, J. S. (1885) *Principles of Political Economy* (New York: Appleton).

Mincer, J. (1958) 'Investment in Human Capital and Personal Income Distribution', *Journal of Political Economy*, vol. 66, no 2, pp. 281–302.

Mincer, J. (1985) 'Intercountry Comparisons of Labor Force Trends and of Related Developments: An Overview', *Journal of Labor Economics*, vol. 3 (Supplement) pp. S1–S33.

Mincer, J. and Polachek, S. (1974) 'Family Investments in Human Capital: Earnings of Women', *Journal of Political Economy*, vol. 82, pp. S76–S108.

Mitchell, D. (1982) 'Gain-Sharing: An Anti-Inflation Reform', *Challenge*, pp. 18–25.

Mitchell, D. J. B. (1972) 'Union Wage Policies: The Ross–Dunlop Debate Reopened', *Industrial Relations*, vol. 11, pp. 46–61.

Mitchell, D. J. B. (1985) 'Shifting Norms in Wage Determination', *Brookings Papers on Economic Activity*, 2, pp. 575–99.

Moore, J. (1984) 'Contracting between Two Parties with Private Information', mimeo, London School of Economics.

Moore, J. (1985) 'Optimal Labour Contracts when Workers have a Variety of Privately Observed Reservation Wages', *Review of Economic Studies*, 52 pp. 37–67.

Moore, W. J. and Pearce, D. K. (1982) 'A Comparative Analysis of Strike Models During Periods of Rapid Inflation: 1967–1973', *Journal of Labor Research*, vol. 3, no 1, pp. 39–53.

Mortensen, D. T. (1986) 'Job Search and Labour Market Analysis', in O. C. Ashenfelter and R. Layard (eds) *Handbook of Labour Economics* (Amsterdam: North-Holland) ch. 15.

Mueller, D. C. (1980) *Public Choice* (Cambridge University Press).

Mundell, R. A. (1968) *International Economics* (New York, Macmillan).

Muth, F. (1966) 'Household Production and Consumer Demand Functions', *Econometrica*, vol. 34, pp. 699–708.

Myrdal, G. (1944) *An America Dilemma: The Negro Problem and Modern Democracy* (New York: Harper & Row).

Narendranathan, W. and Nickell, S. (1985) 'Modelling the Process of Job Search', *Journal of Econometrics*, vol. 28, pp. 29–49.

Nash, J. F. (1950) 'The Bargaining Problem', *Econometrica*, vol. 18, no 2, pp. 155–62.

Newell, A. and Symons, J. S. V. (1985) *Wages and Employment in the OECD Countries*, discussion paper no. 219 Centre for Labour Economics, LSE.

Nickell, S. (1976) 'Wage Structure and Quit Rates', *International Economic Review*, February, 17, 1, pp. 191–203.

Nickell, S. (1979) 'The Effect of Unemployment and Related Benefits on the Duration of Unemployment', *Economic Journal*, 89, pp. 34–49.

Nickell, S. J. (1984) 'The Modelling of Wages and Employment', in D. F.

Hendry and K. F. Wallis (eds) *Econometrics and Quantitative Economics* (Oxford: Basil Blackwell).

Nickell, S. J. and Andrews, M. (1983) 'Unions, Real Wages and Employment in Britain, 1951–79', *Oxford Economic Papers*, 35, (Supplement) pp. 183–206.

Nickell, S. J. and Wadhwani, S. (1987a) 'Unions, Wages and Employment: Tests Based on UK Firm-Level Data', CLE discussion paper no 291.

Nickell, S. J. and Wadhwani, S. (1987b) 'Financial Factors, Efficiency Wages and Employment: Investigations Using UK Micro-Data', CLE discussion paper no 295.

Nordhaus, W. (1986) 'Can the Share Economy Conquer Stagflation?' Yale University, mimeo.

Nuti, D. M. (1986) 'Codetermination, Profit-Sharing and Full-Employment', European University Institute working paper no 228.

Oaxaca, R. (1973) 'Male–Female Wage Differentials in Urban Labor Markets', *International Economic Review*, vol. 14, pp. 693–709.

O'Brien, F. S. (1965) 'Industrial Conflict and Business Fluctuations: A Comment' *Journal of Political Economy*, vol. 73, no 6, pp. 650–4.

Osberg, L., Apostle, R. and Clairmont, D. (1986) 'The Incidence and Duration of Individual Unemployment: Supply Side or Demand Side?, *Cambridge Journal of Economics*, March, 10, 1, pp. 13–33.

Osborne, M. J. (1984) 'Capitalist–Worker Conflict and Involuntary Unemployment', *Review of Economic Studies*, 51, pp. 111–27.

Oster, G. (1978) 'A Factor Analytic Test of the Theory of the Dual Economy, *Review of Economics and Statistics*, February, 61, 1, pp. 33–9.

Osterman, P. (1975) 'An Empirical Study of Labour Market Segmentation', *Industrial and Labour Relations Review*, July, 28, pp. 508–23.

Osterman, P. (1980) *Getting Started: the Market for Youth Labour* (Cambridge, Mass.: MIT Press).

Osterman, P. (ed.) (1984) *Internal Labour Markets* (Cambridge, Mass.: MIT Press).

Oswald, A. J. (1982) 'The Microeconomic Theory of the Trade Union', *Economic Journal*, vol. 92, no 367, pp. 576–95.

Oswald, A. J. (1985) 'The Economic Theory of Trade Unions: An Introductory Survey', *Scandinavian Journal of Economics*, 87, pp. 160–93.

Oswald, A. J. (1986) 'Unemployment Insurance and Labor Contracts under Asymmetric Information: Theory and Facts', *American Economic Review*, 76, pp. 365–77.

Oswald, A. J. (1987) 'Efficient Contracts are on the Labour Demand Curve: Theory and Facts', Discussion Paper no 284, Centre for Labour Economics, London School of Economics.

Oswald, A. and Turnbull, P. (1985) 'Pay and Employment Determination in Britain: What are Labour Contracts Really Like?', *Oxford Review of Economic Policy*, vol. 1, pp. 80–97.

Parsons, D. O. (1972) 'Specific Human Capital: An Application to Quit Rates and Lay-off Rates', *Journal of Political Economy*, November, 80, pp. 1120–43.

282   References

Pencavel, J. H. (1970) *An Analysis of the Quit Rate in American Manufacturing Industry* (Princeton: Industrial Relations Section, Princeton University).
Pencavel, J. H. (1970) 'An Investigation into Industrial Strike Activity in Britain', *Economica*, vol. 37 (new series) no 147, pp. 239–56.
Phelps, E. S. (1968) 'Money Wage Dynamics and Labour Market Equilibrium', *Journal of Political Economy*, 76, pp. 678–711.
Phelps, E. S. (1972) 'The Statistical Theory of Racism and Sexism', *American Economic Review*, vol. 62, pp. 659–61.
Phipps, A. J. (1977) 'Strike Activity and Inflation in Australia', *Economic Record*, vol. 53, nos 142 and 143, pp. 297–319.
Pigou, A. C. (1952) *Essays in Economics* (London: Macmillan).
Pike, M. (1982) 'Segregation by Sex, Earnings Differentials and Equal Pay: An Application of the Crowding Model to UK Data', *Applied Economics*, vol. 14, pp. 503–14.
Pike, M. (1985) 'The Employment Response to Equal Pay Legislation, discussion paper no 2, University of Hull; published in *Oxford Economic Papers*, vol. 37 (1985) pp. 304–18.
Piore, M. J. (1970) 'The Dual Labour Market; Theory and Applications', in R. Barringer and S. H. Beer (eds) *The State and the Poor* (Cambridge, Mass.: Winthrop).
Piore, M. J. (1973) 'Fragments of a "sociological" theory of Wages', *American Economic Review*, May, 63, 377–84.
Piore, M. J. (1975) 'Notes for a Theory of Labour Market Stratification', in Edwards *et al.* (1975).
Piore, M. J. (1975a) 'Notes for a Theory of Labor Market Stratification' in R. C. Edwards, M. Reich and D. M. Gordon (eds) *Labor Market Segmentation* (Lexington, Mass.: D. C. Heath) pp. 125–50.
Piore, M. J. (1982) 'American Labour and the Industrial Crisis', *Challenge*, March, 25, 1, pp. 5–11.
Pissarides, C. A. (1976) *Labour Market Adjustment* (Cambridge: Cambridge University Press).
Pissarides, C. A. (1981) 'Contract Theory, Temporary Lay-offs and Unemployment: A Critical Assessment', in D. Currie *et al.* (eds) '*Microeconomic Analysis*' (London: Croom-Helm).
Pissarides, C. A. (1984) 'Efficient job rejection', *Economic Journal*, 94 (Supplement) pp. 97–108.
Pissarides, C. A. (1985) 'Job Search and the Functioning of Labour Markets', in *Labour Economics* by D. Carline *et al.* (London: Longman).
Pohjola, M. (1986) 'Profit-Sharing, Collective Bargaining and Employment' (Helsinki: Labour Institute for Economic Research) discussion paper no 52.
Pollak, R. A. (1985) 'A Transactions Cost Approach to Families and Households', *Journal of Economic Literature*, vol. XXIII, no 2, pp. 581–608.
Prais, S. J. (1978) 'The Strike Proneness of Large Plants in Britain, *Journal of the Royal Statistical Society* (Series A), vol. 141, Pt 3, pp. 368–84.
Rabinovitch, R. and Swary, I. (1976) 'On the theory of Bargaining,

Strikes, and Wage Determination Under Uncertainty,' *Canadian Journal of Economics*, vol. 9, no 4, pp. 668–84.

Rathbone, E. (1917) 'The Remuneration of Women's Services', *Economic Journal*, vol. 27, pp. 55–68.

Reder, M. W. and Neumann, G. R. (1980) 'Conflict and Contract: The Case of Strikes', *Journal of Political Economy*, vol. 88, no 5, pp. 867–86.

Rees, A. (1952) 'Industrial Conflict and Business Fluctuations', *Journal of Political Economy*, vol. 60, no 5, pp. 371–82.

Reich, M. (1981) *Racial Inequality: A Political Economic Analysis* (Princeton: Princeton University Press).

Reich, M. (1984) 'Segmented Labour: Time-Series Hypotheses and Evidence', *Cambridge Journal of Economics*, March, 8, 1, pp. 63–8.

Robinson, J. (1933) *The Economics of Imperfect Competition* (London: Macmillan).

Roemer, J. E. (1979) 'Divide and Conquer: Microfoundations of a Marxian Theory of Wage Discrimination', *Bell Journal of Economics*, vol. 10, pp. 695–705.

Rosen, S. (1985) 'Implicit Contracts: A Survey', *Journal of Economic Literature*, 23, pp. 1144–75.

Rosenberg, S. (1977) 'The Marxian Reserve Army of Labour and the Dual Labour Market', *Politics and Society*, 7, 2, pp. 221–8.

Rosenberg, S. (1980) 'Male Occupational Standing and the Dual Labour Market', *Industrial Relations*, Winter, 19, 1, pp. 34–49.

Ross, A. M. (1948) *Trade Union Wage Policy* (Berkeley, California: University of California Press).

Rossi, A. S. (ed.) (1970) *Mill, J. S. and Mill, H. T.: On Sex Equality* (Chicago: University of Chicago Press).

Rubery, J. (1978) 'Structured Labour Markets, Worker Organisation and Low Pay', *Cambridge Journal of Economics*, 2, pp. 1–20.

Rubery, J. and Wilkinson, F. (1981) 'Outwork and Segmented Labour Markets', in Wilkinson (1981).

Rubinstein, A. (1982) 'Perfect Equilibrium in a Bargaining Model', *Econometrica*, 50, pp. 97–110.

Rubinstein, A. and Wolinsky, A. (1986) 'Decentralised Trading, Strategic Behaviour and the Walrasian Outcome', *CARESS Working Paper 86–12.*, University of Pennsylvania.

Rumberger, R. and Carnoy, M. (1980) 'Segmentation in the US Labour Market: Its Effects on the Mobility and Earnings of Whites and Blacks', *Cambridge Journal of Economics*, June, 4, pp. 117–32.

Ryan, P. (1977) 'Job Training', unpublished Ph.D. dissertation, Harvard University.

Ryan, P. (1980) 'The Costs of Training for a Transferable Skill', *British Journal of Industrial Relations*, November, 18, 3, pp. 334–52.

Ryan, P. (1981) 'Segmentation, Duality and the Internal Labour Market', in Wilkinson (1981).

Ryan, P. (1987) 'Primary and Secondary Labour Markets', in J. Eatwell, M. Milgate and P. Newman (eds) *The New Palgrave* (London: Macmillan).

Ryan, P., Kumar, M. and Osberg, L. (1986) 'The Sterling Exchange Rate and the Structure of Wages and Prices in the UK, 1970–81', Cambridge Growth Project discussion paper no 2; Department of Applied Economics, University of Cambridge.

Sabourian, H. (1988) 'Wage Norms and Involuntary Unemployment', *Economic Journal* (Conference Supplement) 98, pp. 177–88.

Sapsford, D. R. (1978) 'Employer Resistance and Strikes: A Contradiction Resolved', *Scottish Journal of Political Economy*, vol. 25, no 3, pp. 311–15.

Sapsford, D. R. (1982) 'The Theory of Bargaining and Strike Activity', *International Journal of Social Economics*, vol. 9, no 2, pp. 3–31.

Schiller, B. R. (1977) 'Relative Earnings Mobility in the United States', *American Economic Review*, December, 67, 5, pp. 926–41.

Schmidt, P. and Strauss, R. P. (1976) 'The Effects of Unions on Earnings and Earnings on Unions: A Mixed Logit Approach', *International Economic Review*, 17, pp. 204–12.

Sengenberger, W. (1981) 'Labour Market Segmentation and the Business Cycle', in Wilkinson (1981).

Shaked, A. and Sutton, J. (1984) 'Involuntary Unemployment as a Perfect Equilibrium in a Bargaining Model', *Econometrica*, 52, pp. 1351–64.

Shorey, J. (1976) 'An Inter-Industry Analysis of Strike Frequency', *Economica*, vol. 43 (new series) no 172, pp. 349–65.

Shorey, J. (1977) 'Time-Series Analysis of Strike Frequency', *British Journal of Industrial Relations*, vol. 15, no 1, pp. 63–75.

Shorey, J. (1980) 'An Analysis of Quits Using Industry Turnover Data', *Economic Journal*, December, 90, pp. 821–37.

Siebert, W. S. and Addison, J. (1981) 'Are Strikes Accidental?', *Economic Journal*, vol. 91, no 362, pp. 389–404.

Siebert, W. S., Bertrand, P. and Addison, J. (1985) 'The Political Model of Strikes: A New Twist', *Southern Economic Journal*, vol. 52, no 1, pp. 23–33.

Smith, A. (1776) *The Wealth of Nations* (London: Strahan & Cadell).

Smith, G. (1986) 'Profit-Sharing and Employee Share Ownership in Britain', *Department of Employment Gazette*, vol. 94 (September) pp. 1–21.

Snower, D. J. (1983) 'Imperfect Competition, Underemployment and Crowding-Out', *Oxford Economic Papers*, 35, 245–70.

Solow, R. M. (1985) 'Insiders and Outsiders in Wage Determination', *Scandinavian Journal of Economics*, 87, pp. 411–28.

Sowell, T. (1981) *Markets and Minorities* (Oxford: Basil Blackwell).

Stewart, M. B. and Greenhalgh, C. A. (1984) 'Work History Patterns and Occupational Attainment of Women', *Economic Journal*, vol. 94, pp. 493–519.

Stigler, G. J. (1962) 'Information in the Labour Market', *Journal of Political Economy*, vol. 70, no 1, pp. 94–105.

Stiglitz, J. (1984) 'Theories of Wage Rigidity', mimeo.

Stoikov, V. and Raimon, R. (1968) 'The Determinants of the Quit Rate among Industries', *American Economic Review*, 58, 5, pp. 1283–98.

Strauss, G. (1984) 'Industrial Relations: A Time of change', *Industrial Relations*, Winter, 23, 1, pp. 1–15.

References# References   285

Svejnar, J. (1982) 'On the Theory of A Participatory Firm', *Journal of Economic Theory*, vol. 27, pp. 313—30.

Swindinsky, R. and Vanderkamp, J. (1982) 'A Micro-econometric Analysis of Strike Activity in Canada', *Journal of Labor Research*, vol. 3, no 4, pp. 455–71.

Symons, J. S. V. (1985) 'Relative Prices and the Demand for Labour in British Manufacturing', *Economica*, 52, 37–50.

Symons, J. S. V. and Layard, P. R. G. (1984) 'Neoclassical Demand for Labour Functions for Six Major Economies', *Economic Journal*, 94, 788–90.

Taubman, P. and Wachter, M. L. (1986) 'Segmented Labour Markets', in O. Aschenfelter and R. Layard (eds) *Handbook of Labour Economics* (Amsterdam: Elsevier).

Taylor, J. B. (1980) 'Aggregate Dynamics and Staggered Contracts', *Journal of Political Economy*, 88, pp. 1–24.

Theochorakis, N. (1988) 'The Economics of Responsibility', Ph.D. dissertation in progress, University of Cambridge.

Thurow, L. (1969) *Poverty and Discrimination* (Washington, DC: Brookings Institution).

Thurow, L. (1975) *Generating Inequality* (New York: Basic Books).

Tracy, J. S. (1987) 'An Empirical Test of an Asymmetric Information Model of Strikes', *Journal of Labor Economics*, vol 5, no 2, pp. 149–73.

Turk, C. (1984) 'Strike Activity and Uncertainty', London School of Economics, Centre for Labor Economics, discussion paper no 205.

Turkington, D. J. (1975) 'Strike Incidence and Economic Activity in New Zealand', *New Zealand Economic Papers*, vol. 9, pp. 87–106.

Tzannatos, Z. (1989) 'The Long-Run Effects of the Sex Integration of the UK Labour Market', *Journal of Economic Studies*, vol. 15, no. 1, pp. 5–18.

Tzannatos, Z. (1986) 'Female Discrimination in Britain: Has the State Unshackled the the Market?', *Economic Affairs*, vol. 7, no 2, pp. 26–9.

Tzannatos, Z. (1987a) 'A General Equilibrium Model of Discrimination and Its Effects on Incomes', *Scottish Journal of Political Economy*, vol. 34, pp. 19–36.

Tzannatos, Z. (1987b) 'Equal Pay in Greece and Britain', *Industrial Relations Journal*, vol. 18, pp. 275–83.

Tzannatos, Z. (1989), 'The Greek Labour Market: Current Perspectives and Future Prospects', *Greek Economic Review*, (forthcoming).

Tzannatos, Z. (1989) 'Female Wages and Equal Pay in Greece', *Journal of Modern Greek Studies*, vol. 7, (forthcoming).

Tzannatos, Z. and Zabalza, A. (1984) 'The Anatomy of the Rise of British Female Relative Wages in the 1970s: Evidence from the New Earnings Survey', *British Journal of Industrial Relations*, vol. 22, pp. 177–94.

Tzannatos, Z. and Zabalza, A. (1985) 'The Effect of Sex Discrimination Legislation on the Variability of Female Employment in Britain', *Applied Economics*, vol. 17, pp. 117–34.

Ulman, L. (1965) 'Labour Mobility and, the Industrial Wage Structure in the Post-War United States', *Quarterly Journal of Economics*, February, 79, 1, 81–95.

Ulph, A. M. (1989) 'The Incentives to Make Commitments in Wage Bargaining', *Review of Economic Studies* (forthcoming).

Wachtel, H. and Betsey, C. (1972) 'Employment at Low Wages', *Review of Economics and Statistics*, May, 54, pp. 121–9.

Wachter, M. (1974) 'Primary and Secondary Labour Markets: A Critique of the Dual Approach', *Brooking Papers on Economic Activity*, 3, pp. 637–80.

Wadhwani, S. (1986) 'Profit-Sharing As A Cure for Unemployment: Some Doubts', London School of Economics, Centre for Labour Economics discussion paper no 253, published in *International Journal of Industrial Organisation*, no. 6, pp. 59–68.

Wadhwani, S. (1987a) 'The Macroeconomic Implications of Profit-Sharing: Some Empirical Evidence, *Economic Journal*, vol. 97, pp. 171–83.

Wadhwani, S. (1987b) 'Profit-Sharing and Meade's Discriminating Labour–Capital Partnerships: A Review Article', *Oxford Economic Papers*, vol. 39, no 3, pp. 421–42.

Wadhwani, S. and Wall, M. (1988) 'The Effects of Profit-Sharing on Employment, Wages, Stock Returns and Productivity', London School of Economics, Centre for Labour Economics, mimeo.

Walker, K. E. and Woods, M. E. (1976) *Time Use: A Measure of Household Production of Family Goods and Services* (The American Home Economics Association).

Wallace, M. and Kalleberg, A. (1981) 'Economic Organisation of Firms and Labour Market Consequences: Towards a Specification of Dual Economic Theory', in I. Berg (ed.) *Sociological Perspectives on Labour Markets* (New York: Academic Press).

Walsh, W. D. (1975) 'Economic Conditions and Strike Activity in Canada', *Industrial Relations*, vol. 14, no 1, pp. 45–54.

Webb, B. (1919) *The Wages of Men and Women: Why Should They be Equal?* (London: Fabian Society and Allen & Unwin).

Webb, S. (1891) 'The Alleged Differences in the Wages Paid to Men and Women for Similar Work', *Economic Journal*, vol. 1, pp. 635–62.

Weiniger, O. (1906) *Sex and Character* (London: Heinemann).

Weitzman, M. (1983) 'Some Macroeconomic Implications of Alternative Compensation Systems', *Economic Journal*, vol. 93, pp. 763–83.

Weitzman, M. (1984) *The Share Economy* (Cambridge, Mass.: Harvard University Press).

Weitzman, M. (1985) 'The Simple Macroeconomics of Profit-Sharing', *American Economic Review*, vol. 75, pp. 937–53.

Weitzman, M. L. (1986) 'The Case for Profit Sharing', Public Lecture to Employment Institute, July.

Weitzman, M. L. (1987) 'Steady State Unemployment Under Profit-Sharing, *Economic Journal*, vol. 97, pp. 86–105.

Wilkinson, F. (ed.) (1981) *Dynamics of Labour Market Segmentation* (New York: Academic Press).

Williamson, O. E., Wachter, M. L. and Harris, J. E. (1975) 'Understanding the Employment Relation: The Analysis of Ideosyncratic Exchange', *Bell Journal of Economics*, 6, pp. 250–78.

Willis, R. J. (1973) 'A New Approach to the Economic Theory of Fertility Behaviour', *Journal of Political Economy*, vol. 81, pp. S14–S64.

Woodward, N. and McNabb, R. (1978) 'Low Pay in British Manufacturing', *Applied Economics*, 10, pp. 49–60.

Yellen, J. (1984) 'Efficiency Wage Models of Unemployment', *American Economic Review* (Papers and Proceedings) vol. 74, pp. 200–5.

Zabalza, A. and Arrufat, J. L. (1985) 'The Extent of Sex Discrimination in Britain' in A. Zabalza and Z. Tzannatos, *Women and Equal Pay: The Effects of Legislation on Female Employment and Wages in Britain* (Cambridge: Cambridge University Press).

Zabalza, A. and Tzannatos, Z. (1985a) 'The Effect of Britain's Sex Anti-Discriminatory Legislation on Relative Pay and Employment', *Economic Journal*, vol. 95, pp. 679–99.

Zabalza, A. and Tzannatos, Z. (1985b) *Women and Equal Pay: The Effects of Legislation on Female Employment and Wages in Britain* (Cambridge: Cambridge University Press).

Zabalza, A. and Tzannatos, Z. (1988) 'Reply to the Comments on the Effects of Britain's Anti-Discriminatory Legislation on Relative Pay and Employment', *Economic Journal*, vol. 98, pp. 839–43.

Zeuthen, F. (1930) *Problems of Monopoly and Economic Warfare* (London: Routledge).

Zucker, L. G. and Rosenstein, C. (1981) 'Taxonomies of Institutional Structure: Dual Economy Reconsidered', *American Sociological Review*, December, 46, pp. 869–84.

Name Index

Subject Index

293